'They Were Good Soldiers'

African–Americans Serving in the Continental Army, 1775–1783

John U. Rees

Helion & Company

Helion & Company Limited
Unit 8 Amherst Business Centre
Budbrooke Road
Warwick
CV34 5WE
England
Tel. 01926 499 619
Fax 0121 711 4075
Email: info@helion.co.uk
Website: www.helion.co.uk
Twitter: @helionbooks
Visit our blog at http://blog.helion.co.uk/

Published by Helion & Company 2019
Designed and typeset by Mach 3 Solutions Ltd (www.mach3solutions.co.uk)
Cover designed by Paul Hewitt, Battlefield Design (www.battlefield-design.co.uk)

Text © John U. Rees 2019
Maps by George Anderson © Helion and Company 2019
Cover: Capt. Thomas Arnold's veteran 1st Rhode Island detachment at the Battle of
Monmouth, 28 June 1778. Artwork by Peter Dennis © Helion and Co. 2019

ISBN 978-1-911628-54-5

British Library Cataloguing-in-Publication Data.
A catalogue record for this book is available from the British Library.

For details of other military history titles published by Helion & Company Limited,
contact the above address, or visit our website: http://www.helion.co.uk

We always welcome receiving book proposals from prospective authors.

Dedicated to Linda, Evan, Christian,
Dolli and Bill,
Miriam and Les.

Contents

Preface

My first in-depth exposure to African Americans' contributions in the War for Independence was some 30 years ago, when I first read Benjamin Quarles' 1961 classic *The Negro in the American Revolution*. Professor Quarles introduced me to one of the conflict's many interesting facets, black Revolutionary soldiers and their military service, joined with the conundrum of slavery and American independence. As I continued my own research into the armies of the Revolution, I turned up additional references to soldiers of color, and increasingly realized what a complex and little-known aspect of the war their service was. When approached to do a book, having written two articles on the subject, I almost immediately decided to further examine black Continental soldiers' capacities and experiences during the war.

The story of African American soldiers in the cause for American Independence is tied to the complicated history of English and American enslavement of Africans, the genesis and growth of the abolition movement, and, despite efforts to the contrary, post-war entrenchment of black slavery in the United States. White society's attitude towards African Americans, free and enslaved, is also part and parcel of the soldiers' history. As will be seen, black Americans participated early-on in the militia and New England Army of Observation and, despite some backlash, continued to be accepted as soldiers to the war's end. By and large, commanders treated them as they did other enlisted men; their white fellow-soldiers appreciated their contributions to the cause, and many, perhaps most, valued them as human beings. Despite the waning of Northern slavery, with the ratification of the 1789 United States Constitution, and boosted by the 1794 cotton gin patent, black bondage was cemented as a political and economic fact, and detrimental racial attitudes hardened before, but more especially after, 1800. In the first quarter of the 19th century many citizens either did not know, or willfully forgot, that African Americans had served as soldiers. This societal amnesia was so ingrained that when southern Congressmen questioned black citizenship during the 1820 Missouri debates, northerners had to remind them with ready evidence of African American participation in the Continental Army and militia. Thirty-five years after the war black Revolutionary veterans, along with their white comrades, were eligible for service pensions, but, even in that system, they experienced the effect of increasing bias. When all is said and done, African American military service was a direct challenge to slavery and the racial construct.

Before proceeding to the narrative, some discussion of methodology is in order. Having used African American veterans' pension accounts for an earlier work, two attributes led me to rely on them again. First, they are the best way to hear the men's stories in as close to their own words as is possible – to almost hear them speak. Second, personal details, available nowhere else, are revealed by the veterans themselves or people close to them. In essence, my wish is to present their experiences as soldiers, as citizens, and as individuals, and pension narratives are the best way to accomplish that.

Using pensions as the foundation of my work was a leap of faith. While their narratives can be compelling and eye-opening, many are limited to simple facts, and there was no way of knowing how many informative, usable accounts I would find. To increase the difficulty, my search was narrowed to a subset of a subset: black veterans with some Continental Army service. From the outset quickly locating pension files belonging to black veterans was a large hurdle. The online Southern Campaigns Revolutionary War Pension website contains thousands of transcribed pensions, is fully searchable, and an invaluable resource. Unfortunately, it covers only veterans with southern service and not yet even all of those. After several false starts and dead-ends, I stumbled across Eric Grundset's *Forgotten Patriots: African American and American Indian Patriots in the Revolutionary War* (National Society Daughters of the American Revolution, 2008), a fully searchable digital resource. Though the ability to search Grundset's collection was useful, to ensure accuracy I examined each entry, state by state, to glean all the men listed with pension numbers. Along the way I discovered some few errors and probable duplicates. I also found men I knew had pension files, but were not listed as such. While *Forgotten Patriots* was crucial to my work, undoubtedly some African American veterans and pension accounts were missed.

Two other factors are crucial in studying African American Continental Army service. A discussion of numbers is a must, though the only reliable figures are from the 1778 'Return of the Negroes' in General George Washington's main army. Similar information is available for a few small units, but data on total numbers of black soldiers who served the 'Rebel' cause is lacking, and any statistics are based on educated assumptions rather than hard facts. It is also important we delve into the lineage of the military units black soldiers served in. Men who signed on for more than one year periodically experienced changes in company and regimental organization, even being reassigned en masse to another newly-forming unit with an unfamiliar officer corps. These transformations and transferals were integral to the Continental Army's organizational churn and affected most soldiers at some point during their career. Soldier numbers and black wartime free and slave populations are covered in a dedicated chapter, while unit lineage is included in the chapters covering individual states.

There is more, much more, to be discovered and written on this subject, but this is my small contribution, a supplement to the canon of better historians than myself concerning the African American experience and their contributions to our nation.

John U. Rees, March 2019
Solebury, Pennsylvania,
http://tinyurl.com/jureesarticles

Acknowledgements

My heartfelt appreciation to the following for their contributions, many and varied, to this work: Lawrence E. Babits, Jennifer Bolton, Joseph Lee Boyle, Todd W. Braisted, Justin Clement, Charles H. Fithian, Will Graves, Don N. Hagist, John Hannigan, C. Leon Harris, Joshua B. Howard, Martha Katz-Hyman, Bob McDonald, Philip S. Mead, Philip Morgan, David Niescior, Daniel M. Popek, Todd Post, Christian S. Rees., Evan T. Rees, John K. Robertson, Cat Schirf, Eric H. Schnitzer, Michael C. Scoggins, Robert A. Selig, Matthew Skic, R. Scott Stephenson, Gregory J.W. Urwin, Judith L. Van Buskirk, and Thaddeus J. Weaver. Thanks also to Marvin-Alonzo Greer, Peter Harrington (Anne S.K. Brown Military Collection), Nick Johnson, Daryian Kelton, and Aimee E. Newell (Luzerne County Historical Society), for their help with images, paintings, or photographs of artifacts. Special thanks to Don Troiani for his kindness in allowing me to share his work, and to Bryant White for creating original artwork specifically for this project.

Elsa Gilbertson (Vermont Division for Historic Preservation), and Kate Swisher (DuSable Museum of African American History), kindly provided information on surviving African American soldiers' belongings referred to in my work.

Two Pennsylvania institutions have been inspirational, as well as invaluable resources: the David Library of the American Revolution, Washington Crossing, Pennsylvania, and the Museum of the American Revolution, Philadelphia.

Last, but most certainly not least, I wish to recognize and thank Matthew C. White, my friend, cousin, and alter ego, in the best sense of the phrase. His discovery and study of the role Pennsylvania Revolutionaries had in the through-line of abolitionism, from 1775 to the first third of the 19th century, helped place this study in a much larger context. Many of those men had served in the Continental Army; their zeal is typified by Thomas Forrest, former artillery officer with an outstanding war record, who in 1820 passionately argued against compromise, at one point declaiming in Congress, 'if the extension of slavery grows out of the question before the committee, I shall think the small share I have had in the revolution, was the blackest part of my life'.

Introduction

The first United States veterans' legislation was enacted in 1776, stipulating pensions for soldiers and sailors disabled in service and incapable of making a living, but not until 1818 was a pension act passed that covered all veterans of the War for American Independence.[1] The early 19th century in America was a period of growing racial tension and controversy regarding abolition and the societal role of blacks. In 1836 James Redd of Patrick County, Virginia, wrote the Secretary of War, under whose auspices fell veterans' pension administration:

> To the Secretary of the War … Patrick C. House February 13 1836
>
> D[ea]r Sir Is A Free Negro entitled to a Pension [?] if they are not, There has been an imposition put on you, for there is one James Harris [formerly of the 3rd North Carolina Regiment] of this County who has Just rec'd his Warrant, who I understand [is] receiving thirty dollars per year, he is as Black as half of the Negroes in this county nothing promps me to make this inquiry but to know if that class of the community is entitled to pensions and to detect fraud if there should be any I inquired of the Gentleman who drew his declaration if he stated it that he was a free negro and his answer was no therefor think something is rong
>   Yours respectfully James M. Redd [2]

Mr Redd's query, likely inspired by racial animus, was indicative of the times, but African American Revolutionary veterans were indeed entitled to an annuity, as were their widows after them.

The role of black Americans, most free but some enslaved, in the regiments of the Continental Army is not well-known. The same goes for the fact that the greatest proportion served alongside their white comrades in integrated units and that relatively large numbers were soldiers in southern regiments. This work examines African American Continental soldiers' wartime service, with some

---

1   Anon, *Index of Revolutionary War Pension Applications in the National Archives* (Washington, D.C.: Government Printing Office, 1976), pp.ix-xiii.

2   National Archives (United States), Revolutionary War Pension and Bounty-Land Warrant Application Files (National Archives Microfilm Publication M804), Records of the Department of Veterans Affairs, Record Group 15, Washington, D.C., reel 1199, James Harris (W11223), James M. Redd to Patrick C. House, 13 February 1836 (letter).

comparison as to how blacks were treated in the Crown forces, and their post-war experiences as veterans and second-class citizens in an increasingly intolerant country. As with their white counterparts, soldiers of color who fought for the cause of American Independence by and large served well and honorably. That service was rewarded in the 19th century when both black and white veterans were eligible for pensions. Despite that recognition, the denigration of free blacks and the continuance of slavery belied the Revolution's ideals. Still, the war years were actually a time of possibility, and slavery's demise during that time was not out of the question. A few radicals purchased and freed slaves early in the conflict, some slaveowners voluntarily manumitted their bonds-people, and the abolition movement, largely confined pre-war to members of the Society of Friends, was embraced more widely. Some states even made legislative moves towards ending slavery, though few were of any substance. In fact, arguments against slavery, and the push to recognize African Americans as equal human beings, led to a backlash of vilification, rationalization, and self-justification by slaveowners and those entrenched in a slave-supported society. With the conservative reaction following the Revolution the 'peculiar institution' was cemented in place and detrimental racial attitudes hardened.[3]

Racial Epithets, 1775 and 1863

Given the degrading nature of the epithet featured in the appended discussion, the author hesitated in including it. However, the mere fact of its unfortunate prominence during much of our nation's troubled history, and that it surfaced during research for this book, made its inclusion unavoidable.

After the Battle of Honey Springs on 17 July 1863, where United States Colored Troops first experienced large-scale combat, a Federal soldier who witnessed the action wrote, 'I never believed in niggers before, but by Jasus, they are hell for fighting.'[4]

Coming across that passage led to the realization that in researching and writing this work the N-Word popped up only once in a reference dating to the War of the Revolution. This is not to say the word was not in common use, but – at least from what this author has seen – that racial epithet rarely surfaces in writing during the period. In fact, the closest match in the nineteenth century pension accounts occurred when Cezar Shelton related that 'at the time he went into the Army he resided in Bridgeport [Connecticut] … with a Family

---

3   Winthrop D. Jordan, *White Over Black: American Attitudes Toward the Negro, 1550–1812* (Baltimore, Md.: Penguin Books, Inc., 1971), pp.269–292, 294–301; Gary B. Nash, *Race and Revolution* (Lanham, Boulder, New York, and Oxford: Rowman & Littlefield Publishers, Inc., 2001), pp.6–18; John C. Calhoun, 'Speech on the Reception of Abolition Petitions, Delivered in the Senate, February 6th, 1837,' in Richard R Cralle (ed.), *Speeches of John C. Calhoun, Delivered in the House of Representatives and in the Senate of the United States* (New York: D. Appleton, 1853), pp.625–33. Calhoun in this speech argued 'that in the present state of civilization, where two races of different origin, and distinguished by color, and other physical differences, as well as intellectual, are brought together, the relation now existing in the slaveholding States between the two, is, instead of an evil, a good-a positive good'.

4   Noah Andre Trudeau, *Like Men of War: Black Troops in the Civil War, 1862–1865* (Boston, New York, London: Little, Brown and Co., 1998), p.108.

by whom he was brought up by the name of Shelton. He was then and during the term he was in the Army call'd Ceasar Negro or Ceasar Nig'.[5]

Here then is an excerpt from the parody, 'The Trip to Cambridge,' undoubtedly written by a supporter of the British Government. Benson J. Lossing in his work *American Historical Record* wrote:

> I have before me a small broadside, on which is printed the following burlesque account of Washington's trip to Cambridge, after he received the appointment of Commander-in-Chief of the armies, from the Continental Congress, in June, 1775. It may here be remarked that Washington was not often the butt of ridicule by the Tory writers; the shafts of their wit were usually lavished on the subordinate officers, and the mass of the 'rebels'.
>
> *Trip to Cambridge* ....
> Full many a child went into camp,
> All dressed in homespun Kersey,
> To see the greatest rebel scamp
> That ever crossed o'er Jersey.
> The rebel clowns, oh! what a sight!
> For awkward was their figure:
> 'Twas yonder stood a pious wight,
> And here and there a nigger.
> Upon a stump, he placed himself,
> Great Washington, did he,
> And through the nose of lawyer Close,
> Proclaimed great Liberty.
> The patriot brave, the patriot fair,
> From fervor had grown thinner,
> So off they marched, with patriot zeal,
> And took a patriot dinner.[6]

The Oxford English Dictionary cites 'The Trip to Cambridge' as the first written perjorative use of the word in North America. Undoubtedly used in 18th century American correspondence and other documents, as well as in conversation, the upshot is that the term was more often used as racial animus increased into the nineteenth century. Elizabeth S. Pryor notes, 'Prior to the 1770s, the labels nigger and slave were interchangeable, each describing an actual social category of involuntary black laborers. ... By the 1820s, blackness, not slavery, marked people of color as occupying a fixed social class. Most significantly, the word ... became a slur in ... [relation] with black social aspiration'.[7]

---

5   NA (US), Pension, reel 2168, Cezar Shelton (S19764).

6   Benson J. Lossing, *American Historical Record* (Philadelphia: Chase & Town, Publishers, 1872), p.502. See also, Burton Egbert Stevenson (ed.), *Poems of American History* (Cambridge, Ma.: The Riverside Press, 1922), p.169. Mentioned in Benjamin A. Quarles, *The Negro in the American Revolution* (New York, London: W.W. Norton & Company, 1973), p.51

7   Oxford Englsh Dictionary Online, Third Edition, September 2003 (Oxford University Press, http://www.oed.com/viewdictionaryentry/Entry/126934 (accessed 29 April 2019); Elizabeth Stordeur Pryor, 'The Etymology of Nigger: Resistance, Language, and the Politics of Freedom in the Antebellum North,' *Journal of the Early Republic*, Vol. 36, No. 2 (Summer 2016), p.205.

1

'I do promise to every Negroe … full security … within these Lines': Black Americans in Service to the Crown

Before looking at black soldiers fighting for American Independence, it is important to see how they were treated and utilized by Crown commanders, and in British, Loyalist, and German regiments.

While arming free blacks and slaves for defense had been done by the Spanish and Portuguese in the West Indies and South America, the British home government and others balked at instituting such measures. One major reason was their unwillingness, as a group of 'Gentlemen, Merchants and Traders' in Britain proclaimed in October 1775, to unleash the horrors of a slave rebellion on 'our American brethren'.[1]

Lacking proper instructions, British commanders in America proceeded on their own hook. Lieutenant General Thomas Gage took a hesitant lead. On 12 June 1775 he wrote William, 2nd Viscount Barrington, colonial secretary in London, 'Things are now come to that crisis, that we must avail ourselves of every resource, even to raise the negroes, in our cause'. Lord William Campbell, then Royal governor of South Carolina, advised Gage to not 'fall a prey to the Negroes' and the Massachusetts military governor took no further action on that head. Gage was prompted by John Murray, Earl of Dunmore and Virginia governor, who two months earlier stated that if forced to react against rebellion, he could rely on 'all the Slaves on the side of Government'. On 8 June Dunmore, compelled by growing unrest, quit the capitol city of Williamsburg and moved aboard the armed ship *Fowey* in the

---

1   Jane Landers, 'Transforming Bondsmen into Vassals: Arming Slaves in Colonial Spanish America'; Hendrik Krary, 'Arming Slaves in Brazil from the Seventeenth to the Nineteenth Century'; Philip D. Morgan, and Andrew Jackson O'Shaughnessy, 'Arming Slaves in the American Revolution', all in Christopher Leslie Brown, and Philip D. Morgan (eds.), *Arming Slaves: From Classical Times to the Modern Age* (New Haven and London: Yale University Press, 2006), pp.120, 146, 180; Quarles, *The Negro in the American Revolution*, p.112.

York River. He soon added other vessels and with a force of 300 white soldiers, Loyalists, and seamen, the governor saw his chance to hit at the rebels and gather black recruits for his small army. One Virginian wrote that October, 'Lord Dunmore sails up and down the river and where he finds a defenceless place, he lands, plunders the plantation and carries off the negroes'. These moves alarmed the insurgent Virginians, particularly when word spread and escaped slaves began placing themselves under the governor's protection.[2]

Following a minor victory over local Whig forces in November at Kemp's Landing, near Norfolk (where two black recruits reputedly captured a Virginia officer), an emboldened Governor Murray issued a proclamation composed the week before. His missive declared martial law and announced his intention to use slaves and indentured servants as soldiers: 'I do hereby further declare all indented Servants, Negroes, or others, (appertaining to Rebels,) free that are able and willing to bear Arms, they joining His MAJESTY'S Troops as soon as may be, for the more speedily reducing this Colony to a proper Sense of their Duty …' Despite rumblings in that vein previously, Dunmore's declaration was a thunderbolt that Virginia and the other, mostly southern, large slave population colonies could not ignore. In addition to the ensuing omnipresent fear of British-inspired slave uprisings, when Crown forces later entered any rebellious southern region, slaveowners often moved their black bondspeople en masse to safer precincts. In those same circumstances, numbers of slaves 'stole' themselves and hastened towards Crown forces' protection. These simultaneous pilgrimages, moving in opposite directions, exposed previously cloistered and vulnerable African American populations to various diseases (of which, more later).[3]

On 30 November 1775 Lord Dunmore wrote Major General Sir William Howe, commander-in-chief in America, 'you may observe by my proclamation that I offer freedom to the blacks of all Rebels that join me, in consequence of which there are between two and three hundred already come in, and those I form into Corps … giving them white officers and non commissioned officers in proportion …'. On 2 December the *Virginia Gazette* published the following: 'Since Lord Dunmore's proclamation made its appearance here, it is said he recruited his army, in the counties of Princess Anne and Norfolk, to the amount of about 2000 men, including his black regiment, which is thought to be a considerable part, with this inscription on their breasts:- "Liberty to Slaves."' Along with the exaggerated estimate of Dunmore's army, there is some question whether the use of that motto was

---

2   Gage to Barrington, 12 June 1775, in Michael Lee Lanning, *African Americans in the Revolutionary War* (New York: Kensington Publishing Corp., 2000), p.132; Quarles, *Negro in the American Revolution*, pp.21–22, 111–112.

3   Quarles, *Negro in the American Revolution*, p.23; Lord Dunmore's Proclamation, The Gilder Lehrman Institute of American History, https://www.gilderlehrman.org/sites/default/files/inline-pdfs/01706_fps_1.pdf; Gary, Sellick, '"Undistinguished Destruction": The Effects of Smallpox on British Emancipation Policy in the Revolutionary War', *Journal of American Studies*, vol. 51, no. 3 (2017), pp.865–885.

true or a bit of Whig rabble-rousing; whatever the case, the phrase was supremely evocative.[4]

As the war's first and largest black-centered combat unit, and a forerunner of later events, the Ethiopian Regiment merits further focus. Some black troops had participated in the Kemp's Landing action, but their first real combat was at Great Bridge where Crown and Whig forces had erected fortifications on opposite sides of a causeway. On 9 December 1775 Dunmore, in an effort to forestall a Rebel attack, sent his own forces against the opposing breastworks. The assault, led by the 14th Regiment of Foot, supported by contingents from the Queen's Own Loyal Virginians and the Ethiopian Regiment, was a disastrous failure. Among the casualties were two of Dunmore's newly-freed slaves, now soldiers: wounded and taken prisoner were James Anderson, hit 'in the Forearm – Bones shattered and flesh much torn,' and Casar, wounded 'in the Thigh, by a Ball, and 5 shot – one lodged'. As a result of this action, Lord Dunmore's troops were forced to abandon the mainland and return to their small fleet, occasionally occupying small islands or isolated, defensible land in the area.[5]

Soldier of Dunmore's Ethiopian Regiment, 1775–1776. After smallpox ravaged the unit in 1776 it was disbanded, ending for the remainder of the war any large-scale Crown effort to arm Loyal black Americans. Artwork by Bryant White (Image courtesy of the artist, https://whitehistoricart.com/)

As a side note, William Flora was a free black Virginia militiaman opposing the attack on the bridge, making this the first-known instance in this conflict of African Americans facing each other in battle.

The following months were spent harassing and plundering waterside Whig properties and foraging for food and other necessities. By late winter 1776 there was a new foe for Dunmore's men to reckon with, variola major, otherwise known as smallpox. Compared to Europeans, the inhabitants of North America were especially susceptible. Even more so were the large southern slave populations, usually sequestered in the locale where they lived and worked, rarely travelling far afield. The men of the Ethiopian Regiment were hit hard, as were other former slaves who made their way to British protection. In the face of the disease Dunmore's forces established a camp on

---

4   Dunmore to William Howe, 30 November 1775, in William Bell Clark (ed.), *Naval Documents of the American Revolution* (Washington: U.S. Government Printing Office, 1966), Vol.2, pp.1209–1211; *Virginia Gazette*, 2 December 1775, p.3.

5   Todd W. Braisted, 'The Black Pioneers and Others: The Military Role of Black Loyalists in the American War for Independence', in John W. Polis, (ed.), *Moving On: Black Loyalists in the Afro-Atlantic World* (New York and London: Garland Publishing, Inc., 1999), pp.8–9. Quarles, *Negro in the American Revolution*, pp.13, 23, 27, 28. Peter Copeland, 'Lord Dunmore's Ethiopian Regiment', *Military Collector & Historian*, vol. 58, no. 4 (2006), pp.208–215, online at https://tinyurl.com/EthiopianRegt.

Tucker's Island, near Portsmouth, where it was determined to inoculate the healthy troops. During that lengthy process they needed a more defensible position, so moved to Gwynn's Island, in the Chesapeake Bay, at the end of May 1776. One British captain claimed that most of the black soldiers had been inoculated while still at Norfolk and were felled by an unrelated fever, perhaps typhus, during the spring and summer. Several others noted that inoculations occurred on Gwynn's Island. Whatever the case, they died in great numbers. In June Lord Dunmore wrote, 'Had it not been for this horrid disorder I should have had two thousand blacks …' By the time the Royal governor abandoned his Virginia efforts to sail north in early August 1776, roughly 300 black men, women, and children left with him. Approximately 150 of those served as soldiers.[6]

Smallpox remained a problem for the remainder of the war, not only for American soldiers, Whig and Loyalist, but particularly for blacks who left bondage behind to take their chances with the King's forces. Gary Sellick argues that the fact and danger of smallpox affected British military policy towards harboring African Americans as the war progressed. Lord Dunmore armed and inoculated ex-slaves in 1775 and 1776, but the British high command failed to support or supply either of his Loyalist units, white or black. After 1776, blacks under British protection, especially in the south, were not inoculated. Instead, once infected with smallpox they were left without care and either quarantined or expelled from the lines. From Virginia to South Carolina hundreds, if not thousands, of formerly enslaved African Americans suffered and died as a result of this policy. One reason for this neglect was the 1777 British decision to not accept armed blacks into the Loyalist military establishment and to expel any African American soldiers already serving. Without any military purpose, armed or otherwise, black men and their families were neglected. By contrast, black soldiers in American service were inoculated along with their white comrades when wide-scale Continental Army inoculation was instituted in spring 1777.[7]

After leaving Virginia in August 1776, the Ethiopian Regiment sailed north to Staten Island, likely disbanding soon after arrival. The members dispersed, some perhaps to a remnant of the 'Company of Negroes,' a labor unit formed in Boston in 1775 and evacuated to Nova Scotia during the March 1776 abandonment of that city. Another organization they may have joined was the only black corps to be officially placed on the Loyalist establishment: with that recognition the Black Pioneers were allotted the same pay, clothing quality, provisions, and other necessaries, and served under the same discipline, as British troops. All other corps partly or wholly

---

6 Quarles, *Negro in the American Revolution*, p.29; Copeland, 'Lord Dunmore's Ethiopian Regiment', p.214; Elizabeth A. Fenn, *Pox Americana: The Great Smallpox Epidemic of 1775–82* (New York: Hill and Wang, 2002), pp.3, 58–61; Douglas Egerton, *Death or Liberty: African Americans and Revolutionary America* (New York: Oxford University Press, 2009), p.72; Sellick, 'Undistinguished Destruction', pp.871–872.

7 Quarles, *Negro in the American Revolution*, pp.112–119; Gregory J.W. Urwin, 'When Freedom Wore a Red Coat: How Cornwallis' 1781 Campaign Threatened the Revolution in Virginia', *Army History*, no.68 (Summer 2008), pp.13–19; Fenn, *Pox Americana*, pp.81–134; Braisted, 'The Black Pioneers and Others', pp.9–10; Sellick, 'Undistinguished Destruction', pp.875–884.

manned by African Americans and fighting for the Crown were privately-organized or considered militia, and did not serve under the same strictures or enjoy the benefits of the officially recognized Provincial Corps. The Black Pioneers were first formed in 1776, mostly with men from the Carolinas and a few from Georgia. The unit went north with Lieutenant General Sir Henry Clinton's forces when they abandoned their efforts to capture Charleston, South Carolina in late July. Unarmed, the Pioneers did menial work, from building fortifications, to cleaning streets, and hauling wood, food, and other goods. They served in New York, Philadelphia (where they numbered 72 privates, 15 women, and 8 children), Rhode Island, and, later in the war, back to Charleston. Many other African Americans labored as individuals or in small groups supporting the British war effort.

There were many irregular Loyalist units containing black soldiers. Perhaps the best known was a band of 'refugees' commanded by Colonel Tye, formerly known as Titus when enslaved by a resident of Shrewsbury, New Jersey. Tye freed himself in November 1775 and went on to lead a group of black and white Loyalists operating from the fortified Sandy Hook lighthouse. He and his men (known colloquially as the 'Black Brigade') harassed local Whigs from early 1779 until Tye's death from wounds in autumn 1780. Tye's 'Brigade' disintegrated after his death. but Loyalist African American partisans, with their white counterparts, continued to operate along the New Jersey coast well into 1782.[8]

British policy towards blacks evolved as the war progressed. Early-war middle-states Loyalist units contained some few soldiers of color, but in March 1777 Sir William Howe directed that 'all Negroes, Mollattoes, and other Improper Persons who have been admitted into these Corps be immediately discharged'. However, there was a post-1777 dichotomy between regiments serving around Manhattan and in the middle states, and those stationed elsewhere in the North American theater. Steven Baule notes that at 'least 29 black drummers, fifers or trumpeters were identified as having served with American Loyalist troops during the war. The majority of those joined after the war moved into Georgia and the Carolinas'. (Loyalist units in Canada, too, had a smattering of black soldiers in their ranks.)

British light infantry with a black horn player, October 1777. For most of the war the British Army relegated African Americans to unarmed service. Small numbers were company musicians (playing drums, fifes, or horns), while the majority worked as laborers supporting the troops. Detail from 'The Battle of Germantown' by Xavier della Gatta (circa 1782), painting executed with the assistance of an officer who participated in the battle, likely Richard St George Mansergh St George, 52nd Foot.(Image courtesy of the Museum of the American Revolution, Philadelphia, Pennsylvania)

8   Quarles, *Negro in the American Revolution*, p.134; Braisted, 'The Black Pioneers and Others', pp.3–4, 10–11; Mark M. Boatner (ed. Harold E. Selesky), *Encyclopedia of the American Revolution: Library of Military History* (New York: Charles Scribner's Sons, 2006), Vol.2, p.185. Michael S. Adelberg, *The American Revolution in Monmouth County: The Theatre of Spoil and Destruction* (Charleston and London: The History Press, 2010), pp.75–92. For more on African American service in Loyalist units and their post-war diaspora see, Braisted, 'The Black Pioneers and Others'; John W. Polis (ed.), *Moving On: Black Loyalists in the Afro-Atlantic World* (New York and London: Garland Publishing, Inc., 1999).

Following the 1780 Charleston siege the Queen's Rangers had four former black Continental artillerymen in their ranks as tailors and musicians. Other Loyalist units known to contain African American soldiers were the South Carolina Royalists, American Legion cavalry, and British Legion cavalry. In New York in spring 1782 the newly-raised King's American Dragoons had six troops of horse, each with two men belonging to the Black Pioneers; the unit's trumpeters were also black.[9]

Up to 1777 some Crown regiments had black soldiers in their ranks. Garrisoned in Boston prior to the war, the 29th Foot had black drummers in most or all of its companies. The presence of these soldiers of color had an upsetting effect on the locals, particularly when the drummers performed their duty during military punishments: as one Bostonian related, 'to behold Britons scourg'd by Negro Drummers, was a new and very disagreeable Spectacle'. A week later the same man noted that, 'one Rogers, a New-England Man, sentenced to receive 1000 Stripes… [was] scourged in the Common by the black Drummers, in a Manner…which… was shocking to Humanity'. Steve Baule notes in his work on the subject, 'Ten black drummers were recorded with the [29th] regiment in April 1774. Three of the original blacks were still present in the regiment in 1775. [J.D.] Ellis identifies eleven black drummers as serving in the 29th during the American War …'.[10]

German regiments also took black Americans into service as drummers, again mostly during service in the south. George Jones writes in 'The Black Hessians' that at least 83 African American drummers and 3 fifers served in Hessian corps.[11] Jones also notes:

> Whereas the majority of black Hessians were drummers, a good number were *Knechte* (servants or laborers). Some of these were further designated as *Packknechte* (sumpters, packhands [i.e., packhorseman]) and *Wagenknechte* (carters, teamsters), and it is not always possible to ascertain what duties the Knecht performed. No doubt, in time of need, such as while preparing for Count D'Estaing's attack on Savannah, all hands pitched in to dig trenches. The 'Moor' John Jack replaced Christoph Schmidt as *Packknecht* on 1 March 1780; and the drummer John Hunter was reassigned as *Wagenknecht* on 16 April 1783 after more than three years as a drummer. Sam of Virginia enlisted for the first time, at the age of fourteen, as a drummer; but three years later, having increased in

9   Braisted, 'The Black Pioneers and Others', pp.3–7, 11–29; Steven M. Baule, 'Drummers in the British Army during the American Revolution', *Journal of the Society for Army Historical Research*, vol. 86 (2008), no.346, pp.20–33; Todd W. Braisted, 'Bernard E. Griffiths: Trumpeter Barney of the Queen's Rangers, Chelsea Pensioner – and Freed Slave', *Journal of the American Revolution* (21 February 2019), https://tinyurl.com/Barney-QR.

10 David Niescior, '"to behold Britons scourg'd by Negro Drummers, was a new and very disagreeable Spectacle": The Army, Race, and Slavery in Boston During the Townshend Acts Crisis' (Rutgers University, 2014), pp.11–12, 19 (https://tinyurl.com/Britons-scourged); Baule, 'Drummers in the British Army', pp.20–33; J.D. Ellis, 'Drummers for the Devil? The Black Soldiers of the 29th (Worcestershire) Regiment of Foot, 1759–1843'. *Journal of the Society for Army Historical Research*, 80 (2002), pp.186–202.

11 George Fenwick Jones, 'The Black Hessians: Negroes Recruited by the Hessians in South Carolina and Other Colonies'. *The South Carolina Historical Magazine*, vol. 83, no. 4, 1982, pp.287–302.

age and size, he reenlisted in the same regiment as a *Knecht*.[12]

Another change in British policy occurred when commander-in-chief Sir Henry Clinton issued his Philipsburg proclamation on 30 June 1779:

> Whereas the Enemy have adopted a practice of enrolling Negroes among their Troops; I do hereby give Notice, That all Negroes taken in Arms, or upon any military Duty, shall be purchased [in some versions, 'for the public service'] for a stated Price; the money to be paid to the Captors.
>
> But I do most strictly forbid any Person to sell or claim Right over any Negroe, the Property of a Rebel, who may take Refuge with any Part of this Army; And I do promise to every Negroe who shall desert the Rebel Standard, full Security to follow within these Lines, any Occupation which he shall think proper.[13]

This declaration publicized the offer of freedom to thousands of enslaved Americans of all ages and sexes, an offer that was to effect British civil and military policy to the end of the conflict and beyond. Clinton also referred to and threatened African Americans enlisted in the cause for American Independence. It is their story, often in their own words, we will now examine.

Lieutenant General Sir Henry Clinton's June 1779 Philipsburg proclamation. (*New York Gazette*, 21 July, 1779)

---

12 Jones, 'The Black Hessians', p.295.
13 *New York Gazette*, 21 July 1779; Braisted, 'The Black Pioneers and Others', p.16.

2

'Numbers of Free Negroes are desirous of inlisting': An Overview of African Americans in the Continental Army

The poet Walt Whitman could easily have been referring to the veterans of the eight-year long War for American Independence when he wrote of the conflict and soldiers of 1861–65, 'the real war will never get in the books ...'[1] Portions of their reality are still difficult to know or reconstruct; interactions among messmates, soldiers' musings on nighttime sentry duty, or what went through their minds standing in formation, waiting, under enemy fire, with the prospect of advancing on the enemy or receiving a charge. As for soldiers of color, what was *their* experience of military service? Were African American soldiers treated more or less as equals by their white comrades? Did their officers deal with them differently than white soldiers? Did black soldiers serve as non-commissioned officers (sergeants or corporals) in any units, Continental or militia? What were their post-war experiences, and did they differ north and south?

Regarding equal treatment, at the most basic level, Continental Army soldiers of color (both African and Native Americans) received the same pay, provisions, clothing, and equipment as white soldiers. They suffered together in times of scarcity and jointly enjoyed the rare times of bounty. Were there difficulties due to officers' or fellow soldiers' personal or race animus? Most surely, but to the author's knowledge such instances were few and far between.[2]

Black soldiers *were* singled out at times. At Albany, New York, 21 October 1777 army orders called for 'The Majors of Brigades ... to furnish

---

1   Walt Whitman, *Specimen Days & Collect* (New York: Dover Publications, Inc., 1995; originally published, Glasgow: Wilson &McCormick, 1883), pp.80–81.

2   For a brief but interesting discussion of the relationships between black and white soldiers see, David O. White, *Connecticut's Black Soldiers, 1775–1783* (Chester, Ct.: Pequot Press, 1973), p.35.

0

Colo. Hay D[eputy]. Q[uarter]. M[aster]. Genl. with Sixty Negroes to be employed as a Standing fatigue Party – they are to be paraded & sent with a Non-commissioned officer to the old Dutch Church as soon as possible tomorrow'.[3] The aforementioned 'fatigue' duties likely entailed any number of onerous tasks. It must be said, too, that the 'Negroes' thus chosen had just participated as arms-bearing soldiers in the just-culminated successful operations against Lieutenant General John Burgoyne's British army.

Daniel M. Popek, author of a groundbreaking study of the Rhode Island regiments during the war, 'found no evidence of racial incidents in the [integrated 1781–83] Rhode Island Regiment. Although [black and white soldiers] were segregated into companies … Fatigue and Guard duty was the same [no matter a soldier's color] … [and] Detachments from the [regiment] were usually integrated'. Based on other evidence seen to date, Mr Popek's statement seems to hold true for the generality of relations between white and black soldiers. Still, this question is by no means considered settled.[4]

To delve further into the issue, let us at look at three wartime incidents in which Rhode Island black soldiers were involved in shootings that resulted in the death or wounding of white men, two civilians and one soldier.

Private Prince Greene, a veteran having enlisted in March 1778, was on guard duty in Providence, Rhode Island, after curfew early on the morning of 10 April 1781. A few locals, chafing under martial law and likely under the influence of alcohol, had taken to harassing soldiers on sentry when they thought they could get away with it. Some details are vague, but we know that Private Greene spotted and challenged someone near his post. Calling for the person to halt and not being complied with, Greene fired and killed outright 23-year-old Edward Allen. Greene was arrested by civil authorities and charged with murder. The death of a citizen at the hands of a soldier would have produced a tumult in Providence, but that the soldier was black and his victim white would likely have added to the uproar. The trial was held in county court four days after the shooting and Prince Greene was convicted of manslaughter. His sentence was to receive an M-shaped brand on his hand and to pay all court costs. Afterwards Greene returned to his regiment, then stationed in New York, and served to the end of the war.[5]

A second shooting incident was hardly as controversial. That involved a black soldier on duty protecting a cornfield in northern New Jersey. On the evening of 20 August 1781 Private John Lewis, an alumnus of the 1780 six months Rhode Island Battalion, challenged a white corporal in Colonel Alexander Hamilton's Light Infantry Battalion. When the man fled Lewis shot and wounded him. The corporal was found to have several ears of corn stuffed in his coat. At a Court of Enquiry Private Lewis was exonerated via

---

3   New York Historical Society, Early American Orderly Books, 1748–1817, microfilm edition (Woodbridge, N.J., 1977), reel 5, item 50, Maj. Ebenezer Stevens' order book (artillery).

4   Daniel Popek to author, 15 October 2015, 10:31 p.m. (email). Daniel M. Popek's treatise on Rhode Island soldiers is, They '… fought bravely, but were unfortunate': The True Story of Rhode Island's 'Black Regiment' and the Failure of Segregation in Rhode Island's Continental Line, 1777–1783 (Bloomington: Authorhouse, 2015).

5   Popek, They fought bravely, pp.186, 487, 817–818.

the testimony of three white soldiers from his regiment. John Lewis went on to serve at the Yorktown siege, but died of illness in December 1781.[6]

One last event, another soldier-civilian confrontation, showed the particular perils free black Americans were exposed to. Private Fortune Stoddard also began his military career with the 1780 six months battalion. Reenlisting in the 1781 Rhode Island Regiment, that December he and a number of other Rhode Island soldiers, most of them ill, were quartered on the first floor of a home at Head of Elk, Maryland. Upstairs a group of seamen, with their captain James Cunningham, were celebrating. Much in his cups, Cunningham descended to the first floor and commenced abusing the soldiers, particularly Stoddard who he assaulted with his fists and 'a small round chair'. Private Stoddard called on the captain to cease and threatened to notify his commanding officer. Connecticut Captain Ebenezer Wales then entered and, learning of the incident, confronted Captain Cunningham who, in turn, threatened Wales. Captain Wales had the seamen ousted at the point of the bayonet.

Cunningham and his men returned the following day, presented themselves to the home's owner and demanded alcohol, which she refused. The sound of breaking furniture drew two unarmed Rhode Islanders upstairs. One was quickly knocked to the floor and Benjamin Blanchard, a white private, retreated downstairs. By the time the seamen had followed him down, the rest of the soldiers were ready with loaded muskets and fixed bayonets. One white private aimed at Captain Cunningham's chest, but a seaman seized the weapon from the soldier, upon which the captain grabbed it and struck the soldier's head. At this, Private Stoddard fired, hitting Cunningham in the groin, a wound that proved mortal.

Fortune Stoddard was arrested and tried for murder in a Cecil County, Maryland, civil court. Like Prince Greene he was convicted of manslaughter and sentenced to be branded, but specifically 'burnt in the *brawn* of the left thumb with a hot iron'. That being done, Private Stoddard was still required to pay court costs, but did not have the funds to do so. He remained confined, and at one point the county government settled on the solution that he be sold into slavery to pay his debt. Fortunately, Lieutenant Colonel Jeremiah Olney interceded on Stoddard's behalf with General George Washington, who then wrote Secretary at War Benjamin Lincoln on 5 August 1782:

I have the honor to inclose you a Letter from Colo. Olney with some other Papers relating to a soldier of the Rhode Island Regiment who has been in confinement in the state of Maryland since last Winter. As it will be extremely unjust and cruel that the Soldier should be any longer confined or should be sold to pay the Charges of his Prosecution I request you to take the matter up as soon as possible and procure his release.[7]

6 Popek, *They fought bravely*, pp.689, 831.
7 George Washington to Benjamin Lincoln, 5 August 1782, in John C. Fitzpatrick (ed.), *The Writings of George Washington from the Original Manuscript Sources 1745–1799* (Washington: Government Printing Office, 1938), Vol. 24 p.467.

Stoddard's case was presented to Congress on 21 August:

On the report of a committee consisting of Mr. Howell, Mr. Clark, and Mr. Osgood, to whom was referred a report of the Secretary at War, concerning Fortune Stoddard, a soldier of the Rhode Island regiment:

War Office, August 10th., 1782.
Sir, By the enclosed papers which I have the honor to lay before Congress, they will be informed that on the 22nd. of December last a soldier of the Rhode Island Regiment killed one James Cunningham, for which act he has been tried by the laws of the State of Maryland and acquitted of murder; but found guilty of manslaughter, and is now detained in jail for costs, which amount to about 24 pounds, which sum must be discharged by the public or he will be sold to refund the expence. This I am convinced would be a real injury to the service; besides it will cost much more than that sum to procure a man in his stead to serve during the war--

I beg leave therefore to submit to the consideration of Congress the propriety of passing the following resolve.

Whereas Fortune Stoddard a soldier in the army of the United States has been tried and punished by the civil authority of the State of Maryland for an offence against the laws of that State and is now kept in custody for the fees,

Resolved, That the Executive of the State of Maryland be requested to discharge the said Fortune Stoddard from his confinement and charge the United States with the fees, and that the amount of the said fees be charged by the United States to the State of Rhode Island.[8]

Congress's decision did not conform exactly with Lincoln's recommendation:

Resolved, That the executive authority of the State of Maryland be requested to discharge from confinement Fortune Stoddard, a soldier belonging to the Rhode Island regiment, confined for costs accrued in a late prosecution, and charge such costs to the United States, transmitting to the Secretary at War the account thereof, in order that the same may be charged to the said soldier, and deducted out of his pay.[9]

It is not known when Stoddard was released from confinement. He never reappeared on the regimental muster rolls, but did return to Rhode Island, residing in Newport, where he married, raised a family, and by 1805 was working as a chimney sweep.[10]

The results of these cases are mixed. John Lewis was treated fairly and equitably by the military justice system. At the very least it is odd that Prince Greene and Fortune Stoddard were allowed to be tried by civilian courts, but perhaps understandable given the high command's concern that the

---

8   Worthington Chauncey Ford, (ed.) *Journals of the Continental Congress 1774-1789* (Washington: Government Printing Office, 1914), Vol.23, p.527.
9   Ford, *Journals of the Continental Congress*, Vol.23, p.527.
10   Popek, *They fought bravely*, pp.325, 534–535, 629, 841.

military be subordinate to civil authorities. That the murder charges resulted in convictions for manslaughter but did not require confinement speaks to some fairness in the juries' deliberations, despite the, to us, barbaric sentences of branding. Whether in fact these were fair sentences depends on finding similar cases that involved white soldiers and comparing the verdicts. Unfortunately, to date we have no such cases available. The most telling and horrifying result of any of these trials is the Cecil County government's suggestion that Fortune Stoddard be sold into slavery to pay the owed court costs. Beyond any other opinions on the matter, no white soldier could be subjected to the same 'solution'.

In regard to African Americans serving as non-commissioned officers we have, first, a September 1779 return of 'Colo. [Christopher] Greene's [1st Rhode Island] Reg.' bearing this note:

> This from its Numbers can hardly be called a Regiment consisting only of 147 Negroes in very bad Order. The Non Commiss[ioned] Officers are very bad which must always be the case as they being white Men cannot be reduced or their places supplied from the Ranks – It were to be desired that the state would keep this Regiment with them & replace it in the Line with one of their state Regiments.[11]

In his study of the Rhode Island regiments, 1775–1783, Daniel Popek found three black soldiers who made corporal, all in the 1st Rhode Island. Those men, Pero Mowry, Prince Limas, and David Porter, remained in that rank, the highest attained by African or Native American soldiers in any Rhode Island regiment, only a short time. Porter was reduced to the ranks after being tried for robbery in February 1780. Mowry and Limas were demoted when the 1st Rhode Island was merged with the integrated Rhode Island six months Battalion in July 1780. The reason for the short-term promotions was that enlistments had expired for several white 1st Rhode Island non-commissioned officers and those vacant positions needed to be filled. With the July 1780 unit merge and company consolidation that need ended.[12]

Only a few other soldiers of color are known to have attained non-commissioned rank. The greatest number were Native Americans, most serving in a special company comprising about 75 men from a number of tribes, including Tunxis, Mohegans, Pequots, and Stockbridge Mohicans, Wappingers, and Oneidas. The 'Indian Corps' was formed in summer 1778 of men already serving with Massachusetts and Connecticut Continental regiments. The company's command contingent included Sergeants Timothy Yokun and Thomas Hikumon, and Corporals Jacob Tusnuck and Aaron Sausonkhok, all Stockbridge Mohicans. A Montauk Indian, Joshua Sampson, was a corporal in Col. Henry Knox's Artillery Regiment in 1776. As for African Americans, Sampson Coburn, noted to be a 'colored' soldier in a 1922 town history of Dracut, Massachusetts, was corporal in Captain Oliver

---

11 NA (US), Revolutionary War Rolls (National Archives Microfilm Publication M246), Record Group 93, Miscellaneous, Returns of Brigades, Divisions, Armies, etc., folder 9, frame 55, 'Return of the Brigade of Foot Commanded by Brigadier General Stark … Sept. 6 1779'.
12 Popek, *They fought bravely*, p.314.

Parker's company of Colonel William Prescott's 1775 Massachusetts regiment. Another black sergeant, claimed, but uncorroborated, is Virginia soldier Isaac Brown. If these last two claims prove true, Coburn and Brown would have been eligible to give orders to white soldiers. Six non-commissioned officers in Captain David Humphrey's segregated 1782 4th Connecticut company are mistakenly listed as men of color in Eric Grundset's work. Thus far, only a few black sergeants and corporals are known, more the exception than the norm.[13]

From the first, black Americans were in the fight against British infringement of the American colonies' rights. On 19 April 1775 Massachusetts militia men of color, free and enslaved, along with their white comrades opposed British troops during the operations intended to seize American arms that ended in a harried retreat to the safety of Boston. Blacks served in Minute companies, as well as the normal embodied militia. To date we have the names of 35 black men present that day, at least 18 seeing combat: one, Prince Estabrook, was wounded while with Captain John Parker's company on Lexington Green. John Hannigan notes that, given incomplete records, it is likely that as many as 40 to 50 African Americans were with the militia on the war's first day.[14] Another was 26-year-old Cuff Whittemore, slave to William Whittemore. A 1907 history of Arlington, Massachusetts recounted a supposed eyewitness account from 19 April:

> Cuff was on the hill with the Menotomy militia [under Captain Benjamin Locke] … Solomon Bownan was lieutenant, and on the opening of the fight at that point … [Whittemore] acted cowardly, and in his alarm turned to run down the hill. But the lieutenant threatened to shoot him with a horse pistol, and pricked him in the leg with the point of his sword. This brought Cuff to his senses and the negro

---

13 Richard S. Walling, *Patriots' Blood: The Indian Company of 1778 and its Destruction in the Bronx* (Privately printed, 2000), pp.6, 9, 30–34; Eric G. Grundset, (ed.), *Forgotten Patriots: African American and American Indian Patriots in the Revolutionary War* (Washington, D.C.: National Society Daughters of the American Revolution, 2008), pp.116, 129, 134, 137, 276, 289, 292–293, 336; NA (US), Pension, reel 2113, Joshua Sampson (W16953); Fred Anderson Berg, *Encyclopedia of Continental Army Units - Battalions, Regiments and Independent Corps* (Harrisburg, Pa.: Stackpole Books, 1974), p.58; George Quintal, Jr., *'A Peculiar Beauty and Merit': African Americans and American Indians at the Battle of Bunker Hill* (Privately printed: 2006), p.30; Lawrence E. Babits, and Joshua B. Howard, *Long, Obstinate, and Bloody: The Battle of Guilford Courthouse* (Chapel Hill: University of North Carolina Press, 2009), p.75; NA (US), Revolutionary War Rolls, folder 13, frames 7–19, 4th Connecticut Regiment, David Humphrey's company, muster rolls, 16 June 1782, 23 July 1782, 6 August 1782, 10 September 1782, 15 October 1782. Sergeants Gamaliel Terry and Edmond 'Ned' Fields, and corporals Phineas Strong, Heman Rogers (Robers), and Jesse Vose (Vorse), of Capt. David Humphrey's 4th Connecticut company, at first thought to be black, were in fact white.

14 John Hannigan, 'How many men of color served on April 19, and from which towns? Were they slaves or free men?' *Patriots of Color*, Paper 4, https://www.nps.gov/mima/upload/PoC-Paper-4-SoC-on-April-19-Final-for-Web.pdf. Hannigan, 'Soldiers of Color on April 19, 1775,' *Patriots of Color*, Appendix, https://www.nps.gov/mima/upload/PoC-Appendix-FINALfor-WEB.pdf. Data gleaned from Quintal, *'A Peculiar Beauty and Merit': Bunker Hill*, and Office of the Massachusetts Secretary of State, *Massachusetts Soldiers & Sailors of the Revolutionary War*, (Boston: Wright & Potter Printers, 1896–1904).

'about facing' fought through the contest, as the colonel [Ebenezer Thompson] said, like a wounded elephant, making two 'cuss'd Britishers' bite the dust.[15]

At the end of the day's action Lieutenant Frederick Mackenzie, 23rd Regiment of Fusiliers, noticed another black participant:

As soon as the troops had passed Charlestown Neck the Rebels ceased firing. A Negro (the only one who was observed to fire at the Kings troops) was wounded near the houses close to the Neck, out of which the Rebels fired to the last.[16]

This detail from John Trumbull's 1786 painting 'The Battle of Bunker's Hill, June 17, 1775' was long thought to portray Peter Salem, one of the many African American participants at that action. The man pictured is actually Asaba, slave to Lieutenant Thomas Grosvenor of Connecticut. (Artwork by permission of Yale University Art Gallery)

Private Whittemore enlisted in the newly formed New England army on 4 June 1775, and fought at Bunker Hill two weeks later. An 1826 book on the battle included this passage:

[Cuff Whittemore] fought bravely in the redoubt. He had a ball through his hat ... fought to the last, and when compelled to retreat, though wounded, the splendid arms of the British officers were prizes too tempting for him to come off empty handed, he seized the sword of one of them slain in the redoubt, and came off with the trophy, which in a few days he unromantically sold.[17]

The Bunker Hill battle took place on 17 June 1775, 16 days before General George Washington formally assumed command of the troops surrounding Boston. The names of 88 black and 15 Indian soldiers who fought at that battle are known. George Quintal, Jr. estimates the total may be as high as 150, roughly five percent of American troops involved.[18]

There are several other mentions of black soldiers at the 17 June action. Aaron Smith was positioned at a rail fence 'strengthened' with bundles of new-cut hay. He told of,

a man at his side, a negro, so crippled by a shot in the leg that he could not rise up to discharge his gun, but he could load and re-load, which he continued to do, both Smith's and his own, and then hand them to Smith to fire, until their ammunition was expended, when he

15 Quintal, 'A Peculiar Beauty and Merit': Bunker Hill, p.201; Charles Parker, Town of Arlington, Past and Present: A Narrative of Larger Events and Important Changes in the Village Precinct and Town from 1637 to 1907 (Arlington, Ma: C. S. Parker & Son, Publishers, 1907), p.197.
16 Frederick Mackenzie (ed. Allen French), A British Fusilier in Revolutionary Boston (Cambridge: Harvard University Press, 1926), p.58.
17 Quintal, 'A Peculiar Beauty and Merit': Bunker Hill, p.201; Samuel Swett, History of Bunker Hill Battle: With a Plan (Boston: Monroe and Francis, 1826), p.24.
18 Quintal, 'A Peculiar Beauty and Merit': Bunker Hill, pp.26, 34, 39–41.

undertook to carry the negro off the field on his back, but was obliged to leave him to his fate ... [19]

Massachusetts Fifer John Greenwood noted another man:

> Everywhere the greatest terror and confusion seemed to prevail ... as I ran along the road leading to Bunker Hill it was filled with chairs and wagons, bearing the wounded and dead ... Never having beheld such a sight before, I felt very much frightened ... I could positively feel my hair stand on end.
>
> Just as I came near the place, a negro man, wounded in the back of his neck, passed me and, his collar being open and he not having anything on except his shirt and trousers, I saw the wound quite plainly and the blood running down his back. I asked him if it hurt him much ... he said no, that he was only going to get a plaster put on it, and meant to return. You cannot conceive what encouragement this immediately gave me; I began to feel brave and like a soldier from that moment, and fear never troubled me afterward during the whole war.[20]

Despite their proven ability African-Americans were early on deemed unfit for Continental service. A 20 May 1775 Massachusetts Provincial Committee of Safety resolution said nothing of free blacks, only 'that no slaves be admitted into this army upon any consideration whatever'. By contrast an October 1775 council of general officers 'Agreed unanimously, to reject all slaves, and, by a great majority, to reject negroes altogether,' while 12 November army orders stated, 'Neither Negroes, Boys unable to bare [sic] Arms, nor old men unfit to endure the fatigues of the campaign, are to be inlisted ...'. Signaling a change of policy, at the end of December Washington told of 'Numbers of Free Negroes [who] are desirous of inlisting,' giving 'leave to the recruiting Officers to entertain them ...'. On 16 January 1776 Congress relented slightly, admitting that black soldiers already contributed, resolving 'That the free negroes who have served faithfully in the army at Cambridge, may be re-enlisted therein, but no others'.[21]

Given the desperate need to fill Continental regiments, the American army began as, and remained, a racially integrated organization to the war's

19 Quintal, 'A Peculiar Beauty and Merit': Bunker Hill, p.37; Andrew H. Ward, History of the Town of Shrewsbury, Massachusetts from its Settlement in 1717 to 1829 ... (Boston: S.G. Drake: 1847), pp.55–56.

20 Isaac J. Greenwood (ed.), The Revolutionary Services of John Greenwood of Boston and New York, 1775–1783 (New York: The De Vinne Press, 1922), pp.12–13.

21 Jesse J. Johnson (ed.), The Black Soldier (Documented, 1619–1815): Missing Pages in United States History (Hampton, Va.: Hampton Institute, 1969), p.32 (citing 'Proceedings of the Committee of Safety of Massachusetts Bay. Cambridge, 20th May, 1775,' Mass. Ms Archives, vol. 138, p.67): 'Resolved, that it is the opinion of this Committee, as the contest now between Great Britain and the Colonies respects the liberties and privileges of the latter, which the Colonies are determined to maintain, that the admission of any persons, as soldiers, into the army now raising, but only such as are freemen, will be inconsistent with the principles that are to be supported, and reflect dishonor on the colony, and that no slaves be admitted to this army, upon any consideration whatever'. General orders, 12 November 1775; Fitzpatrick, Writings of George Washongton, Vol.4, p.86; Ford, Journals of the Continental Congress, Vol.4, p.60.

end. Many observers noted the fact, not always favorably. In June 1776 Pennsylvania Captain Alexander Graydon generally described New England regiments as 'miserably constituted bands' of soldiers, but complimented Colonel John Glover's Massachusetts Marblehead Regiment as 'the only exception …'. Graydon continued, 'even in this regiment there were a number of negroes, which, to persons unaccustomed to such associations, had a disagreeable, degrading effect'. Major General Philip Schuyler in August 1777 wrote of the regiments involved in the loss of Fort Ticonderoga, 'I wish one third of them had not been little Boys and Negroes, perhaps the Disaster we have experienced would not have happened …'. The previous month Schuyler asked Major General William Heath, 'Is it consistent with the Sons of Freedom to trust their all to be defended by slaves?' That opinion is nicely juxtaposed with the situation of New Hampshire Captain William Whipple's slave Prince, a veteran of the 1776 Delaware River crossing, who replied to his master's questioning of his sad mood, 'you are going to fight for your freedom, but I have none to fight for'. Having no answer, Whipple freed him. In a similar manner, in 1778 Rhode Island slaves, African and Native American, were manumitted in return for military service.[22]

On 5 October 1775 John Adams had written Major General Heath about his and others' concerns:

> [I]t makes an unfriendly Impression upon Some Minds, that in the Massachusetts Regiments, there are great Numbers of Boys, Old Men, and Negroes, Such as are unsuitable for the service, and therefore that the Continent is paying for a much greater Number of Men, than are fit for Action or any Service. I have endeavoured to the Utmost of my Power to rectify these Mistakes as I take them to be, and I hope with some success, but still the Impression is not quite removed.
>
> I would beg the favour of you therefore sir, to inform me Whether there is any Truth at all in this Report, or not.
>
> It is natural to suppose there are some young Men and some old ones and some Negroes in the service, but I should be glad to know if there are more of these in Proportion in the Massachusetts Regiments, than in those of Connecticutt, Rhode Island and New Hampshire, or even among the Rifle Men.[23]

Heath's measured reply is significant considering that he seems to have been battling personal prejudice, based on a later remark (given below) he made concerning black troops.

> Camp at Cambridge Octr. 23rd: 1775 … It is not Surpriseing that Jealousies do Subsist, and that Misrepresentations have been made, respecting our Colony by

---

22 Alexander Graydon (ed. John Stockton Littell), *Memoirs of His Own Times* (Philadelphia: Lindsey & Blakeston, 1846), pp.148–149; Johnson, *The Black Soldier (Documented)*, item no. 60; Library of Congress, George Washington Papers, series 4, General Correspondence, 1697–1799, Library of Congress, Presidential Papers Microfilm (Washington, D.C.: Library of Congress, 1961), reel 42, Philip Schuyler to George Washington, 18 July 1777; Quarles, *Negro in the American Revolution*, p.72; Egerton, *Death or Liberty*, p.96.

23 NA (US), John Adams Papers, Founders Online, John Adams to William Heath, 5 October 1775, https://founders.archives.gov/documents/Adams/06-03-02-0093.

some, But Such will be despised, by the Wise the Generous and Brave, who will be rightly Informed before they Censure ... There are in the Massachusetts Regiments Some few Lads and Old men, and in Several Regiments, Some Negroes. Such is also the Case with the Regiments from the Other Colonies, Rhode Island has a Number of Negroes and Indians, Connecticut has fewer Negroes but a number of Indians. The New Hampshire Regiments have less of Both. The men from Connecticut I think in General are rather stouter than those of either of the other Colonies, But the Troops of our Colony are Robust, Agile, and as fine Fellows in General as I ever would wish to see in the Field.[24]

Massachusetts Brigadier General John Thomas had the last word in this line of correspondence. The prejudice he mentions was aimed at the New England army as a whole.

I am Sorrey to hear that any Prejudice Should take Place in any of the Southern Colony's with Respect to the Troops Raised in this; I am Certain the Insinuations you Mention are Injurious; if we Consider with what Precipitation we were Obliged to Collect an Army. The Regiments at Roxbury, the Privates are Equal to any that I Served with Last war, very few Old men, and in the Ranks very few boys, Our Fifers are many of them boys, we have Some Negros, but I Look on them in General Equally Servicable with other men, for Fatigue and in Action; many of them have Proved themselves brave ... [25]

Heath's referred-to derogatory remark occurred in August 1777 in the midst of recriminations following the loss of Fort Ticonderoga. Writing in regard to the Massachusetts troops, he sounds like a man battling his own biases:

As to the ability of body of the men I can not fully determine. The greater part that I saw appeared able, but it is more than probable that there were some men advanc'd in life, and some lads and a number of negroes (the latter were generally able bodied, but for my own part I must confess I am never pleased to see them mixed with white men).[26]

The presence of black Continental troops was noted, often favorably, by foreign observers. In December 1777 a German officer wrote of the American Revolutionary forces, 'The negro can take the field in his master's place; hence you never see a regiment in which there are not a lot of negroes, and there are well-built, strong, husky fellows among them.'[27] The situation had not changed by 1781 when *Sous-Lieutenant* Comte Jean-Francois-Louis

24 NA (US), Adams Papers, Founders Online, William Heath to John Adams, 23 October 1775, https://founders.archives.gov/documents/Adams/06-03-02-0118,.

25 NA (US), Adams Papers, Founders Online, John Thomas to Adams, 24 October 1775, https://founders.archives.gov/documents/Adams/06-03-02-0123.

26 William Heath to Samuel Adams, 27 August 1777, 'The Heath Papers,' *Collections of the Massachusetts Historical Society*, 7th series, (Boston: Published by the Society, 1904), Vol.4, p.148.

27 Letter by an anonymous staff officer with Burgoyne's Convention Army, from Kinderhook, New York, 18 December 1777 Ray W. Pettengill (ed. and trans.), *Letters from America 1776–1779:*

de Clermont-Crevecoeur, of the French Auxonne Royal Artillery Regiment, recorded:

> On 8 July General Washington reviewed the two armies. I went to the American camp, which contained approximately 4,000 men. In beholding this army I was struck, not by its smart appearance, but by its destitution: the men were without uniforms and covered with rags; most of them were barefoot. They were of all sizes, down to children who could not have been over fourteen. There were many Negroes, mulattoes, etc.[28]

Baron Ludwig von Closen, aide–de–camp to French *Lieutenant-Général* Jean Baptiste Donatien de Vimeur, Comte de Rochambeau, wrote later the same month, following the Franco–American Grand Reconnaissance of British dispositions:

> I had a chance to see the American Army, man for man. It is really painful to see those brave men, almost naked with only some trousers and little linen jackets, most of them without stockings, but, would you believe it, very cheerful and healthy in appearance … It is incredible that soldiers composed of men of every age, even children of fifteen, of whites and blacks, unpaid and rather poorly fed, can march so fast and withstand fire so steadfastly'.

As for numbers, Closen claimed, with some hyperbole, 'A quarter of [Washington's army] were negroes, merry, confident, and sturdy'.[29]

For the war's entirety integrated units were the rule, with just a few military organizations containing only black common soldiers. One such was the Bucks of America, a Massachusetts militia company commanded by Boston freeman George Middleton, about which very little is known. Another was Captain David Humphrey's company, of Colonel Zebulon Butler's 4th Connecticut Regiment. Formed at the beginning of 1782 and consisting of African-American privates with white officers and non-commissioned officers, the company seems to have been disbanded and the men dispersed by the following January. Two other companies comprising only black enlisted personnel were formed at the beginning of 1781 when the 1st and 2nd Rhode Island regiments were combined into a single unit. The new Rhode Island Regiment had two 'black' companies, again with white command staff; African-American fifers and drummers served in some of the white companies. The best-known unit, the 1st Rhode Island Regiment, beginning in summer 1778 was composed largely of enslaved African-Americans and Indians promised their freedom in return for

---

Being Letters of Brunswick, Hessian, and Waldeck Officers with the British Armies during the Revolution (Port Washington, N.Y.: Kennikat Press, 1964), p.119.

28 Journal of Jean-Francois-Louis, Comte de Clermont–Crevecoeur (*sous-lieutenant*, Auxonne Regiment, Royal Artillery) in Howard C. Rice and Anne S.K. Brown (eds. and trans.), *The American Campaigns of Rochambeau's Army 1780, 1781, 1782, 1783* (Princeton, N.J. and Providence, R.I.: Princeton University Press, 1972), Vol. I p.33.

29 Evelyn M. Acomb, (ed.), *The Revolutionary Journal of Baron Ludwig von Closen, 1780–1783* (Chapel Hill: University of North Carolina Press, 1958), pp.90–92, 102.

enlistment. (That regiment will be examined in detail in Chapter 8.) Another 'black' company has long been ignored by historians. Captain Thomas Arnold's consolidated company of veteran black soldiers from both Rhode Island regiments was formed in May 1778. Arnold's men were attached to the 2nd Regiment at Valley Forge and went on to fight in the Battle of Monmouth in late June, before marching to join the 1st Regiment at Rhode Island in July.[30]

The matter of slave soldiers begs attention. Rhode Island bondsmen were enlisted in 1778 with the promise of freedom and that pledge was kept. Some slave owners personally promised manumission in return for military service, and it seems most, if not all, kept their word. Other slave-soldiers did not receive such promises and went back to bondage following their military stints.[31]

John Hannigan wrote a focused examination of enslaved soldiers in Massachusetts, and the state's policy, or lack thereof, in accepting their service. While colonies and states differed, the study's findings mirror practices elsewhere. Mr Hannigan poses three queries: 'Was it legal for slaves to enlist in the army? Could slaves receive their freedom for doing so? And did military service function as "practical emancipation?"' Regarding the legality of enlisting slaves, the laws varied from state to state, but any ban was often overlooked. In Massachusetts, the 1709 militia law, in effect until 1776, was silent on the subject. Thus, when fighting broke out on 19 April 1775 both free and enslaved African Americans took up arms and answered the call. These combatants went on to serve in the 1775 New England army, only to be banned by the high command that autumn. That decision was partially reversed, barring enslaved men but allowing free African Americans already serving. In 1776 state statutes had exempted African and Native Americans from the militia draft, but not from service. The following year the Massachusetts legislature decided to augment the state's Continental regiments with militia levies, with no differentiation as to color. The first outright ban of blacks occurred in June 1778 when Massachusetts was embodying militia for operations in Rhode Island. On that occasion 'Indians, Negroes and Molattoes' were purposely excluded, but drafted men were given the option of finding another man as a substitute. One draftee, Nathan Coolidge, contracted with free black Medfield resident James Arcules to serve in his stead. By and large, free blacks were allowed to enlist and slave-soldiers were accepted under certain conditions.[32]

---

30 Charles Patrick Neimeyer, *America Goes to War: A Social History of the Continental Army* (New York and London: New York University Press, 1996), pp.76–77, see also page 191, endnote 54; George Middleton House, 'Boston African–American Sites,' http://www.nps.gov/boaf/site2.htm; NA (US), Revolutionary War Rolls, folder 13, frames 7–19, David Humphrey's company, 4th Connecticut Regiment, muster rolls, 16 June 1782, 23 July 1782, 6 August 1782, 10 September 1782, 15 October 1782; Popek, *They fought bravely*, pp.81–84, 86, 169–178, 209–211, 421–432, 442–453.

31 For examples see, White, *Connecticut's Black Soldiers*, pp.19–27.

32 Hannigan, 'Massachusetts laws concerning the enlistment of men of color in the military' (including emancipation of slaves in return for service, and owners use of enslaved men as substitutes in military service), *Patriots of Color*, Paper 3 (National Park Service, 2014), pp.1–3, https://www.nps.gov/mima/upload/PoC-Paper-3-Enslaved-Enlistment-FINAL-for-web.pdf.

Given that slaves did serve, John Hannigan notes that 'military service offered enslaved men limited opportunities to negotiate their freedom, either with white owners, with local officials, or with army officers'.[33] Among several instances he discusses, the following two serve as examples.

On June 15, 1776, Pomp Jackson, a slave owned by prominent Newburyport merchant Jonathan Jackson, enlisted in Colonel Edmund Phinney's Regiment. Four days later, Jonathan manumitted Pomp, offering as his reasons 'the impropriety I feel... in beholding any person in constant bondage—more especially at a time when my country is so warmly contending for the liberty every man ought to enjoy...' Although the manumission document does not make an explicit connection between Pomp Jackson's enlistment and his subsequent freedom, the timing of the two events only four days apart can hardly be coincidental. In November 1776, Pomp Jackson reenlisted for the duration of the war and served as a fifer in Colonel Joseph Vose's Regiment until his discharge in June 1783.[34]

Another man's case may not have ended in immediately in freedom, but he was allowed to continue as a soldier:

In March 1781, a nineteen-year-old enslaved man named Richard Hobby enlisted to serve three years in the Continental Army. Hobby marched to West Point where he remained until the winter of 1783 when his owner, Jonathan Hobby, appeared in camp to retrieve his wayward servant. Claiming that Richard had enlisted without permission, Jonathan demanded the slave be released from the army into his custody. A military court composed of white officers determined that Richard had legally enlisted and any prior claims on his servitude were secondary to the army's claim on his soldiering. Frustrated, Jonathan Hobby left West Point empty handed and Richard Hobby remained in the army.[35]

In the end the 1783 Quock Walker litigation made slavery all but illegal in Massachusetts. By 1790 the state's census returned no enslaved people in the state.[36]

Many southern regiments, too, enlisted blacks early on with little compunction, and African Americans were a common sight in Continental, state, and militia units from Maryland to Georgia, with some little variation. Judith Van Buskirk writes, 'the state government of North Carolina certainly supported a black man's sanguine expectation of full citizenship by stipulating that *all* men between the ages of sixteen and fifty had to serve in

---

33 Hannigan, 'Massachusetts laws,' p.8.
34 Hannigan, 'Massachusetts laws,' p.5. William Cooper Nell, *Colored Patriots of the American Revolution* (Boston: Territon and Sons, 1855), pp.42–43.; Office of the Massachusetts Secretary of State, *Massachusetts Soldiers & Sailors*, Vol.8, p.685.
35 Hannigan, 'Massachusetts laws,' p.6; Richard Hobby, Office of the Massachusetts Secretary of State, *Massachusetts Soldiers & Sailors*, Vol.8, p.21; LOC, Washington Papers, series 4, 'Proceedings of a Court of Inquiry', 3 February 1783; LOC, Washington Papers, series 4, David Humphreys to Jonathan Hobby, Newburgh, 7 February 1783.
36 'Massachusetts Constitution and the Abolition of Slavery,' https://www.mass.gov/guides/massachusetts-constitution-and-the-abolition-of-slavery

the militia. Unlike its neighbors to the north and south, North Carolina did not distinguish between white and black men when it came to militia service'. Despite any difference in militia eligibility, South Carolina and Virginia did allow African Americans to serve as soldiers. Regarding Virginia, Michael McDonnell notes that while indentured servants and slaves were initially barred from enlisting, 'at some point between 1775 and early 1777 … desperate recruiters began allowing free blacks into the Virginia line'. This practice led some enslaved blacks to pass themselves off as free and join the military, with varied success. Admittedly, numbers of black soldiers remained relatively small, but, unlike many New England soldiers of color, it seems most southern black Continentals were free rather than slave. In one instance an intoxicated Virginia farmer, Rolling Jones, was induced to enlist; regretting his action when sober, he sent his slave Tim in his place. Tim Jones (taking his master's last name) served with the 3rd Virginia Regiment, seeing action at the battle of Camden and the Yorktown siege, where he 'lost his leg by a musket ball'. He 'was given his freedom by the Country for the faithful discharge of his duty as a soldier'.[37]

In 1777 Virginia felt the need to counter the use of enslaved men, the General Assembly resolving that 'whereas several negro slaves have deserted from their masters, and under pretence of being free men have enlisted as soldiers … Be it enacted, that it shall not be lawful for any recruiting officer within this commonwealth to enlist any negro or mulatto into the service of this or either of the United States, until such negro or mulatto shall produce a certificate … for the county wherein he resides that he is a free man'. That slaves had served as soldiers was recognized in October 1783 when the legislature passed 'An act directing the emancipation of certain slaves who have served as soldiers in this state'. The law attempted to redress slaveowners' wrongs, declaring that 'many persons in this state had caused their slaves to enlist in certain … corps … as substitutes for free persons … at the same time representing to … recruiting officers that the slaves so enlisted … were freemen … that on expiration of the term of enlistment of such slaves that the former owners have attempted again to force them to return to a state of servitude, contrary to the principles of justice, and to their own solemn promise'. Since those slaves had 'contributed towards the establishment of American liberty and independence, [they] should enjoy the blessings of freedom as a reward for their toils and labours'. As a result, the men in question were to be 'fully and compleatly emancipated, and shall be held and deemed free in as full and ample a manner as if each and every of them were specially named in this act'. It is not known how diligent the

---

37 Judith L. Van Buskirk, 'Claiming Their Due: African Americans in the Revolutionary War and Its Aftermath,' in John Resch and Walter Sargent, (eds.), *War & Society in the American Revolution: Mobilization and Home Fronts* (DeKalb: Northern Illinois University Press, 2007), pp.134, 135, 136–137; Michael A. McDonnell, '"Fit for Common Service?": Class, Race, and Recruitment in Revolutionary Virginia,' in Resch and Sargent (eds.) *War & Society in the American Revolution*, p.108. See also Michael A McDonnell, *The Politics of War: Race, Class, & Conflict in Revolutionary Virginia* (Chapel Hill: University of North Carolina Press, 2007), pp.261, 282, 338, 417–418.

government was in finding the slaves concerned, nor how many were freed as a result.[38]

Massachusetts Brigadier General John Glover's personal soldier-slaves were also returned to bondage. In August 1782 Glover wrote Washington from Marblehead:

I had the Honor of receiving your Excellencys Letter of the 30th Ulto Covering a Resolve of Congress, permiting me to retire … and yours of the 7th. instant Directing my public Servants, and Waggon, to be Sent on to Camp, I have Sent on two Soldiers who Served Me as Steward & Waggoner, Vizt. Wm. Crowningfield, of ye first Massachusetts Regt. & [Toney?] Cartright of ye 4th; my other two are Negro boys, Slaves, & my Owne Property – Boston Black 17 years of Age, & Merrick Willson, 15, boath of the 7th Massachusetts Regt.; they were ingagd. for three years, from Feby 1781; to Send them on to Camp, will be much against my intrest, [they] being my house Negros, and are much wanted in my family; besides this, to be in ye army unless I was With them, will Totally Spoile them for Servants hereafter, I must therefore beg it as a particular favor, your Excellency would please to permit them to be Discharg'd, or if that Cannot be don, & peace not take place soon, and Soldiers wanted the next Campaine, that I may be permitted to hire two men to Serve in their romes [rooms] for the time they were ingagd. – the Horses that Drew my Baggage Waggon were my owne property, have therefore sent the waggon to the Care of Colo. Hatch D.Q.M. in Boston, which hope will meet your Excellencys Approbation.[39]

After being opposed at the war's beginning to using blacks as soldiers, by 1782 Washington had long relented due to manpower needs, and his pragmatism was set in stone:

Sir … In the present State of the Army, and the Difficulty attendg the Recruitg Service in all the States, it is impossible for me to comply with your Request for discharging your two Servants, Soldiers in the Massa[chusetts] Line. Neither, for the same Reasons, can I consent to their remaing longer out of Service. You will therefore please to order them immediately to join their Regiments or send on two others of equal goodness and to the Acceptance of the Musterg Officers, as Substitutes to take their places.[40]

Thus, the soldiers' value to the army, be they black or white, trumped personal need. Glover's final missive was sent 6 October, again from Marblehead:

38 'An act for the more, speedily completeing the Quota of Troops to be raised in this commonwealth for the continental army, and for other purposes', May 1777, William Waller Hening, *The Statutes at Large Being a Collection of all the Laws of Virginia, from the First Session of the Legislature, in the Year 1619* (Richmond: J&C Cochran, Printers, 1821), Vol.IX, pp.275, 280; 'An act directing the emancipation of certain slaves who have served as soldiers in this state, and for the emancipation of the slave Aberdeen,' October 1783, *ibid.*, Vol XI, pp.308–309.
39 LOC, Washington Papers, series 4, John Glover to George Washington, 24 August 1782.
40 George Washington to John Glover, 23 September 1782, Fitzpatrick, *Writings of George Washington*, Vol.25, p.197.

Sir I … am very sorry the Difficulty attending the recruiting service, renders it impossible for your Excellency to grant my request, in Discharging my two Negro Servants. It will be attended with very Great inconvenience to me, in my present ill state of helth, with the almost total Loss of the use of my right arm & hand, to send them on to Camp, haveing no other men Servants in my family; besides this, they being Slaves, its ten Chances to one, if ever I see them again. I have therefore, as your Excellency has been pleased to indulge me in keeping them at home (on Conditions of Sending on two others of equal Goodness), sent a man into the Country to hire two men, to serve as Substitutes, for the time they were Ingaged. As soon as they Can possiblely be procured, Shall present them to ye mustering officer of the State, and no time shall be Lost, in sending them on to their respective regiments … Your Excellencys most Obt Hble. Servant

Jno. Glover[41]

Despite the inclusion and acceptance of African Americans in the ranks and little to no indication of animus from white soldiers, black Continentals were generally allowed only to serve as privates and may have been channeled into such roles as waiter or laborer more often than their white comrades. Added to that, black soldiers lived under the shadow of slavery, with freedmen liable to seizure (lawful or unlawful) by their former owners, or the possibility of being sold into bondage by British authorities if captured.

41 LOC, Washington Papers, series 4, John Glover to Washington, 6 October 1782.

3

Analysis: 'Return of the Negroes in the Army,' August 1778

At the onset of the War for Independence approximately 500,000 African-Americans lived in the colonies, of whom some 450,000 were enslaved. Blacks fought in provincial regiments prior to the war, and roughly 7,000 African-American soldiers and sailors, free and slave, served the Revolutionary cause.[1]

Given that total numbers of African Americans who served the cause for Independence are an approximation, as a counterpoint we have a 24 August 1778 'Return of the Negroes in the Army,' listing 755 black soldiers in fifteen brigades of George Washington's main army at White Plains, New York. The 1778 return not only provides hard numbers for a specific timeframe, but, as well, strikingly illustrates the service of African–American soldiers alongside their white counterparts.

---

1   Hard numbers for black population in the American colonies, circa 1775, are difficult, but a number of sources give a good idea. Perhaps the most recent is Ray Raphael, *A People's History of the American Revolution: How Common People Shaped the Fight for Independence* (New York: Perennial, 2002), pp.311, 355) which gives the following totals: slaves, about 430,000 in the southern colonies, approximately 50,000 in the north. About 10 percent of blacks in the north (5,000) were free as opposed to 3 percent (12,900) in the south. Northern slaves enumerated at circa 6,000 in Pennsylvania, 9,000 in New Jersey, 20,000 in New York, and 13,500 in New England. Following those numbers, 55,000 blacks, free and slave, resided in the northern colonies/states, and 442,900 in the south; total 497,900. See also table of 'Whites, Free Blacks, and Slaves, 1790–1800,' based on the 1790 and 1800 censuses in Egerton, *Death or Liberty*, p.173. Total population (white and black) in all the British American colonies was 2.5 million to 3 million. Robert Middlekauff, *The Glorious Cause – The American Revolution, 1763–1789* (New York and Oxford: Oxford University Press, 1982), pp.28, 32. Tallying the number of African Americans who served in the Continental army, navy, and state militias, and numbers have ranged from 5,000 to 10,000. John Hannigan attempted to enumerate those who served solely for Massachusetts and arrived at a total of 2,100, in his words, 'a conservative estimate that in all likelihood will be revised upwards with further research'. John Hannigan, 'How many men of color from Massachusetts fought in the American Revolution?', https://www.nps.gov/mima/upload/PoC-Paper-1-Final-Version-for-Website.pdf.

Table 1: Manpower Analysis August 1778[2]

Brigades	Present	Sick Present	On Command	Total	% of Brigade Rank and File Strength	Notes
North Carolina	42	10	6	58	4.8	
Woodford	36	3	1	40	3.2	Virginia
Muhlenberg	64	26	8	98	6.8	Virginia
Scott	20	3	1	24	1.6	5 Regts. Virginia; 1 Regt. Delaware
Smallwood	43	15	2	60	4.0	Maryland
2nd Maryland	33	1	1	35	2.0	3 Regts. Maryland; German Regt.
Wayne	2	0	0	2	0.15	Pennsylvania
2nd Pennsylvania	0	0	0	0	0	
Clinton	33	2	4	39	2.8	New York
Parsons	117	12	19	148	8.6	Connecticut
Huntington	56	2	4	62	4.7	Connecticut
Nixon	26	0	1	27	1.6	Mass., including 1 militia levy regt.
Patterson	64	13	12	89	5.7	Massachusetts
Late Learned	34	4	8	46	3.9	Massachusetts
Poor	16	7	4	27	1.8	3 Regts. New Hampshire; 2nd Canadian Regt.
Total	586	98	71	755	3.56	21,209 army rank and file total

Notes to Table:

Percentage of black soldiers among the rank and file in each brigade listed is given in Richard S. Walling, *Men of Color at the Battle of Monmouth, June 28, 1778: The Role of African Americans and Native Americans at Monmouth* (Hightstown, N.J.: Longstreet House, 1994), pp.26–27. Unfortunately, Mr Walling's proportions are incorrect and also do not include Scott's Brigade. He also erroneously gives the proportion of blacks in the 2nd Pennsylvania Brigade as six percent when that brigade in fact had none at all. The recalculated figures here are based on the following brigade rank and file strengths (from a strength return (dated 29–30 August 1778) calculated by taking total regimental strength and subtracting the numbers of field, company, and staff officers): North Carolina, 1207 rank and file; Woodford, 1263; Muhlenberg, 1444; Scott, 1476; Smallwood, 1493; 2nd Maryland, 1723; Wayne, 1219; 2nd Pennsylvania, 1072; Clinton, 1384; Parsons, 1717; Huntington, 1318; Nixon, 1667; Patterson, 1560; Late Learned, 1183; Poor, 1483.

While the August 1778 return does not include black soldiers sick absent, sick absent numbers are included in total brigade strengths above. If sick absent totals in each brigade are deducted, percentages of black soldiers in each brigade are as follows: North Carolina, 6.5%; Woodford, 4%; Muhlenberg, 8.5%; Scott, 2%; Smallwood, 5%; 2nd Maryland, 2.3%; Wayne, 0.18%; 2nd Pennsylvania, 0%; Clinton, 3.4%; Parsons, 9.3%; Huntington, 5.5%; Nixon, 2%; Patterson, 6.3%; Late Learned, 4.3%; Poor, 2.3%. New overall strength for fifteen brigades, 17,981; revised proportion of black soldiers in fifteen brigades, 4.2%.[3]

New Jersey and Rhode Island are the only states not represented that had units serving with Washington's army. The number of blacks serving in New Jersey's four Continental regiments is uncertain, but likely no more than 40, possibly as few as 20. Rhode Island had just reconstituted one of its regiments, filling it with approximately 180 black soldiers, mostly former slaves, black and Indian.

---

2   LOC, Washington Papers, series 4, 'Return of the Negroes in the Army,' 24 August 1778.

3   Charles H. Lesser, *Sinews of Independence: Monthly Strength Reports of the Continental Army* (Chicago, Il. and London: The University of Chicago Press, 1976), pp.80–81.

All the brigades listed in the table were integrated organizations; the only segregated unit having only African American privates (with white officers and non-commissioned personnel) was the newly re-formed 1st Rhode Island Regiment, then serving in its home state. Reciprocally, the only purposely segregated whites-only unit was the 2nd Rhode Island Regiment, after Capt. Thomas Arnold's company of black privates was transferred to the 1st Rhode Island in July 1778. (These units are examined in-depth later in this study.)

Comparing northern and southern brigades provide additional insights on numbers of African Americans in the ranks. Two southern brigades ranked among the top four with the highest average numbers of African Americans per regiment.

Average Number of Black Soldiers Per Regiment Within Each Brigade (In descending order)
(At this time 8 companies per regiment)

(N) Northern brigade; (S) Southern brigade
(N) Parsons (3rd, 4th, 6th, 8th Regts.) Ct.
    average of 37 black soldiers per regiment
(S) North Carolina (1st and 2nd Regts.)
    average of 29 black soldiers per regiment
(N) Patterson (10th, 11th, 12th, 14th Regts.) Mass.
    average of 22.25 black soldiers per regiment
(S) Muhlenberg (1st/5th/9th, 14th Regts., Grayson's Additional, and 1st & 2nd State Regts.) Va.
    average of 19.5 black soldiers per regiment or battalion
(N) Huntington (1st, 2nd, 5th, 7th Regts.) Ct.
    average of 15.5 black soldiers per regiment
(N) Late Learned (2nd, 8th, 9th) Mass.
    average of 15.3 black soldiers per regiment
(S) Smallwood (1st, 3rd, 5th, and 7th Regts.), Md.
    average of 15 black soldiers per regiment
(S) Woodford (2nd/6th, 3rd/7th, 11th/15th Regts.) Va.
    average of 13 black soldiers per regiment or battalion
(N) Clinton (1st, 2nd, 4th, and 5th Regts.), N.Y.
    average of 9.75 black soldiers per regiment
(S) 2nd Maryland (2nd, 4th, 6th Md. and German Regt.)
    average of 8.75 black soldiers per regiment
(S) Scott (4th/8th/12th, 10th Va. and Delaware Regts.)
    average of 8 black soldiers per regiment
(N) Nixon ((3rd, 5th, 6th Mass. and Wood's Mass. Militia Levy Regt.)
    average of 6.75 black soldiers per regiment
(N) Poor (1st, 2nd, 3rd N.H. and 2nd Canadian Regt.)
    average of 6.75 black soldiers per regiment or battalion

(Note: The two Pennsylvania brigades are not included, as they contain so few black soldiers.)

A New England brigade had the highest percentage of black soldiers, but of the six brigades (of 15) reporting the highest proportions, again, three were from southern states:

- Parsons' (Connecticut) 8.6 % of rank and file
- Muhlenberg's (Virginia) 6.8 % of rank and file
- Patterson's (Massachusetts) 5.7 % of rank and file
- North Carolina 4.8 % of rank and file
- Huntingdon (Connecticut) 4.7 % of rank and file
- Smallwood (Maryland) 4 % of rank and file

For comparison, the estimate of blacks, free and enslaved, in 1775 was 41 percent of the Lower South's population, and 37 percent for the Upper South (see table below). By contrast, the Mid-Atlantic states' black population was approximately six percent, and New England's was three percent of their regional population.

Table 2: White and Black Population by Region, 1775 (in percentages)[4]

	White	Black	Regional Population as a % of Total
Lower-South	59	41	17
Upper-South	63	37	31
Mid-Atlantic	94	6	24
New England	97	3	26
West	83	17	1
Total Population	79%	21%	100%
Population in Millions	1.94	0.52	2.46

Lower South: Georgia, South Carolina, North Carolina. Upper South: Virginia, Maryland, Delaware.
Mid-Atlantic: Pennsylvania, New Jersey, New York. New England: Connecticut, Rhode Island, Massachusetts, New Hampshire, (Vermont). West: Kentucky, Tennessee.

Note: 1775 interpolated from 1770 and 1780 figures. Percentages do not add to 100 because of rounding.

Total estimated population for those regions in 1780, the closest year for which we have information, is as follows: Lower South, 506,209; Upper South, 828,863; Mid-Atlantic, 678,133; New England, 616,076 (no information for the West in 1780). If the 1775 percentages held true, the number of blacks in 1780 would have been 207,546 for the Lower South, for the Upper South 306,679; Mid-Atlantic, 40,688; New England, 18,482. With the exception of New England, these figures are near matches to the 1780 estimates (see following table).

4   James T. Lemon, 'Colonial America in the Eighteenth Century,' in Robert D. Mitchell, and Paul A. Groves, (eds.), *North America: The Historical Geography of a Changing Continent* (Totowa, New Jersey: Rowman and Littlefield, 1987), pp.121–146.

Table 3: Black (Free and Enslaved), and White Population, 1780 (estimate)[5]

	State	Population	Black	Black as %	White	White as %
North	New York	210,701	21,054	10	189,645	90.0
	New Jersey	139,627	10,460	7.5	129,167	92.5
	Pennsylvania	327,805	7,855	2.4	319,950	97.6
	Middle States Total	**678,133**	**39,369**	**5.8**	**638,762**	**94.2**
	Connecticut	206,701	5,885	2.8	200,816	97.2
	Rhode Island	52,946	2,671	5	50,275	95.0
	New Hampshire	87,802	541	0.6	87,261	99.4
	Massachusetts	268,627	4,822	1.8	263,805	98.2
	New England Total	**616,076**	**13,919**	**2.3**	**602,157**	**97.7**
	North Total	**1,294,209**	**53,288**	**4.1**	**1,240,291**	**95.9**
South	Virginia	538,004	220,582	41	317,422	59.0
	Maryland	245,475	80,515	32.8	164,959	67.2
	Delaware	45,385	2,996	6.6	42,389	93.4
	Upper South Total	**828,864**	**304,093**	**36.7**	**524,770**	**63.3**
	North Carolina	270,138	91,000	33.7	179,138	66.3
	South Carolina	180,000	97,000	53.9	83,000	46.1
	Georgia	56,071	20,831	37.2	35,240	62.8
	Lower South Total	**506,209**	**208,831**	**41.3**	**297,378**	**58.7**
	South Total	**1,335,072**	**512,924**	**38.4**	**822,148**	**61.6**

If we assume the 1790 percentages of nonwhite free and enslaved people apply to those in 1780, we come up with the following proportions:

Table 4: 1780 Percentages of Nonwhite Free and Enslaved American People (Based on 1780 Population Estimates)[6]

			Nonwhite Free		Nonwhite Enslaved	
	State	Black	Number	Percentage	Number	Percentage
North	New Hampshire	541	433	80	108	20
	Massachusetts	4,882	2,465	*	2,357	*
	Connecticut	5,885	3,009	51.1	2,876	48.9
	Rhode Island	2,671	2,095	78.4	576	21.6
	New York	21,054	3,810	18.1	17,244	91.9
	New Jersey	10,460	2,037	19.5	8,423	80.5
	Pennsylvania	7,855	5,011	63.8	2,844	36.2
South	Delaware	2,996	931	30.5	2,083	69.5
	Maryland	80,515	5,833	7.2	74,682	92.8
	Virginia	222,582	9,297	4.2	211,285	95.8
	North Carolina	91,000	4,336	4.8	86,664	95.2
	South Carolina	97,000	1,605	1.7	95,395	98.3
	Georgia	20,831	280	1.3	20,515	98.7
Total		**568,272**	**41,142**	**7.2**	**525,052**	**92.8**

Note to Table:
* Massachusetts figures estimated using using 1790 Connecticut percentages.

---

5   Terry Bouton, University of Maryland, Baltimore County, http://userpages.umbc.edu/~bouton/History407/SlaveStats.htm
6   1790 census, 'Population of the Original Thirteen Colonies, selected years by type,' EH,net (Economic History Association) https://eh.net/encyclopedia/slavery-in-the-united-states/.

Comparing these estimated statistics with those from the August 1778 army 'Return of the Negroes' we see the known Northern brigade percentages are significantly lower than the 1780 state proportions of free nonwhite citizens, while for two southern brigades (Virginia, and North Carolina), the opposite is true.

One final comment on black soldier numbers. With available research several resources are lacking. Unlike eyewitness accounts available for Washington's main army, to date none have been found specifically commenting on the presence of black soldiers in southern regiments at any period of the war. Luckily, we know that relatively sizeable numbers did serve thanks to muster rolls, pension accounts, and the August 1778 return of brigades. Additionally, in the years after 1778, we have no certain idea of numbers for black Continentals, north or south, but several suppositions can be made based on information at hand. From known trends and available sources, it seems likely the number and/or proportion of black citizens, and perhaps numbers of slaves or former slaves, serving in Continental regiments, grew as the war went on. Manpower shortfalls became more troublesome, and many states increasingly relied on the draft of short-term soldiers serving terms from as low as six to as high as 18 months. Similarly, due to poor recruiting returns made worse by yearly attrition, and in the south by heavy losses when Charleston fell to Crown forces, from 1778 onward each state's official allotment of regiments fell. With fewer regiments in the field and those often created by consolidating two or more older units, in the later war years the proportion of black soldiers in each regiment was likely higher in relation to white soldiers, whether numbers of African-American Continentals remained stable or increased.[7]

---

7   For troop shortages and the draft see John U. Rees, '"The pleasure of their number": 1778, Crisis, Conscription, and Revolutionary Soldiers' Recollections'; Part I. 'Filling the Regiments by drafts from the Militia: The 1778 Recruiting Acts' http://tinyurl.com/blz2gjw; Part II. '"Fine, likely, tractable men".: Levy Statistics and New Jersey Service Narratives', http://tinyurl.com/cttrxe8; Part III. '"He asked me if we had been discharged ...": New Jersey, Massachusetts, New York, Maryland, and North Carolina Levy Narratives, http://tinyurl.com/cayayg5, in *ALHFAM Bulletin*, vol. XXXIII, no. 3 (Fall 2003), pp.23–34; no. 4 (Winter 2004), pp.23–34; no. 1 (Spring 2004), 19–28.

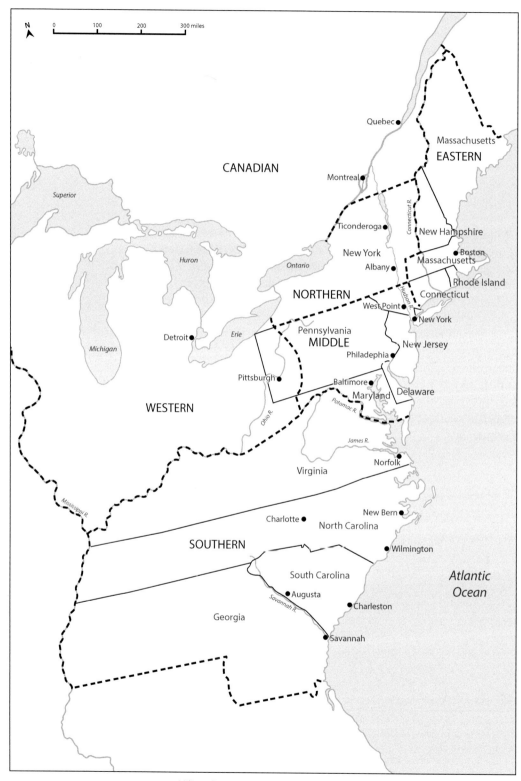

Military Departments, Continental Army.
(Map by George Anderson, based on Robert K. Wright, Jr., *The Continental Army*
(Washington: Government Printing Office, 1984), p.83)

4

Soldier Narratives and Regimental Service

Unit Lineage and Why it Matters

To fully appreciate an individual Continental soldier's experience, especially long-term, it is necessary to understand how the unit, or units, he served in changed over time. Any study of each state's Continental regiments must account for the reduction of the number of regiments/battalions due to recruiting shortfalls, as well as when units were combined, on a temporary or permanent basis.

The number and composition of regiments allotted to each state changed as the war progressed. The war's first two years witnessed the formation of the early Continental regiments, usually enlisted for a single year or less. With the prospective dissolution of most states' regiments at the turn of the new year, Congress enacted legislation in autumn 1776 calling for the raising of 88 battalions with long-term enlistments. Beginning in January 1777 most states' existing units were reorganized and reenlisted, others formed anew. Each state had a unit quota, apportioned according to population. All enlistments spanned three years or the war's duration, in what became known as the Continental Army Second Establishment. There were several exceptions, including six North Carolina and nine Virginia regiments, all formed in 1776, with enlistments expiring in 1778 or early 1779. Besides these, there were organizations like the stateless 1st and 2nd Canadian Regiments, or the German Battalion, the latter formed in 1776 of three-year soldiers in companies enlisted in either Maryland or Pennsylvania. Also included in the new arrangement were 16 Additional regiments, only 13 of which were actually formed, with varying success.[1]

---

1   Robert K. Wright, Jr., *The Continental Army* (Washington: Government Printing Office, 1984), pp.15–18, 51–65, 68–82, 92–93.

Table 5: 1777 State Quotas (Infantry Regiments Actually Raised)[2]

	Regular	Additional (not included in state quota)
New Hampshire	3	0
Massachusetts	15	3
Rhode Island	2	2½
Connecticut	8	1½
New York	5 (quota was 4)	½
New Jersey	4	2
Pennsylvania	13 (quota was 12)	2½ (plus half of German Battalion)
Delaware	1	0
Maryland	7 (quota was 8)	(half of German Battalion)
Virginia	15	3
North Carolina	9	1
South Carolina	5	0
Georgia	4	0

Following the formation (or reformation) of the 1777 regiments, most of which were never fully recruited at the outset, unit strengths gradually began to fall due to sickness, accident, desertion, and combat losses. By 1778 some states' Continental regiments were so small they were dissolved and the men absorbed by the units remaining. In other state lines, smaller single regiments were retained but combined with another understrength unit for field service. As will be seen in the ensuing pages, all the state lines were reduced year by year. By 1781 some state regiments existed on paper, while the enlisted men and officers were apportioned to provisional field battalions. For many southern states, the 1780 capture of Charleston and other disasters shattered their Continental lines leaving them to be rebuilt from scratch. For example, a veteran (black or white) who noted service with the 1st Virginia Regiment in 1780, was in an organization bearing little resemblance to the 1777 1st Virginia. Sometimes early and late-war units with the same regimental number retained some of the same field and company officers, as well as a shared lineage in company personnel. However, such a shared connection cannot be taken for granted; knowing how and why a unit was formed, its field officers, where it served, and whether the enlisted men were wholly or in part short-term levies or long-term soldiers, tells us much about the experience of the men who served with it.

1775 Regiments of Foot and the 1777 Additional Regiments

There were at least two instances when missteps were made with regard to unit designations or regimental formation. One of these cases did in fact add a number of regiments to the Continental contingent, and those units are important in any discussion of the Continental Army.

---

2   Wright, *Continental Army*, p.93.

The 1775 New England Army began forming in late April of that year, and by the time George Washington, the newly appointed commander-in-chief from Virginia, assumed command the various provincial regiments were already at least partially organized and many in service. Wishing to recognize the Continental Congress's adoption of the already-formed army, he asked that body to determine the seniority of the existing units and re-number them accordingly without regard to state affiliation. Only regiments assigned to the army around Boston were to be assigned numbers, leaving out any units serving in the northern department or to the southward. Congress formed a special Board who completed their work on 20 August. In all 39 regiments were affected (28 from Massachusetts, five from Connecticut, and three each from New Hampshire and Rhode Island). Colonel James Frye's Massachusetts Regiment became the 1st Regiment of Foot and Colonel Charles Webb's Connecticut Regiment the 39th Regiment of Foot. All in all, this was well-intentioned but doomed to go by the wayside as the same numbering and naming system was used in the British Army. The new numbers were used only occasionally in army orders, but on army returns units continued to be listed by their commanders' names with no other designation.[3]

On 2 September 1776 Congress passed a resolution reorganizing the Continental Army based on long-term enlistments and revising each state's unit allotment. This statute became known as the 88-battalion resolve and formed the army's basic structure for the rest of the conflict. At General Washington's request at the end of the year 16 additional foot regiments were added, as well as five artillery regiments and four regiments of light dragoons. While each of the added units had an affiliated state to recruit from those states generally had no responsibility for supplying clothing or equipment, they having to come from Congress and Continental stores. Artillery and cavalry, being specialized units and crucial to military operations, seem to have been relatively well taken care of. The foot regiments were catch-as-catch-can, depending largely on the ingenuity of their commanding officers. While Colonel Henry Jackson's and Samuel Webb's Additional Regiments were well-run and equipped, others such as David Forman's and William Grayson's suffered from poor supply, lack of manpower, or both. Here, then, are the sixteen Additional regiments, with state affiliations, plus some miscellaneous organizations.[4]

- Col. David Forman's Regiment (New Jersey)
- Col. Nathaniel Gist's Regiment (Maryland and Virginia)

---

3   General orders, 5 August, 25 August, and 5 September 1775, Fitzpatrick, *Writings of George Washington*, Vol.3, pp.402, 472, 448; Harold L. Peterson, *The Book of the Continental Soldier* (Harrisburg, Pa.: Stackpole Company, 1968), p.256; 'Massachusetts Bay Provincial Regiments, 1775', http://www.wikitree.com/wiki/Category:Massachusetts_regiments_of_the_Continental_Army; 'Connecticut Provincial Regiments, 1775', https://en.wikipedia.org/wiki/Connecticut_Line; NA (US), Revolutionary War Rolls, Army returns (Jul 19, 1775–Dec 1782), folder 137, frame 28, 'Returns of the Army under General Washington)', 18 November 1775.

4   Wright, *Continental Army*, pp.91–107, 215–216, 238, 303, 317–318, 319–325, 335–342 (artillery).

- Col. William Grayson's Regiment (Maryland, and Virginia)
- Col. Thomas Hartley's Regiment (Maryland and Pennsylvania)
- Col. David Henley's Regiment (Massachusetts and New Hampshire)
- Col. Henry Jackson's Regiment (Massachusetts)
- Col. William Lee's Regiment (Massachusetts)
- Col. William Malcolm's Regiment (New Jersey and New York)
- Col. John Patton's Regiment (New Jersey and Pennsylvania)
- Col. Moses Rawlings' Regiment (formerly the Maryland and Virginia Rifle Regiment)
- Col. Abraham Sheppard's Regiment (North Carolina)
- Col. Henry Sherburne's Regiment (Connecticut and Rhode Island)
- Col. Oliver Spencer's Regiment (New Jersey and Pennsylvania)
- Col. Charles Thruston's Regiment (Virginia)
- Col. Seth Warner's Regiment (New York/Vermont)
- Col. Samuel Webb's Regiment (Connecticut)

Plus, the German Regiment (Maryland and Pennsylvania, eventually transferred wholly to Maryland's care) and the 1st and 2nd Canadian Regiments (Unaffiliated with any state).

There are many units that must be left unremarked in an abbreviated study such as this. They range from independent companies, many of which entered Continental service as part of a larger organization, to mixed cavalry and infantry legions, such as those commanded by Colonel Charles Armand-Tuffin, Marquis de La Rouerie, and Lieutenant Colonel Henry 'Light Horse Harry' Lee.[5]

Commentary: Veterans' Pension Accounts

To gain additional insight into soldiers' service and experiences this study makes extensive use of black veterans' pension narratives. Despite the vicissitudes of remembering, it is remarkable how much some of these veterans did recollect, and, when verifiable, the proportion of events and details recalled quite accurately. Carefully evaluated pension depositions can be invaluable and are often the only way we get to 'hear' these now voiceless men and women speak in their own words.[6]

---

5   Wright, *Continental Army*, pp.347–349.
6   African American northern veterans' pensions were largely found via gleaning applicants listed in Grundset, *Forgotten Patriots*, supplemented by Ancestry Search, U.S., Revolutionary War Pension and Bounty-Land-Warrant Application Files, 1800–1900, https://search.ancestry.com/search/db.aspx?dbid=1995. Grundset's work is an excellent resource, but it did become apparent by doing a first search on Ancestry that some black veterans were not listed as such. The initial search was for given names generally linked to 18th century black Americans, such as Africa, Boston, Brister, Caesar, Cato, Cicero, Cuff, Fortune, Liberty, London, Nero, Pomp, Pompey, Prince, Samson, Sampson, Scipio, Tertius, Titus. Some of these names, such as Prince and Titus, returned white veterans as well; some accounts were gleaned using this method, but, given that glitch and that many black veterans had names indiscernible from their white brethren, switched to the DAR study. For a good resource of regional names associated with black Americans, free and enslaved, see, George Quintal, Jr., *'A Peculiar Beauty and Merit': African Americans and*

John C. Dann, editor of *The Revolution Remembered: Eyewitness Accounts of the War for Independence*, noted:

> To qualify for a pension under the 1832 act, a soldier had to indicate in his application the time and place of service, the names of units and officers, and engagements in which he had participated. The narrative was presented and sworn to in a court of law, and it had to be supported by the statements of two or more character witnesses ... The regulations governing applications under the 1832 act urged that veterans lacking strong documentary evidence or the testimony of contemporary witnesses submit "a very full account" of their service.
>
> A relatively small percentage of the applicants wrote out narratives themselves. In many cases the soldier would go to the courthouse and tell his story to a clerk or court reporter. Some of them seem to have presented their stories in open court ... Many others went to a lawyer, related their experiences, and attested to the narratives in court. The 1832 act also encouraged the multiplication of pension agents who sought out veterans, took down narratives, and filled out applications as a regular business. In reality, then, the pension application process was one of the largest oral history projects ever undertaken, with thousands of veterans being interviewed.[7]

Note: Further discussion of veterans' pension legislation is included in Chapter 18.

American Indians at the Battle of Bunker Hill (Privately printed: 2006), 22; lists 108 names connected to New England black inhabitants. Most of the southern pensions used were found at the fully searchable website, Southern Campaign Revolutionary War Pension Statements & Rosters (http://www.southerncampaign.org/pen/). Soldiers' pension records accounts may also be sought by name via *Index of Revolutionary War Pension Applications in the National Archives* (Washington, D.C.: Government Printing Office, 1976). Copies of depositions and related materials are in National Archives Microfilm Publication M804 (2,670 reels), Record Group 15, National Archives Building, Washington, D.C. Microfilmed copies are housed at the David Library of the American Revolution, Washington Crossing, Pa., or available online at https://www.fold3.com/.

7   John C. Dann (ed.), *The Revolution Remembered: Eyewitness Accounts of the War for Independence* (Chicago: The University of Chicago Press, 1980), Introduction, p.xvii.

5

Massachusetts: 'The Person of this … Negro Centers a Brave & gallant Soldier'

Note: Soldiers' identities as men of colour are crucial to this study. In many cases, personal descriptions are given in the narrative or are evident from the context. In cases where their identity is not clear, a brief description is posted at first mention of the soldier's name in the associated page note.

Immediately following the 19 April 1775 actions at Lexington and Concord, the Massachusetts Provincial Congress authorized a voluntary force of over 13,000 soldiers, at the same time asking New Hampshire, Connecticut, and Rhode Island to contribute to a 30,000-man New England army. With that the stage was set for a siege of British-held Boston, and the inception of the Continental Army. That year Massachusetts fielded 27 regiments, with men enlisting for eight months; they were initially numbered and in August they were assigned totally different numeric designations but, by and large, were known by the name of their commanders (i.e., Ward's Regiment, Thomas's Regiment, etc.). The Massachusetts regiments were renumbered and designated Continental regiments for the 1776 campaign, but again were filled with only short-term men, with one-year enlistments. The 3rd, 4th, 6th, 7th, 12th, 13th, 14th, 15th, 16th, 18th, 21st, 23rd, 24th, 25th, 26th, and 27th Continental regiments were all recruited in Massachusetts. It is difficult to link 1775 regiments to their counterparts of the year following, as the 1776 regiments were built on components of various previously existing Massachusetts units. For example, the 3rd Continental Regiment comprised the remains of Learned's and Danielson's 1775 regiments, one company of Cotton's Regiment, and was commanded by Colonel Ebenezer Learned. Many of the 1776 regiments served with Washington's main army, others went north to oppose a British invasion via Canada. Some of the latter marched to Pennsylvania during the December 1776 military and political crisis in time to participate in the Battles of First and Second Trenton, and Princeton.[1]

---

1   Wright, *Continental Army*, pp.216–224; 'Massachusetts Line,' https://en.wikipedia.org/wiki/Massachusetts_Line.

The 1777 army reorganization assigned to Massachusetts 15 regiments, plus three additional regiments, the latter to be recruited wholly or in part in that state. The 1777 Massachusetts Continental regiments were not at first numbered, but, again, known by their commanders' names. Not until August 1779 did they receive official numerical designations. Once again, unit lineage is difficult to trace; Colonel Joseph Vose's Regiment (designated the 1st Massachusetts in 1779), in 1777 was formed from the 6th Continental Regiment of 1775, and part of the 18th Continental Regiment. In July 1780 Henry Jackson's Additional Regiment was designated the 16th Massachusetts, having the previous year absorbed the other two additional regiments. The 11th through 16th regiments were disbanded in January 1781 and their men dispersed to the state's remaining 10 regiments.[2]

In January 1783 the Massachusetts contingent was reduced to eight regiments, and that June the men of the 5th, 6th, 7th, and 8th Regiments were given their final furlough, though those corps were not yet formally disbanded. In November 1783 the four remaining Massachusetts units were furloughed and then, along with all the northern and southern Continental regiments, disbanded.[3]

Massachusetts Soldier Narratives

Peter Salem is perhaps the best-known Massachusetts African American Revolutionary soldier, largely because he is often credited with killing Marine Major William Pitcairn at Bunker Hill. Though not the most senior British officer lost in that battle, Pitcairn was notorious as being the officer in command at Lexington and blamed for ordering his men to fire on the assembled militia. As John Bell writes, Major Pitcairn was likely blameless and, in truth, no one really knows who shot him during the bloody 17 June 1775 battle. A 1787 account claimed that 'a negro man belonging to Groton [Connecticut], took aim at Major Pitcairne, as he was rallying the dispersed British Troops, & shot him thro' the head …'. Early 19th century historian Samuel Swett, likely without access to the 1787 document, wrote of Pitcairn's shooting, 'a black soldier named Salem, shot him through and he fell'. Eight years after Swett's 1818 publication a Worcester historian first claimed a local man as the soldier who shot the British major. While Salem did fight at Bunker Hill, the claim has never been confirmed. Since 1818, other shooters, white and black, have been posited. In the end, several men may have shot Pitcairn that day, considering Rev. John Eliot's 1775 published statement that the major 'received four balls in his body'.[4]

The likely misidentification in no way detracts from Peter Salem's service record. He was out for four days during the April 1775 Lexington alarms, after which he immediately enlisted for eight months in Colonel John Nixon's

2   Wright, *Continental Army*, pp.203–216; ''Massachusetts Line' (Wikipedia).
3   'Massachusetts Line' (Wikipedia).
4   J.L. Bell, 'Peter Salem – Salem Poor, Who Killed Major John Pitcairn', *Journal of the American Revolution* (18 June 2018), https://allthingsliberty.com/2018/06/peter-salem-salem-poor-who-killed-major-john-pitcairn/.

Massachusetts regiment. In September 1776 he again signed up and fought with Lieutenant Colonel Thomas Nixon's Regiment at the White Plains battle, where his company commander was killed. The ensuing January he joined Nixon's 6th Massachusetts Regiment and served through the 1777 Saratoga campaign. In 1779 he was a member of Captain John Holden's light infantry company and likely took part in the assault and capture of Stony Point, New York, on 16 July 1779. Salem was discharged from the army on 1 March 1780, returned to his home state, and passed away in Framingham in 1816.[5]

Salem Poor was another soldier put forward as the man who killed Major Pitcairn, but, again, there is no solid proof. Still, Poor performed some extraordinary action at Bunker Hill, as evidenced by this testimonial signed by Colonel William Prescott, who oversaw the construction of the redoubt and commanded its garrison, and 13 officers from five different regiments. The document was addressed to 'The Honorable General Court of the Massachusetts Bay':[6]

> The Subscribers beg leave, to report to your Honble House, (which wee do in justice to the Caracter of So Brave a Man) that under Our Own observation, Wee declare that A Negro Man Called Salem Poor of Col Fryes Regiment Capt Ames Company in the late Battle at Charlestown, behaved like an Experienced officer, as Well as an Excellent Soldier, to Set forth Particulars of his Conduct Would be Tedious, Wee Would Only beg leave to Say in the Person of this Sd Negro Centers a Brave & gallant Soldier. The Reward due to So great and Distinguisht A Caracter, Wee Submit to the Congress ___ Cambridge Decr 5th 1775 [7]

In addition to Prescott, the signatories were Colonel Jonathan Brewer, Lieutenant Colonel Thomas Nixon, Captains Jonas Richardson, William Hudson Ballard, and William Smith, Lieutenants Joseph Baker, Joshua Read, Eliphalet Bodwell, Josiah Foster, Ebenezer Varnum and Richard Welsh, and Surgeon John Martin. George Quintal pondered the nature of the actions that earned Poor such an encomium and provided a possible answer:

> It is a strong [unsubstantiated] local tradition in Andover that he shot Lieutenant Colonel James Abercrombie of the grenadiers, the highest-ranking British officer to have been killed ... that day. To have performed this act, Salem Poor would have had to remain in the front ranks in the redoubt probably much longer than was prudent ...[8]

Salem Poor's subsequent military career mirrors Peter Salem's. Freed in 1769, in 1771 he married Nancy Parker, a free mulatto woman. Poor served at Bunker Hill with Colonel James Frye's Regiment, though no record of his enlistment survives. He does appear on a September 1775 company return and a December clothing voucher. In 1776 he joined a Maine militia

5   Quintal, 'A Peculiar Beauty and Merit': Bunker Hill, pp.172–173.
6   Quintal, 'A Peculiar Beauty and Merit': Bunker Hill, pp.159–160.
7   Quintal, 'A Peculiar Beauty and Merit': Bunker Hill, pp.159.
8   Quintal, 'A Peculiar Beauty and Merit': Bunker Hill, pp.153, 159–161.

50

regiment garrisoned at the lower end of Lake George, New York. In May of the following year he signed a three-year enlistment in Colonel Edward Wigglesworth's 13th Massachusetts Regiment. Poor was with his regiment during the Saratoga campaign, at the Valley Forge winter camp, and took part in the 1778 Monmouth campaign as well. By the time Private Poor was discharged in March 1780 he and his regiment had been stationed for some months in the Hudson highlands, in and around West Point, New York.[9]

Many veterans applying for pensions provided a mere outline of their wartime service, but even those sometimes contain compelling or poignant details. Some early annuities were issued prior to the nineteenth century Federal acts. Caesar Spragues, formerly of the 4th Massachusetts Regiment, had been placed on the pension list in 1794, he having had 'his left foot shot off by a cannon at Monmouth in June 1778'. Spragues' discharge date was listed as 15 April 1780, which is odd given his 1778 wounding. It turns out he was transferred to the Corps of Invalids after his recovery, and 15 April 1780 was actually the day he deserted from the army. When this was discovered his payments were halted. For the later pension laws, to our benefit, a number of men provided more information than was necessary. Pomp Magus enlisted in Colonel Loammi Baldwin's Regiment in 1775 and served during the Boston siege. In 1776 he reenlisted in the 25th Continental Regiment and implied that soldiers of color were sometimes singled out for menial tasks: 'I continued in said Regiment and proceed[ed] with it in to the [city] of New York, and … being a man of colour myself and some others were left on fatigue there, & there continued until regularly discharged …'.[10] Three years later he was drafted for nine months service in the 8th Massachusetts Regiment, overwintering with that unit. He noted in his pension narrative,

> A few days before the expiration of said term of service I was taken prisoner and carried to New-York and was in confinement for ten or eleven months … When I gave my deposition in April last [1818] of being in the service I had been confined to the house by sickness for three months and was at the time very feeble and did not recollect whether the service of nine months was at the time of taking Burgoyne or a later period. I am now convinced that I served the term of nine months when I was taken prisoner … to the best of my recollection … in February A.D. 1780.[11]

A July 1780 muster roll shows that Magus's discharge date was 15 April 1780. He may have been in the action at Four Corners, Westchester County, New York, where a mixed force of Massachusetts troops was attacked and captured on 3 February, though none of the 8th Regiment companies are known to have been present. It is also possible Magus was captured on 16 April, during the swift assault and capture by German and Loyalist troops of the Continental Army post at Hopperstown, New Jersey. That garrison

---

9 Quintal, 'A Peculiar Beauty and Merit': Bunker Hill, pp.153–156.
10 NA (US), Pension, reel 2261, Caesar Spragues, African American (no pension number assigned); Ibid., reel 1614, Pomp Magus (S33059).
11 NA (US), Pension, reel 1614, Pomp Magus, 'a man of colour', (S33059).

comprised a mixed force from several regiments, including Massachusetts men like Josiah Willard of Colonel Henry Jackson's Additional Regiment, wounded and captured at Hopperstown. Willard was released from captivity the following November and possibly, too, was Magus.[12]

Slavery was sometimes mentioned by black veterans. Prince Bailey wrote in June 1819:

> when I was about eight years of age, I was stolen from Africa, my native country, and brought to America; my native name was Prince Dunsick – but on my arrival I was called by my master's name which was Bailey. By this name of Prince Bailey, I enlisted and served in the Revolutionary War … and was discharged by the same name. I never lived with my old master Bailey afterwards, and resumed my former name of Dunsick.[13]

Cuff Ashport's widow Lydia noted in her 1836 deposition her husband at one time had been called Cuff Mitchell, that he 'was formerly the slave of Nathan Mitchell of … Bridgewater, that he bought his freedom in the spring of the year 1775'. Scipio Bartlett enlisted in Colonel Ebenezer Francis's Regiment in February 1777 and fought at the battle of Hubbardton in Vermont that July, where Colonel Francis was killed. Bartlett added this postscript, 'I further on oath declare that I was emancipated at the commencement of the Revolutionary War – and was a free man during my whole term of service … I am a Black Man – but free – and of the age of sixty seven years'. A white comrade repeated the statement in a supporting deposition; there being no stipulation that soldier-slaves were denied pensions, the fact of his freedom before and during service was obviously important to Mr Bartlett.[14]

No matter their rank, officers wanted and needed servants and that role was filled by both black and white common soldiers. Quamony Quash enlisted in the 1775 eight months service and served as waiter to Colonel Theophilus Cotton for the entire term. He then signed on with the 16th Massachusetts Regiment in late 1780 for three years, serving that time in the ranks as a common soldier. Thomas Haszard spent his entire enlistment as servant to Lieutenant Colonel Ebenezer Sprout of the 12th Massachusetts Regiment, later with the 2nd Regiment, as did Prince Sayward. Sayward was waiter to Major Samuel Darby, first of the 7th Massachusetts beginning in 1778, moving to the 8th Regiment in January 1783.[15]

12 NA (US), Revolutionary War Rolls Muster roll, folder 11, frame 103, 8th Massachusetts Regiment, Lieutenant Colonel Tobias Fernald's company, muster roll, 22 July 1780; NA (US), Pension, reel 2582, Josiah Willard (S44082); 'Battle of Young's House', Four Corners, Westchester County, New York, https://en.wikipedia.org/wiki/Battle_of_Young%27s_House; John U. Rees, '"Had all the Cavalry been in the front … not one man could have escaped …": Hopperstown, New Jersey, 16 April 1780', *Military Collector & Historian*, Vol.65, No.1 (Spring 2013), pp.28–42, https://tinyurl.com/Hopperstown.
13 NA (US), Pension, reel 111, Prince Bailey (W17230).
14 NA (US), Pension, reel 83, Cuff Ashport (W27332); *Ibid.*, reel 165, Scipio Bartlett, (W4010).
15 NA (US), Pension, reel 1990, Quamony Quash, African American (R18097); *Ibid.*, reel 1219, Thomas Haszard, African American (S29213); *Ibid.*, reel 2129, Prince Sayward, 'a man of Colour' (W27467).

Primus Hall (also called Primus Trask), had wartime experiences many and varied, from the Boston siege to success at Yorktown, Virginia. Hall stated in 1832,

That he … was born in the City of Boston on the twenty ninth day of February Anno Domini 1756 in the family of David Walker in Beacon Street in said Boston, and at the a[ge] of one month old was given to Mr Ezra Trask of Beverly in the Cou[nty] of Essex who subsequently removed to the town of Danvers … in whose family he continued to live until the commencement of the revolutionary War, and that forepart of the month of January in [the] year … [1776] he … enlisted in the town of Cambridge … as a soldier in the army of the Revolution for the term of one year in a company commanded by Capt Joseph Butler of Concord … of the fifth Massachusetts Regiment commanded by Colo [John] Nixon. The Majors name was Scammell. The name of the Lieutenant was Silas Walker, and Ensign Potter, Gad Smit[h?] and Wheeler were Sergeants … [he] served the full period of one year … During [his] service … he was at the following stations and in [the] following battles to wit, First at Winter Hill near Boston, the winter of 1776, where were also stationed on said Hill and the vicinity of the same several Regiments to wit, Colonel Hite['s], Colonel [John] Glover's, Colonel [John] Stark's, [John] Graton's and others … after the British troops evacuated that City [7] March 1776 … he marched to New York with the Army, and was stationed in the Bowery and was employed for some time in erecting Fortifications near Byards Hill. About [that] time Colonel Nixon was … promoted to a Brigadier General and his brother, [Thomas] Nixon who was Lieutenant Colonel assumed [the] command of the said fifth Regiment. After this period he was [stationed] on Governor's Island in the harbour of New York, but was [ob]liged to evacuate the same, when the British took possession of [the] Island. He distinctly remembers that Major Walcott was Bearer of a flagg of truce demanding the surrender of the place [w]hich demand was disregarded and a cannonade commenced – that two of the Vessels of the enemy came beating up the narrows and that by General Washington's orders they were taken off the Island and in passing over to New York the Cockswain was killed by a chain shott fired from the *Asia* Man of War belonging to the enemy. Said Primas was after this stationed at the grand Battery in New York, but soon joined the Maine Army at Rattle-[sn]ake hills, and there had an action. After the engagement retreated [to] Harlem Heights and there had a skirmish [16 September 1776] – thence to Miles [Sq]uare and had another skirmish – thence to White Plains, and there had a Battle [28 October] – thence crossed the Hudson River at Kings Ferry, and marched into New Jersey, and was under General [Charles] Lee at the time that General was surprised at Basking Ridge and taken prisoner [13 December]. Then General [John] Sullivan took command, and marched the troops to Pennsylvania, to a place called Bristol and after remaining at Bristol a few days recrossed the Delaware, and attacked the Hessians at Trenton & Burlington and took them prisoners [26 December], the Regiment to which said Primas belonged being station[ed] at the former place when his term of service of one year expired, but [a]t the earnest request of General Washington he volunteered for the further term of six weeks, and during said service he was at the taking of Princetown [3 January 1777], and soon thereafter marched to Morristown in New Jersey and there received an honorable discharge from the Army signed by General Washington and returned home to Danvers in the Spring of 1777.[16]

That was the end of Hall's service as a Continental soldier, but his military experience continued:

… he again enlisted in the fall of the 1777 in the town of Danvers for three months, into a Militia Company commanded by Capt. Samuel Flint of said town and Lieutenant Herrick of Beverly and Colonel Johnson of Andover, and marched to Saratoga to join the Army under General [Horatio] Gates, who w[as t]hen acting against General [John] Burgoyne; that he was in the second engagement between the two armies when the Hessian Brigade was together with eight pieces of British Artillery – that he distinct[ly] recollects the death of Captain Flint who together with L[ieutenant] Herrick [possibly Joseph Herrick] were both killed in said Battle. [T]hat he was standing near his Captain when he received his mortal wound, and caught him in his arms to prevent his falling, but on observing that [he] bled profusely set him down against a tree when he expired immediately. This battle was fought in October 1777 … After the surrender of Burgoyne he with the Regiment marched to Albany crossed the river at that place to Greenbush, continued down the Hudson River on the east side till they arrived at a place called East Chester on the shore of Long Island Sound, when his term of thr[ee] months service expired, and he was a second time discharged, again returned to the town of Darien.

He further testifies that in the year [1778] … he enlisted at Danvers for a further period of three months under Capt Woodbu[ry] of Cape Ann … and … marched with the company to Rhode Island, and was stationed on the North part of said Island oppo[site] Tiverton, and was employed in building a Fort and keeping [edge of page worn] until his term had again expired and he was a third time disc[harged] from service. The French Fleet and Army under Count Rocham[beau] were at Rhode Island [landed 11 July 1780], the French troops being stationed on land above New Port on said Island at the time of his last tour … himself with another coloured man by the name of Manual were detached from Captain Woodbury's company and p[er]formed service with the French Corps of Sappers & Miners, and that the time he performed military duty in the three foregoing tours was nineteen months and a half.[17]

Hall closed out the war serving with the army's quartermaster general:

He further testifies that in the years 1781 and 1782 he served twenty two months as Steward to and under Colonel Timothy Pickering of the United States Quarter Master department, and was with that Officer at Verplan[cks] Point [Westchesterr County, New York], Philadelphia, Baltimore & other places, and was at Yorktown

---

16 Will Graves and C. Leon Harris, Southern Campaign Revolutionary War Pension Statements & Rosters, Primus Hall (Trask), 'coloured man' (W751) (http://www.southerncampaign.org/pen/); copies of depositions and related materials in National Archives Microfilm Publication M804 (2,670 reels).

17 Graves and Harris, Southern Campaign Pension, Primus Hall (W751).

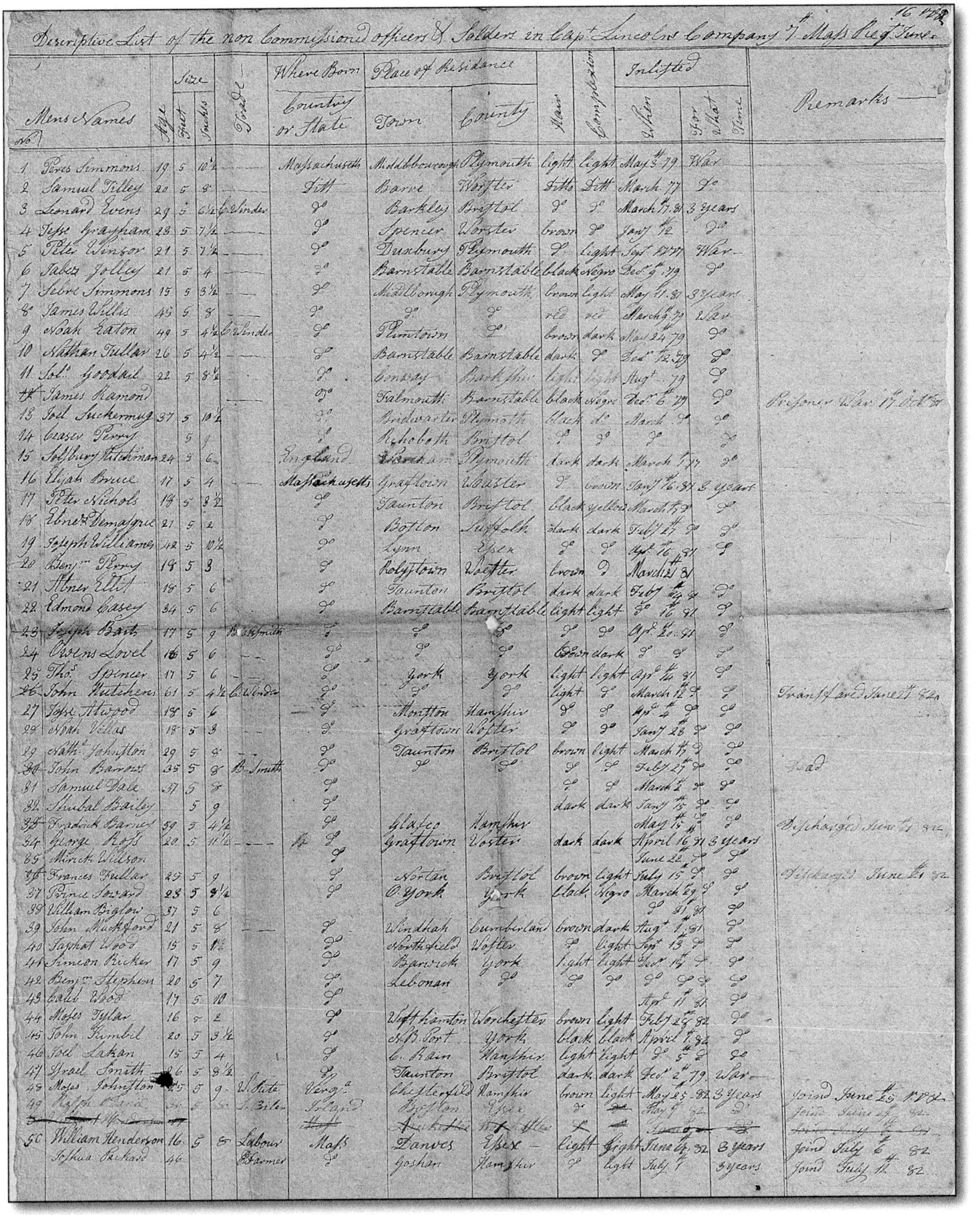

16 172

No. Mens Names	Age	Size (feet)	(inches)	Trade	Where Born Country or State	Place of Residence Town	County	Hair	Complexion	Enlisted When	For what Time	Time	Remarks
1 Peres Simmons	19	5	10½		Massachusetts	Middleborough	Plymouth	light	light	May 3 79	War		
2 Samuel Tilley	20	5	8		Ditt	Barre	Worster	ditto	Ditt	March 77	Do		
3 Leonard Evens	29	5	6½	slender	Do	Barkley	Bristol	Do	Do	March 8 3	3 years		
4 Jesse Grapham	23	5	7½		Do	Spencer	Worster	brown	Do	Jany 82	Do		
5 Peter Winsor	21	5	7½		Do	Duxbury	Plymouth	Do	light	Sept 1277	War		
6 Jabez Jolley	21	5	4		Do	Barnstable	Barnstable	black	Negro	Decr 9 79	Do		
7 Jesse Simmons	15	5	3½		Do	Middleborough	Plymouth	brown	light	May 4 80	3 years		
8 James Willis	45	5	8		Do	Do	Do	red	red	March 79	War		
9 Noah Eaton	49	5	4½	slender	Do	Plimton	Do	brown	dark	May 24 79	Do		
10 Nathan Fuller	26	5	4½		Do	Barnstable	Barnstable	dark	Do	Feb 12 39	Do		
11 Solo. Goodhall	22	5	8½		Do	Conway	Barkshire	light	light	Aug 79	Do		
12 James Ramond					Do	Falmouth	Barnstable	black	Negro	Dec 6 79	Do		Prisoner War 17 Oct 81
13 Joel Suckermug	37	5	10½		Do	Bridwater	Plymouth	black	do	March Do	Do		
14 Ceaser Perry					Do	Rehoboth	Bristol	Do	Do	March 79	Do		
15 Solbury Hutchman	24	5	6		England	Bridwater	Plymouth	dark	dark	March 79	Do		
16 Elijah Bruce	17	5	4		Massachusetts	Graftown	Worster	Do	brown	Jany 16 81	3 years		
17 Peter Nichols	18	5	3½		Do	Taunton	Bristol	black	yellow	March 81	Do		
18 Ebner Demasque	21	5	2		Do	Boston	Suffolk	dark	dark	July 81	Do		
19 Joseph Williams	42	5	10½		Do	Lynn	Essex	Do	Do	Apl 16 81	Do		
20 Benjn Perry	19	5	3		Do	Holystown	Worster	brown	Do	March 21 81			
21 Abner Elliot	18	5	6		Do	Taunton	Bristol	dark	dark	Feby Do	Do		
22 Edmond Casey	34	5	6		Do	Barnstable	Barnstable	light	light	Do 26 81	Do		
23 Joseph Bart	17	5	9	Blacksmith	Do	Do	Do	Do	Do	Apl 20 81	Do		
24 Owens Lovel	16	5	6		Do	Do	Do	brown	dark	Do 81	Do		
25 Thos Spincer	17	5	6		Do	York	York	light	light	Apl 20 81	Do		
26 John Hutchens	61	5	4½	Cutler	Do	Do	Do	light	Do	March 12 81	Do		Transfered June 1 82
27 John Atwood	18	5	6			Houlton	Hampshir	Do	Do	Apl 81	Do		
28 Elijah Vellis	18	5	3		Do	Graftown	Worster	Do	Do	Jany 28 81	Do		
29 Nathl Johnston	29	5	8		Do	Taunton	Bristol	brown	light	March 81	Do		
30 John Barnes	35	5	8	B. Smith	Do	Do	Do	Do	Do	Feby 25 81	Do		Dead
31 Samuel Hale	57	5	8		Do	Do	Do	Do	Do	March 81	Do		
32 Shubal Bailey		5	8		Do	Do	Do	dark	dark	March 81	Do		
33 Fredrick Barnes	59	5	4½		Do	Glasco	Hampshir	Do	Do	May 81	Do		Discharged June 1 82
34 George Ross	20	5	11½		Do	Graftown	Worster	dark	dark	April 16 81	3 years		
35 Minch Willson					Do	Do	Do			June 22 81	Do		
36 Frances Fuller	25	5	9		Do	Norton	Bristol	brown	light	July 15 81	Do		Discharged June 1 82
37 Prince Soward	28	5	8½		Do	O. York	York	black	Negro	March 29 81	Do		
38 William Biglow	37	5	6		Do	Do	Do	Do	Do	Apl 81	Do		
39 John Mackford	21	5	8		Do	Windham	Cumberland	brown	dark	Aug 81	Do		
40 Josiah Wood	15	5	1½		Do	Northfield	Worster	Do	light	Sept 13 81	Do		
41 Simeon Ricker	17	5	9		Do	Berwick	York	light	light	Sept 14 81	Do		
42 Benjr Stephen	18	5	7		Do	Lebonan	Do	Do	Do	Do	Do		
43 Caleb Root	17	5	10		Do	Do	Do	Do	Do	Aug 17 81	Do		
44 Moses Fuller	16	5	4		Do	West Hampton	Worchester	brown	light	Feby 29 82	Do		
45 John Kimbal	20	5	3½		Do	S. B. Port	York	black	black	April 7 82	Do		
46 Joel Lakan	15	5	4		Do	C. Rain	Hampshir	light	light	Do 5 82	Do		
47 Israel Smith	26	5	8½		Do	Taunton	Bristol	dark	dark	Decr 2 79	War		
48 Moses Johnston	45	5	9	U. State	Vergea	Chesterfield	Hampshir	brown	light	May 25 82	3 years		Joind June 1 82
49 Ralph Davis				S. Bilee	Scotland	Brighton							Joind Same 82
50 William Henderson	16	5	8	Labour	Mass	Danvers	Essex	light	light	June 1 82	3 years		Joind July 4 82
51 Joshua Packard	46			Farmer	Do	Goshen	Hampshir	Do	light	July 7	3 years		Joind July 12 82

'Descriptive List of the non Commissioned officers & sold[i]ers in Capt. [Rufus] Lincoln's Company 7th. Mass Regt June 16th 1782' (Image courtesy of the Museum of the American Revolution, Philadelphia, Pennsylvania). Of fifty-one men listed, five (ten percent) were African American: Jabez Jolley, 'Negro', 21 years old, 5 feet 4 inches tall, black hair, born in the town of Barnstable, Barnstable County, Massachusetts, enlisted for the war, 9 December 1779; James Ramond, 'Negro', black hair, born in the town of Falmouth, Barnstable County, Massachusetts, enlisted for the war, 6 December 1779, prisoner of war 17 October 1781 (likely at Croton River, New York); Joel Suckermug, 'Negro', 37 years old, 5 feet 10½ inches tall, black hair, born in the town of 'Bridwater', Plymouth County, Massachusetts, enlisted for the war, March 1779; Ceaser Perry, 'Negro', 5 feet 9 inches tall, born in the town of Rehoboth, Bristol County, Massachusetts, enlisted for the war, March 1779; Prince Soward (Seward), 'Negro', 23 years old, 5 feet 8½ inches tall, black hair, born in the town of York, York County, Massachusetts, enlisted for the war, 29 March 1781.

at the time that place surrendered to the American Army, un[der] General Washington & the French forces [19 October 1781], and went into [the] British Garrison in said town with Colonel Pickering and there assis[ted] him in taking an account of the enemy's specie deposited in the milita[ry] chests ... after the troops marched to the norther[?] and were stationed at or near a place called Rattle snake hill near Newburg in the State of New York he received a final discharge from the Army and in the month of December 1772 [1782] he returned home to Danvers Massachusetts. He further testifies that while serving as Steward in the army ... at a place called Dumfries in the state of Virginia his pocket book was stolen from him containing his several discharges from [the] Army and he has not to this day heard any thing of them, and [th]at he has also lost his last discharge.[18]

Like Primus Hall and other soldiers, at the end of his enlistment term Lewis Shepherd received his hard-earned discharge: 'West Point Jany 20th 1780. Lewis Shepard late of the Eleventh Massachusetts Regiment in the service of the United States's term of Inlistment is expired (he being a good soldier while in said Regt. & service) therefore is discharged ... and has liberty to return home to Scarborough, Massachusetts state'.[19]

---

18 Graves and Harris, Southern Campaign Pension, Primus Hall (W751).
19 NA (US), Pension, reel 2170, Lewis Shepherd, African American (W24944).

6

Connecticut: 'He … entered the service upon condition of receiving his freedom …'

Of the New England colonies, Connecticut was second only to Massachusetts in size and population. The state quickly answered the Bay colony's April 1775 call for more troops, and eventually fielded eight provincial regiments that year. As with the 1775 Massachusetts units, each Connecticut regiment was manned by eight-months men and largely known by its commanding officer's name, with the first being called Wooster's Regiment, the second Spencer's Regiment, and so on. Wooster's, Benjamin Hinman's, and David Waterbury's regiments were assigned to the northern department, while the other Connecticut units served in the Boston siege. In 1776 the state contributed five regular one-year regiments, but these were given national rather than state designations: the 10th, 17th, 19th, 20th, and 22nd Continental regiments were Connecticut's contingent. These units were reformed from the 1775 regiments, in order: Parson's (10th), Huntington's (17th), Webb's, (19th) Putnam's (20th), and Spencer's (22nd) regiments, all of which had served with the main army at Boston.[1]

In 1777 the state's Continental contingent was increased to eight units, designated the 1st through 8th Connecticut regiments. The first five were reorganized versions of the 1776 Continental regiments, with many of the same command staff and a good portion of reenlisted veterans. The 1776 10th, 17th, 19th, 20th, and 22nd regiments became the 5th, 1st, 2nd, 4th, and 3rd Connecticut regiments. The Connecticut line was increased in July 1780 when Webb's Additional Regiment was added and renamed the 9th Connecticut. The state corps were reduced to five regiments in January 1781. The 1781 1st Connecticut was formed by consolidating the old 3rd and 4th Regiments; 1781 2nd Connecticut from the old 5th and 7th Regiments; the 1781 3rd Connecticut from the old 2nd and 9th Regiments; the 1781 4th Connecticut was merely the renumbered 6th Regiment, and the 1781 5th

1   'Connecticut Provincial Regiments, 1775', 'Numbered Continental Regiments, 1776, https://en.wikipedia.org/wiki/Connecticut_Line; Wright, *Continental Army*, pp.233–240.

Connecticut formed from the old 1st and 8th Regiments. At the beginning of 1783 the state's regiments were further reduced by disbanding the 4th and 5th Connecticut and adding their enlisted personnel to the 1st, 2nd, and 3rd Regiments. In June 1783 most of the army was furloughed, never to be recalled to service. The 2nd and 3rd Regiments were then disbanded and the 1st renamed the Connecticut Regiment. That unit was disbanded on 15 November 1783.[2]

Connecticut Soldier Narratives

In order to qualify for a veteran's pension old soldiers needed to recount their Revolutionary service and provide documentation or reliable witnesses. Robin Starr, a 'man of colour', began his career with the 2nd Connecticut in January 1777 and was discharged June 1783. In the intervening years he claimed to have participated in six battles and one siege; 'the first was on lake Champlain' (11–13 October 1776), the others were Danbury, Connecticut (25–28 April 1777), Germantown (4 October 1777), Monmouth (28 June 1778), Norwalk, Connecticut (11 July 1779), Stony Point (16 July 1779), and the Yorktown siege (28 September to 17 October 1781). A comparison with Starr's dates of service and claimed actions shows why pension accounts need to be read with a wary eye. Unless there was another stint he neglected to mention, the Lake Champlain battle was before his military service; the actions at Norwalk and Stony Point were only four days apart, leaving us to wonder which one, if either, he took part in; and the only Connecticut troops at Yorktown were with the light infantry battalions or the Sappers and Miners. It is certainly possible he was sent south with the light troops, but we have yet to confirm that. Still, Private Starr undoubtedly saw some combat during the war, and as noted in his pension papers, 'Robin Starr has been honoured with the Badge of Merit for six years faithful service H. Swift Colo 2nd Connecticut Regt.'[3]

Some men stayed with the same unit during their entire enlistment, others had a varied military career. In April 1844 Cezar Shelton related,

> served in the Revolutionary Army about three years ... under Col. John Durkee ... At the time of his enlistment he was a slave to John Shelton and entered the service upon condition of receiving his freedom when he should be discharged ... he remembers only two of his fellow soldiers – Mr. Avery and one John Patten – he distinctly remembers being in the battle of Germantown – in the attack on the fort at Red Bank by the Hessians – and in the battle of Monmouth which he thinks was about a year after he enlisted – he is confident he enlisted in the spring of 1777 and thinks Monmouth battle was in the summer of 1778, it was very hot weather and he remembers the army expected to fight again next day – but the enemy went off ... Before he enlisted, he was in the Militia in the place of his old masters

---

2   'Connecticut Line, 1777', 'Reorganization of the Connecticut Line, 1781', 'Demobilization of the Connecticut Line', https://en.wikipedia.org/wiki/Connecticut_Line. Wright, *Continental Army*, pp.233–238.

3   NA (US), Pension, reel 2274, Robin Starr (S36810).

son. he was wound[ed] at Horse Neck [Landing, Greenwich Connecticut], he was just relieved from guard and had lain down with his pack on & fell asleep when he was awaked by an order, surrender[,] he jumped out of the window and escaped to the bushes, but received one blow with a cutlass across his back [described in a February1840 account as, 'by the sword of a Refugee Light Horseman'], he was also struck by a [musket] ball on the skin at the same time and that was the only time during his service that he was wounded.[4]

Prince Hull

'first enlisted in April 1775 for eight months in Capt [Joshua or Oliver] Parker's company & Colo Prescott's Regt of Massts troops & served throughout that campaign, was engaged in the Battle of Bunker Hill & … in December 1775 he enlisted for one year in the Con[nnecticu]t line, in Capt [William] Hull's company & Colo Webb's [19th Continental] Regt & at the expiration thereof he was enlisted again at Fishkill N. York for three years [but due to long-term illness did not join his regiment] … In August 1777 he again enlisted into Capt [Jonathan] Wadsworth's company & Col [Thaddeus] Cook's Regt [of Connecticut militia] for three months & was wounded at the battle of Saratoga & having faithfully served out his time was honorably discharged –'[5]

Cook's Battalion was attached to Brigadier General Enoch Poor's brigade and was heavily involved at both Saratoga actions, Freeman's Farm on 19 September 1777 (where Captain Wadsworth was killed) and Bemis Heights on 7 October.[6] Another man, Edward Pellom, enlisted in Colonel Jedediah Huntington's Regiment in 1775 for eight months, reenlisted in the same unit, then called the 17th Continental Regiment, in 1776. Discharged,

after the battle at Trenton … he again enlisted … in a Regiment Commanded by Col John Durkee in the spring of … 1778 & continued to serve therein until Novr. 1778 when he was selected as one of the guard for Clement Biddle Esq. forage Master Genl. [Commissary General of Forage from July 1777 to June 1780] & having been stationed as a Guard for some time s[ai]d Biddle employed him as a Wagoner from November 1778 untill April AD 1779 at which time he gave him a discharge … he served thirteen Months at this time & recvd. his pay as a soldier Wagoner … he again joined the Army after remaining home some time … he still served in sd Regiment … being [the] 5th. Connecticut … in the year 1780 Col Hemon Swift was Commdg & from him on the 9th. Day of December AD 1780 he was finally discharged …'.[7]

Pellom's discharge from Biddle was included in his pension file, as follows:

4   NA (US), Pension, reel 2168, Cezar Shelton (S19764).
5   NA (US), Pension, reel 1364, Prince Hull, African American (S36596).
6   Eric H. Schnitzer, 'The Tactics of the Battles of Saratoga', in William A. Griswold and Donald W. Linebaugh (eds.), *The Saratoga Campaign: Uncovering an Embattled Landscape* (Hanover and London: University Press of New England, 2016), pp.50, 63.
7   NA (US), Pension, reel 1935, Edward Pellom, 'Mulatto' (S3621).

Edward Pellom (Mulatto) having served faithfully as a waggoner in the Continental service in driving my Baggage wagon since November last, he is paid [page torn] wages & is hereby discharged & permitted to return to his home at Coventry in Connecticut

Given under my hand at Camp Middlebrook this 15th. of April 1779 Clement Biddle [8]

Black soldiers, Continental and militia, took part in every battle of the war and most, if not all, minor actions. Timothy Prince testified in April 1818,

in the month of December 1775 or January 1776 … I Enlisted … for the term of thirteen months under Capt. [James] Chapman of New London Connecticut who was afterwards appointed to Majr. and was killd [15 September] in the retreat from new york in 1776 and a few Days after I Enlisted I joind. Colo. [Samuel] Parsons [10th Continental] Regiment at Roxbury near Boston … Colo. [Samuel] Parsons was appointed a Brigadier General and Commanded our Brigade and Colo. [John] Tyler Commanded our Regiment. I was in the retreat from Long island to new York & out of new York to Harlam plains near Kingsbridge … [in] March 1777 I again Enlisted … for nine months under Capt. [James] Eldridge [Lieutenant] Colo. [Samuel] Prentiss's [1st Connecticut] Regiment and Genl. Parsons [actually Jedediah Huntington's] Brigade. I immediately joind. the regiment at Newhaven and I Believe in the month of June [actually late September] following joind. the main army under General Washington at a Place calld. Whitemarsh in Pennsylvania Near Philadelphia and Put up for winter quarters at Valley forge … was Discharged and Returned home – in the month of August 1778 was again one month in the service and in the Retreat with Genl. Sullivan from Rhode island …[9]

In old age William Tracy related, 'he went to New York was on Long Island at the battle near New York … [and] was with the Army at Trenton at the time of the battle there … he knows he served in the Continental Army & for one year at least in a company commanded by Capt Jedediah Waterman in Col John Durkee['s] [20th Continental] Regiment …'[10]

Hundreds of white men and women, old soldiers and others, provided evidence to help African-American veterans procure pensions. William Tracy's file contains Silas Goodell's deposition, stating he 'was a Lieutenant in Col John Durkees Regiment in the year 1776 … he recollects … said Will a black man to have belonged to the … Regiment in that year … he saw him in October or November 1776 off against Fort Washington in New Jersey & that he believes he saw him at the battle at Trenton …'[11] David Gardner, a white veteran of Durkee's regiment, submitted this testimony for Caesar Clark:

8   NA (US), Pension, reel 1935, Edward Pellom (S3621).
9   NA (US), Pension, reel 1978, Timothy Prince, African American (S41079).
10 NA (US), Pension, reel 1978, reel 2407, William Tracy, 'a black man' (S35362).
11 NA (US), Pension, reel 2407, William Tracy (S35362), deposition of Silas Goodale (Goodell).

a black Man now present before me ... sometime in the Fall (he thinks in October) 1777 a Detachment was made from [the 4th] Regiment to go into Mud Fort & this Deponent was detached and accordingly went into Mud Fort in a Company commanded by Captain Brown of the same Regiment who was killed in that Fort ... he well recollects ... Caesar was on Mud Fort at the same time that he belonged to the same Detachment under Captain Brown ... He well recollects that at the Battle of Germantown in the Fall of 1777 – this same Caesar was there in the Regiment – That afterwards when the Army went into Huts at Valley Forge he was also there in the Regiment – That at the Battle of Monmouth in June 1778 – this same Caesar was ... there with the Regiment ...[12]

Some supporting accounts reveal mundane details or insights. Black veteran Pomp McCuff noted in his affidavit for a fellow soldier, 'I was well acquainted with Prince William, alias Stearkweather ... saw him many times during the war was stationed with said Prince Williams at Frogg Neck Near New York and many times played ball with him on the grand parade'. Three white veterans recalled that Prince Crosley was a musician, a distinction that set him apart from others. Samuel Lord said, 'Capt. Christopher Ely [1st Connecticut] had a company in the same Regiment and he joined us at New Haven. In Capt. Ely's company there was a negro by the name of Prince or Prentiss Crosley ... He was there when the company joined us at New Haven and when I came away three years after. I am enabled to recollect the fact more distinctly as he always carried a fiddle with him and was well known throughout the Regiment'. Gamaliel Tracy noted, 'I very well recollect Prince from this circumstance that he most always carried a Fiddle in the top of his knapsack which he used when at liberty ...'. Prince Crosley served first with the 7th Connecticut for three years, from 1777 to 1780, then for six months in the 4th Regiment in 1782.[13]

Connecticut's Continental contingent had many enslaved soldiers, perhaps as many or more than Massachusetts. Cezar Shelton 'served in the Revolutionary Army about three years ... At the time of his enlistment he was a slave to John Shelton and entered the service upon condition of receiving his freedom when he should be discharged ...'.[14] Jack Freeman, also known as Jack Rowland, deposed in 1833,

he was born in Fairfield ... March 1753 ... his age is received from his Master Hezekiel Sanford ... who kept a record ... He was born the slave of one Burritt ... at the age of seven – years he was purchased by [Jonathan?] Booth of Newtown ... he lived [there] in servitude until he became of the age of thirteen years when he was purchased by ... Hezekiel Sanford and serv'd him until he entered the service of the United States of America ... in the month of January 1777 ... he enlisted

12 NA (US), Pension, reel 550, Caesar Clark, 'a black Man' (S37871), deposition of David Gardner.
13 NA (US), Pension, reel 2584, Prince William, 'a negro man' (R10076), deposition of Pomp McCuff; *Ibid.*, reel 701, Prince Crosley (W24833), depositions of Samuel Lord, John Say, and Gamaliel Tracy.
14 NA (US), Pension, reel 2168, Cezar Shelton (S19764).

for the term of during the War ... in the Company commanded by Captain Ezekiel Sanford in the [5th Connecticut] Regiment commanded by Colonel Philip Bradley ... on the 1st day of June 1777 he joined the said Regiment at Crump Pond ... New York and from thence marched south with said Regiment to Peekskill on the Hudson River where he continued serve with the Continental Troops there then under the command of General McDougal ... until the month of September ... when he marched south [to Pennsylvania] ... He was engaged in the battle of Germantown in the month of October ... afterwards marched ... to Philadelphia from thence ... into Winter quarters at Valley Forge ... He participated with the rest of the Army in all the hardships and distress endured by the soldiers during that memorable winter – On the opening of the spring the said Regiment was marched to Princeton. There he was discharged under the following circumstances – Having enlisted as aforesaid he was by the laws of Connecticut emancipated and being sick, enfeebled and desirous of returning home he agreed with his former master through ... Captain Ezekiel Sanford who was a Brother of Hezekiel [and] that notwithstanding he was emancipated he would labor in his service for the term of three years, if his said master would employ or procure a substitute His master did ... procure such substitute to enlist in his stead ...[15]

Hezekiel Sanford's son corroborated Freeman's account:

I William Sanford of Redding ... say that Jack a couloured Man (a slave to my Father) enlisted in the United States service ... under Capt. Ezekiel Sanford & that he went of[f] in the spring 1777 & that he was gone one year ... sd. Capt. came home in the course of the year & told how home sick Jack was & wanted his old Master to hire a Man in his room & he would come back and be a good slave, my Father did hire a Man I understood took his place, Jack came home & served I think three years for his freedom ...[16]

Nathan Buckingham told of Prince Crosley's bondage:

a year before the commencement of the Revolutionary war the father of this deponent Benjamin Buckingham bought of the former Gov. [Matthew] Griswold a negro man of the name of "Jim" [Prince Crosley's brother]. And soon after that Samuel Platt who lived about half a mile from sd Benjamins residence purchased of sd Gov Griswold the brother of sd Jim whose name was 'Prince' ... Jim enlisted for 'during the war' and died in the service ... [after Jim's enlistment] Prince desired to enlist for [the] purpose of getting his freedom ... his master (Mr Platt) was opposed to it ... Prince being discontented with his situation Mr Platt sold him, and he enlisted for three years.[17]

Several men told of their African origins. Cezar Shelton stated, 'He was born at sea as he has always been told when his mother was being brought from

---

15 NA (US), Pension, reel 2093, Jack Freeman, 'a couloured Man' (S17058).
16 NA (US), Pension, reel 2093, Jack Freeman (S17058), deposition of William Sanford.
17 NA (US), Pension, reel 701, Prince Crosley (W24833), deposition of Nathan Buckingham.

Africa'; Richard Leet, 'a man of Colour … is a native of Guinea … brought to the United States when he was about five years old & sold as a slave …'.[18]

Jeffrey Brace (or Stiles), called Pomp London during the war, recorded his enslavement and military service in an extraordinary 1810 autobiography, as well as via his pension recollections. Both garble his military career, highlighting the problem of relying on unverified memories. He begins his 1810 work with an account of his natal land of Bow-Woo in Africa, claimed in one work to be modern-day Mali, adjacent to and northwest of Guinea. He describes his capture, ill-treatment, and eventual brief service as a British seaman during the Seven Years War. Making landfall at Boston, Brace, as he was later called, was sold to a man residing at Milford, Connecticut, near the Oyster River. From that time until the war's onset he was transferred by purchase six times and ill-treated by most of his owners.[19]

Brace's autobiography contains a lively account of his military service, with wonderful stories, but the context is problematic. For example, he says 'I was in the battle at Cambridge, White plains, Monmouth, Princeton, Newark, Froggs-point, Horseneck where I had a ball pass through my knapsack'. Some of this is likely true, but there was no battle at Cambridge, unless one counts the 1775 Boston siege, and no record of his serving at that time or during the period of the White Plains or Princeton actions in 1776. He himself notes his first service was when 'Benjamin and David [Stiles], were drafted to fight in the revolution' David, Joseph, and Nathan Stiles served with the 13th Connecticut (militia) Regiment from mid-August to mid-September 1777. While there is no record of Jeffrey Brace/Stiles or Pomp London in the company, it is possible he accompanied David as a servant. Brace's first confirmed military stint as Pomp London was in Captain Eli Leavenworth's company, Colonel Return Jonathan Meigs' 6th Connecticut Regiment, from 17 June to December 1778. In May 1779 London enlisted with the 8th Connecticut, commanded first by Colonel Giles Russell, and then by Lieutenant Colonel Isaac Sherman for three years. He ended that enlistment in August 1781 serving with Captain Nehemiah Rice's company of Sherman's 5th Regiment.[20]

18 NA (US), Pension, reel 2168, Cezar Shelton (S19764); *ibid.*, reel 1544, Richard Leet, 'a man of Colour' (S38908).

19 Kari J. Winter (ed.), *The Blind African Slave, or Memoirs of Boyrereau Brinch, Nick-Named Jeffrey Brace, as told to Benjamin F. Prentiss* (Madison: University of Wisconsin Press, 2004), p.4.

20 Benjamin F. Prentiss, *The Blind African Slave, or Memoirs of Boyrereau Brinch, Nick-Named Jeffrey Brace* (St. Albans, Vt.: Harry Whitney, 1810), pp.143–156, https://docsouth.unc.edu/neh/brinch/brinch.html; NA (US), Compiled Service Records of Soldiers who Served in the American Army During the Revolutionary War (National Archives Microfilm Publication M881), Record Group 93 (Connecticut), Thirteenth Militia Regiment. David Stiles, Joseph Stiles, Nathan Stiles; NA (US), Revolutionary War Rolls, folder 181, frames 12, 20, 13th Regiment (Connecticut) Militia, David, Joseph, and Nathan Stiles, 1777. NA (US), Compiled Service Records (Connecticut), Pomp London, 6th Connecticut Regiment, enlisted 17 June 1778 for 10 months, discharged 31 December 1778 (17 pages); 8th Connecticut Regiment, enlisted 18 May 1779 for three years, served in the companies of Capt. Samuel Sanford and Capt. Nehemiah Rice (39 pages); 5th Connecticut Regiment, Capt. Nehemiah Rice's company from January to 3 August 1781 (7 pages).

Old soldier Ansel Patterson, formerly of Zebulon Butler's 2nd Connecticut Regiment, testified in 1821 that he

> can not at this length of time Identify this person as [belonging to] Capt [Samuel] Barkers Company in said [4th] Regement [which] was composed of Colored persons & the deponent had but little intercourse with said Company ... [he] does not recollect the name of the Captain who commanded the Colored men ... the Company of Negroes [in the 4th Connecticut in 1782] was generally paraded on the right of the sixth Company ... this deponent in conversing with Jeffery is well persuaded that he was a Soldier of Col. Butlers Regement & belonged to the Negro Company from his narrating so many transactions which took place ... which he could not have done had he not been in the service he narrates ... the [circumstances?] of many tricks performed by a Negro boy necked named [nicknamed] the Cat he also states many circumstances of the Negro [boxing?] which the deponent recollects – also the diferent movement of the regement that I have no doubt in my mind but what he was a Soldier in said Regement ... [21]

Silas Strong noted in 1820,

> he was the owner of a Negro slave called Jeffery Stiles, was well acquainted with Jeffery – that he then well understood that Jeffery was enlisted in the army to obtain his freedom ... [he] remembers that he saw Jeffery a number of times after his enlistment in a soldiers Uniform with a Leather Cap he further recollects that some time in the War ... thinks it must be in the year 1780 he was in the State of New York near West Point – met a Seargeants Guard all in Uniform – among the Guard was Jeffery & conversed with him – I am now acquainted with a Colored man calling himself Jeffery Brace & know him to be the same person then known by Jeffery Stiles – Jeffery sometimes was necked named Pomp London.[22]

Only in his memoirs does Brace mention wearing a leather cap, headgear that Colonel Meigs' 6th Connecticut Regiment (in 1781 renumbered the 4th Regiment) was famous for wearing. Relating an incident he said occurred near Hackensack, New Jersey, Brace claimed have killed a British light horseman and captured his horse. Being pursued, he mounted the horse and fled,

> but having no spurs, and not being so good a horseman they gained upon me. I looked forward and saw my Capt. in full view, almost a mile distant. This encouraged me, and the long shanked negro, soldier with a leather cap, mounted on an elegant english gelding light horse, made all whistle again. When I came in about twenty or thirty rods, I heard the Captain say, 'there come one of our leather caps, and it is Jeffrey –reserve your fire so as not to kill him; however the men fired, and three balls cut my garments, one struck my coat sleeve, the next hit my bayonet belt, and the third went through the back side of my leather-cap.

---

21 NA (US), Pension, reel 313, Jeffrey Brace (S41461), deposition of Ansel Patterson.
22 NA (US), Pension, reel 313, Jeffrey Brace (S41461), deposition of Silas Strong.

They were so close upon me, that the same fire killed four of the British and five horses--and wounded some more …[23]

The commander in chief mentioned the 6th Connecticut's caps in a January 1781 letter to the Board of War, 'We have so constantly experienced the want of Hats, than which no part of dress is more essential to the appearance of a soldier, that I have been endeavouring to find out a substitute for them, which could be procured among ourselves. I have seen none so likely to answer the purpose, and which at the same time of so military an air as a leather Cap which was procured in the year 1777 for the 6th. Connecticut Regt. …'. Leather caps were still being worn in the 6th Regiment in 1779, and the practice likely continued into 1782 when it became the 4th Regiment. Brace served under the name Pomp London in Meigs' 6th Connecticut only in 1778. He is not on the rolls of Captain Humphrey's 1782 4th Connecticut 'Negro Company'; it is possible he served under a name other than those already given, but he himself makes no such claim.[24]

One last Connecticut soldier needs to be addressed. As told by his widow Phillis, Cuff Saunders, also known as Cuff Wells,

was commonally calld Doctr Cuff … a slave of Israel Wells … and … in order to obtain his freedom enlisted into the Army of the United States in the Winter of 1777 … for the term of during the War, and was placd In a Regt. [4th Connecticut] commanded by Colo. John Durkee … where he did duty as a private and was waiter to the Surgeon of sd Regt and it having been discovered by the Officers … that … Cuff possessd considerable medicinal skill by having some years before been a Slave of Doct. [Thomas] Langrel of Hartford who was a Physician and kept an apothecary store where … Cuff Learnt the art of preparing & mixing medicine, he was accordingly placd in the Hospital as a waiter & assistant to the Surgeon and part of the time he acted as an assistant in the apothecary store belonging to the Continental Army at Danbury … where he continued till late in the Fall of 1783… we had agreed to marry each other before he went into the Army … he returnd home in the month of May 1783 on a furlough dressd in Uniform with red facings and the U.S.A. on his buttons…[25]

23 Prentiss, *The Blind African Slave*, pp.164–165.
24 George Washington to the Board of War, 10 January 1781, Fitzpatrick, *Writings of George Washington*, Vol.21, p.83; 'In July 1779 Colonel Walter Stewart of the 2nd Pennsylvania Regiment sent one of his officers to Middletown, Connecticut, there to have leather caps made for his regiment. The caps were to have white leather binding around the edges, and came in different patterns for light infantry, grenadiers, battalion [troops], sergeants and musicians, and officers. In his letter of instruction to his officer, Stewart wrote, *…the [caps] … must be made in the form of the Battalion [caps] w[hi]ch is the same Pattern as Colo. Megg's.* The only colonel in the Continental Army at the time with a name anything like *Meggs*, was the 6th Connecticut Regiment's commander Return Jonathan Meigs': Philip Katcher, *Uniforms of the Continental Army*, (York, Pa.: George Shumway Publisher, 1981), p.75; NA (US), Revolutionary War Rolls, folder 13, frames 7–19, 4th Connecticut Regiment, David Humphrey's company, muster rolls, 16 June 1782, 23 July 1782, 6 August 1782, 10 September 1782, 15 October 1782.
25 NA (US), Pension, reel 2528, Cuff Wells, 'coloured man' (W18103), deposition of Phillis Tatton.

Others added their own stories of Mr Saunders. John Isham relayed an interview with Ephraim White:

> I enquir'd of him if he ever knew a colour'd person that went by the name of Doctr. Cuff that belong'd to the army, he readily said he did perfectly well, that he was a Waiter the latter part of the War to the Surgeons at … Danbury … several of whom roomd. at his Fathers House that he recollected the Colour'd Men had a drawing for the choice of a Capt. near the close of the War and that us Boys advis'd them to choose Doctr. Cuff, as he knew more about [the] Military than any one of them having belong'd to the Army so long – he went on further and described his person as being rather under size, very polite & mannerly, that he was generally dress'd in Uniform &c … [26]

John Say was a veteran of Zebulon Butler's 1781 4th Connecticut Regiment. He 'became acquainted with a coloured man by the name of Cuff, who generally in the army, went by the name of "Doct Cuff" … on one occasion … he came to me with a powder horn filled with camphor, and asked me to smell of it – I did, and asked him what it was – He said camphor, he expected that Phyllis was going to be sick that fall, and he was going home if he could'. John Watrous noted in February 1840, 'I saw him [Cuff Wells] occasionally in the Camp, also at the public Hospital in Danbury … where he officiated as a Waiter to one of the Surgeons … (viz.) Doct. Philip Turner, also to other Physicians in the Hospital – and from his activity, honesty and good understanding, he was employed as an assistant to prepare compositions of medicine prescribed by Physicians attending on the sick …'[27]

In December 1840, John Isham, a vigorous advocate for Cuff's widow, wrote Congressman Thomas W. Williams, 'I can't but believe that Phillis is fully entitled to a Pension agreeable to the Report made by the Hon. Mr Brockway – Phillis is a remarkable intelligent Colour'd. Woman has always sustaind. a fair character for Honesty & industry she was the mother to the noted Prince Saunders who died at Hayti [illegible] 1840 and was Atty General of the Island at the time of his death …' Prince Saunders, the son of Cuff and Phillis Saunders, was indeed a remarkable individual in his own right. Raised in Vermont by lawyer George Oramel Hinckley, absented from his family to ensure he would be a free man when grown, Prince was for a while a schoolteacher, then educated at Dartmouth College in 1807 and 1808. He was a member of Boston's African Masonic Lodge and founded a school for black children in the city. His obituary notes, 'with the backing of

---

26 NA (US), Pension, reel 2528, Cuff Wells (W18103), deposition of John Isham (with Ephraim White interview).

27 NA (US), Pension, reel 2528, Cuff Wells (W18103), depositions of John Say and John Watrous. Camphor (*Cinnamomum camphora*) is obtained from the wood of camphor tree. It has been used for centuries, throughout the world as a remedy for treating variety of symptoms such as inflammation, infection, congestion, pain, irritation, etc., Rafi Hamidpour, Soheila Hamidpour, Mohsen Hamidpour, Mina Shahlari, Camphor (Cinnamomum camphora), 'A traditional remedy with the history of treating several diseases', *International Journal of Case Reports and Images* (2013), vol. 4., no. 2, pp.86–89, http://www.ijcasereportsandimages.com/archive/2013/002-2013-ijcri/001-02-2013-hamidpour/ijcri-00102201311-hamidpour-full-text.php.

Abolitionist friends he made while in London he went to Haiti to aid King Henri Christophe by setting up school systems on the English model. He wrote The Haytian Papers, a translation and commentary on the laws of Haiti. He was involved in promoting black emigration to Haiti and for abolition of slavery'. Prince Saunders passed away in Port-au-Prince in 1839.[28]

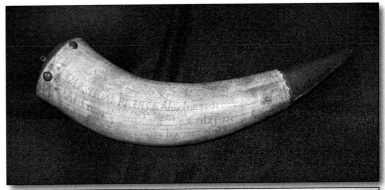

'Garshom Prince his horn made at Crownpoint Septm ye 3rd day 1761/ Prince+Negro his horn M'. (Gift of Edith Angeline Dennis, collection of the Luzerne County Historical Society, 80.8.709.) Gershom (Garshom) Prince's powder horn, worn when he was killed at the Battle of Wyoming in Pennsylvania, 3 July 1778. He was identified solely because the horn was found with his body. Prince was a veteran of the French and Indian War, and reputed to have enlisted with Colonel Zebulon Butler's 4th Connecticut Regiment during the Revolution. Unfortunately, he does not appear on any of 4th Regiment muster rolls, nor those of the three Wyoming Valley independent companies serving with that regiment and detached in June to return and defend their homes. It is likely Gershom Prince was a member of a militia company present at the July 1778 action. Other African American soldiers' belongings survive: Connecticut soldier Barzillai Lew's powder horn is on display at the DuSable Museum of African American History, Chicago; the horn belonging to Prince Simbo, another Connecticut veteran, is held at the Smithsonian Institution. Aaron Oliver of New Hampshire fought at the battle of Hubbardton, Vermont, 7 July 1777. He was wounded and captured, only to die in 1778 after his release from captivity. His wooden canteen, mirror, musket ball bag, and small horn (for priming powder or carrying salt) were donated to the State of Vermont and are displayed at the Hubbardton Battlefield visitor center.[29]

28 NA (US), Pension, reel 2528, Cuff Wells (W18103), deposition of John Isham and Prince Saunders obituary, newspaper cutting (undated); White, Arthur, 'Prince Saunders: An Instance of Social Mobility Among Antebellum New England Black', *The Journal of Negro History*, vol. 40, no. 4 (1975), pp.526–535.
29 For information on Gershom Prince's legacy see, Dennis Farm Charitable Land Trust, http://thedennisfarm.org/; National Archives (United States), Revolutionary War Rolls (National Archives Microfilm Publication M246), Record Group 93, Robert Durkee's company, 4th Connecticut Regiment (1777–80), frame 14, folder 73; Samuel Ransom's company, 4th Connecticut Regiment (1777–80), frame 18, folder 74; Simon Spaulding's company, 4th Connecticut4th Regiment (1777–80), frame 103, folder 74; (Prince Simbo) Alex Palmer, 'The Revolutionary War Patriot Who Carried This Gunpowder Horn Was Fighting for Freedom—Just Not His Own', 22 June 2016, https://www.smithsonianmag.com/smithsonian-institution/patriot-who-carried-revolutionary-war-era-gunpowder-horn-was-fighting-freedomjust-not-his-own-180959385/; Information on other African American soldier artifacts thanks to, Elsa Gilbertson, Vermont Division for Historic Preservation, and Michael Barbieri (Aaron Oliver), and Kate Swisher, DuSable Museum (Barzillai Lew).

7

New Hampshire: 'I was in the battles of Harlem-heights & Monmouth'

With the Massachusetts call for reinforcements, in May 1775 the New Hampshire provincial Congress authorized raising three units, the 1st, 2nd, and 3rd New Hampshire regiments. All three corps were enlisted to the end of the year and served at the Boston siege. A third organization, Major Timothy Bedel's Corps of Rangers, served in the northern (New York) department. In 1776 the three New Hampshire regiments were reformed and renamed the 5th, 8th, and 2nd Continental Regiments. The ranger corps was expanded to form Bedel's Regiment; all four New Hampshire regiments served that year in northern New York and Canada. A fifth unit, Colonel Pierse Long's Regiment was organized in August 1776 and disbanded in northern New York in July 1777.[1]

With the comprehensive Continental Army 1777 reorganization, the New Hampshire regiments reverted to their former numbering and were reenlisted for three years or the war. The 1st, 2nd, and 3rd New Hampshire were commanded by (respectively) Colonel Joseph Cilley, Colonel Enoch Poor (after Poor was promoted to brigadier general, by Nathan Hale, captured at the July Battle of Hubbardton), and Colonel Alexander Scammell. After Hale's capture, Lieutenant Colonel George Reid commanded the 2nd Regiment. All three regiments fought in the northern New York-Saratoga campaign and were transferred to the main army in October. In 1781 the 3rd Regiment was disbanded and the men absorbed by the 1st and 2nd regiments. The New Hampshire contingent was reduced in March 1783 to a regiment plus a four-company battalion, then again that June to the five-company New Hampshire Battalion. In January 1784, the remaining unit was disbanded at New Windsor, New York.[2]

---

1   Wright, *Continental Army*, pp.197–200; 'New Hampshire Provincial Regiments, 1775', 'Numbered Continental Regiments, 1776', https://en.wikipedia.org/wiki/New_Hampshire_Line
2   Wright, *Continental Army*, pp.197–199; 'New Hampshire Line, 1777', 'Reorganization of the New Hampshire Line, 1781', 'Demobilization of the New Hampshire Line', https://en.wikipedia.org/wiki/New_Hampshire_Line

New Hampshire Soldier Narratives

The New Hampshire regiments served in the Boston siege, the 1777 northern campaign (including the Saratoga battles), wintered at Valley Forge, and went on to see action at the 1778 Battle of Monmouth. Moving north, they participated in Major General John Sullivan's 1779 campaign against the Iroquois. Re-joining General Washington's main army, they occupied northern New Jersey and the New York highlands in 1780. In 1781 two light infantry companies marched to Virginia under Major General Marie Joseph Paul Yves Roch Gilbert du Motier, Marquis de Lafayette, opposing British forces there that summer. Additional New Hampshire soldiers moved south that autumn with Colonel Alexander Scammell's light infantry battalion, on their way to besiege Cornwallis at Yorktown.

Only a few pertinent pensions for New Hampshire African American soldiers have been found. Prince Light,

> a free man of Colour … in the year 1776 served six months in a New Hampshire Regiment at Ticonderoga and elsewhere at the Northward, & three months in the Militia, at the taking of General Burgoyne's army in 1777, and afterwards in June 1780 … enlisted in … Capt. [Caleb] Robinson's Company in the [3rd New Hampshire] regiment … for the Term of nine months … he … faithfully served … at West Point … & elsewhere … & at the expiration [of his enlistment] … was honourably discharged at a place called Soldier's Fortune in [the] State of New York.

Mr Light actually served as a six months levy with the 2nd New Hampshire, joining the regiment between 10 July and 28 August 1780. No confirmation has been found for his earlier claimed enlistments.[3]

Robert Glines was another 1780 six-months man, drafted to reinforce the Continental Army. He

> enlisted early in the month of June … as one of three men who were called for out of the militia … [who] would [serve] in place of three years men, whose time had …run out … he went to Kingston [New Hampshire] … passed muster … & went on from there to West Point joined the [3rd] regiment under command of Lieut. Colo Henry Dearborn [later Secretary of War, 1801–1809] … remained a while at West Point went from there to New Jersey was at Orangetown Hackensack Ridge & other places returned soon after General [Benedict] Arnold defected … went into winter quarters at a place called Soldiers Fortune & was there till the sixth of December 1780 when I was discharged.[4]

Caesar Wallace rather laconically described his service, stating he enlisted 'sometime in the year 1777' in Caleb Robinson's company, Colonel George

---

3   NA (US), Pension, reel 1562, Prince Light (S44511); NA (US), Revolutionary War Rolls, folder 24, frames 76–82, 2nd New Hampshire Regiment, Muster rolls, Capt. Caleb Robinson's company, 10 July, 28 August, and 2 November 1780.

4   NA (US), Pension, reel 1082, Robert Glines, African American (R4069).

Reid's 2nd Regiment, and served to June 1783. He ended by noting 'he was in the battle of Monmouth and at horse neck and at Newtown', where he fought against the Iroquois and their allies.[5] Veteran Anthony Gilman nicely provided more details:

> in the latter part of December 1775 I enlisted as fifer … for the term of one year … in Capt. Gilman's Company, in Colonel [John] Nixon's [4th Continental] Regiment of the Massachusetts line … [for] one year, when I again entered in Capt. [Nathaniel] Hutchin's Company in Colonel Joseph Cilley's [1st New Hampshire] Regt. … & served therein till when … [Lieutenant Colonel William] Hull [3rd Massachusetts Regiment] was sent [on 22 January 1781] in the command of a detach-ment of about 1500 men to go to Morrisania [the Bronx,] in N. York state to drive out the Cow-boys or Refugees [Lieutenant Colonel James De Lancey's Loyalist Westchester County militia] as they were called … [I] was with about 40 men taken by the british & carried into New York, & there kept a few weeks prisoner, & then being a man of colour was sold for a slave to one John Falkinham, & was left as a slave more than a year there & then sent to St. John's & to Anapolis-Royal [Nova Scotia], from whence after about 6 or 7 months I made my escape & came away. The war was then over. I was in the battles of Harlem-heights & Monmouth.[6]

Two New Hampshire men are known to have served as officers' servants. Daniel March testified that Pomp Sherburne 'served from sometime in 1780 untill the fall of … 1783 … while in the service … Pomp Sherburn was serving a part of the time a[s] cook or waiter for our Colonel George Reid and I belonged to the same family or mess [squad] …'. Daniel Gookin, former 2nd Regiment lieutenant, related that 'Prime a Blackman … in the Second New Hampshire Regiment in the years 1777 1778 & 1779 for three years … was honorably discharged … Part of the time he was my waiter or servant …' Gookin also noted 'He says he was called and mustered by the name of Prime Lane. I am uncertain by what name he was known except Prime. I have seen a Sergeant who served in the Regiment who says he was called Prime Coffin. He was a slave before the Revolutionary war, and was owned by sundry persons … Being a blackman he was generally called and known by the name of Prime'.[7]

Miscellaneous documents and service records reveal at least four other New Hampshire black soldiers. Fortune Negro was included on a March 1776 list of firearms and accoutrements issued to Colonel Timothy Bedel's Regiment, receiving one musket and bayonet, and a bayonet belt. Having enlisted that February, in June 1776 he was with his company at Île aux Noix, an island on the Richelieu River, Quebec province. 'Dan a Negro' received

5   NA (US), Pension, reel 2479, Caesar Wallace, 'man of colour' (S43250).
6   NA (US), Pension, reel 1076, Anthony Gilman, 'a man of colour' (S32729); Mark M. Boatner (ed. Harold E. Selesky), *Encyclopedia of the American Revolution: Library of Military History*, (2nd Edition, Charles Scribner's Sons, 2006), Vol. 2, pp.754–755.
7   NA (US), Pension, reel 2171, Pomp Sherburne, 'a man of colour' (W17297). Ibid., reel 1521, Prime Lane (S44499).

a bounty in November 1776 upon enlisting in Capt. Benjamin Titcomb's company, 1st New Hampshire Regiment. Prince Negro was noted to be 'with Genl Gates' on a 10 January 1778 'Size Roll of the Absentees Belonging to the First New Hampshire Regiment …' Lastly, 'Peter a Negro' in August 1779 volunteered or was drafted from the 4th Regiment (militia) for the town of Epping to serve one year in the 'New Hampshire battalions in the Continental Army'.[8]

---

8   NA (US), Revolutionary War Rolls, folder 49, frame 41, Bedel's Regiment (Fortune Negro), 'Capt. Samuel Youngs Company in Col Timothy Bedels Regiment … received … the following Fire Arms …', 19 March 1776; *Ibid.*, folder 178, frame 23, New Hampshire regiments (Dan Negro), 'Samuel Nute … 1776 Novr To the Continental Bounty paid the following Soldiers who were enlisted by me …'; *Ibid.*, folder 174, frame 14, New Hampshire regiments (Peter Negro), 'Muster Roll for the Men raised in the fourth Regiment of Militia … to fill up the New Hampshire battalions …', 12 August 1779. NA (US), Compiled Service Records (New Hampshire), Fortune Negro, Prince Negro.

8

Rhode Island: 'Very much crippled in one arm ... [by] a wound received ... [at] Monmouth'

As the state with the only 'black' regiment, Rhode Island's military organizations will be discussed in some detail. The state's Continental cohort was small, beating only Delaware in size. Still, during the *rage militaire* of 1775 the colony contributed three one-year regiments (commanded by colonels James Varnum, Daniel Hitchcock, and Thomas Church) to the New England army. Varnum's and Hitchcock's units were retained in 1776 and respectively renamed the 9th and 11th Continental Regiments. Two existing state regiments, William Richmond's and Christopher Lippett's, were added to the national army in September 1776. Lippett joined Washington's forces at New York that October, while Richmond's men remained in Rhode Island. With the Continental Army's 1777 rebirth only the 1st and 2nd Rhode Island Regiments remained, recruited with men enlisted (or reenlisted) for three years or the duration of the war. All these regiments, from 1775 through 1777, contained black soldiers serving alongside their white comrades.[1]

The 1777 Philadelphia campaign took a toll on the entire army, with men being lost for various reasons. The Rhode Island regiments were particularly hard-hit and the state had to consider how to recruit them. James Varnum, now a brigade commander, wrote General Washington in early January 1778: 'The Battalions from the State of Rhode Island being small ... The Field Officers have represented to me the Propriety of making one temporary Battalion from the two, so that one entire core of officers may repair to Rhode Island, in order to receive and prepare Recruits for the Field. It is imagined that a Battalion of Negroes can be easily raised there'. The legislature met in early February and resolved that any 'negro, mulatto, or Indian man slave in this State may inlist into either of the ... two battalions to serve during the

---

1   Popek, *They fought bravely*, pp.9–15, 39–43, 51, 69–73.

continuance of the war …'. It was eventually determined that these recruits would join only the 1st Rhode Island Regiment and that unit would contain only black or Native-American privates, with white commissioned officers, sergeants, and corporals. Governor Nicholas Cooke noted in late February, 'The number of slaves in this state is not great, but it is generally thought that three hundred, and upwards, will be enlisted …'. Any slaves accepted received their freedom and their owners were remunerated. Unpopular with many residents, in early May the legislature set a 10 June 1778 cut-off date for slave recruiting, though free blacks could continue to enlist. Another obstacle in filling up Colonel Greene's regiment was Brigadier General Ezekiel Cornell's contingent of state troops. The state regiments of Colonels Archibald Crary and John Topham, enlisted for a maximum of 15 months, contained a number of blacks, free and enslaved. In all, only 117 bondsmen were purchased by the Rhode Island legislature in 1778. Despite Governor Cooke's assurances, at best less than 200 African Americans ever joined the 1st Regiment and it was never able to form a full battalion for service with Washington's main army.[2]

While the 1st Rhode Island command staff repaired to their home state to recruit slaves under the new act, the enlisted personnel remaining at Valley Forge were incorporated into the 2nd Regiment. At the same time, the veteran black soldiers from both regiments were formed into a single segregated company under Captain Thomas Arnold. Arnold's large company (5 officers, 3 sergeants, 4 corporals, 6 musicians, and 60 privates) belonged to the absent 1st Regiment, but while with the main army fielded with Colonel Israel Angell's 2nd Rhode Island. When Washington's Continental troops confronted the British at the 28 June 1778 Battle of Monmouth, Captain Arnold's 'black' company marched with Varnum's Brigade in Major General Charles Lee's Advance Force. During the ensuing withdrawal Arnold's men fought with the rest of the brigade at the Hedgerow position in a heavily contested defensive action. Thomas Arnold was severely wounded there, his leg later having to be amputated.[3]

Here is Lieutenant Colonel Jeremiah Olney's narrative of the 2nd Rhode Island at Monmouth. Advancing that morning with Lee's detachment,

We … took a road through the wood on our left, which brought us into the cleared land, in full view of the plains in front of the Court-House, where we discovered a large body of the enemy, paraded in the edge of the wood on the further side of the plain. We were halted, and a small body of men appeared in front on the plain near the wood, who the General took to be the enemy, and accordingly detached me with Colonel Angell's regiment, with orders to go through the wood on our left and attack them; but on a near approach I found them to be our men. I then marched the regiment out on the plain and formed the line in view of the enemy,

2   Popek, *They fought bravely*, pp.81–83, 102–103; 'At the General Assembly … of the State of Rhode-Island … begun on the Second Monday in February', 1778; William Sumner Jenkins (ed.), *Records of the States of the United States of America: A Microfilm Compilation* (Washington: Library of Congress, 1949), Session Laws, B.2, reel 4, pp.14–17. 'At the General Assembly … of the State of Rhode-Island …', begun 6 May 1778, *ibid.*, p.15.

3   Popek, *They fought bravely*, pp.86–87, 169–178, 206–211.

where I halted a few minutes; but seeing the enemy were advancing in column from their left, and our troops retiring, I then wheeled the regiment by platoons to the right, and marched off to join the brigade [Brigadier General James Varnum's, then commanded by Colonel John Durkee] … I then fell in … by this time we had two men killed and two wounded in Colonel Angell's regiment, which, however, did not disorder or confuse the troops.[4]

Nearing the van of the main army, Major General Lee encountered Washington, who questioned the withdrawal and then placed Lee in charge of an ad hoc holding action. Varnum's Brigade was positioned behind a hedgerow and fence line, where they were almost immediately attacked.

After retiring something more than a Mile [under Major General Lee], the main Army made its Appearance, formed on the Heights [Perrine Hill], when Gen. Varnum's brigade was ordered to halt, and form by a cross Fence, to cover two pieces of artillery [under Lieutenant Colonel Eleazar Oswald], which were in Danger of being lost. We there exchanged about ten Rounds, and were then obliged to retire with considerable Loss, but not until the Enemy had out-flanked us, and advanced with charged Bayonets to the Fence by which we had formed. Our Brigade suffered more than any that was engaged: The Loss in our Regiment was Lieutenant [Nathan] Wicks, a Sergeant and 8 Privates killed; Captain Thomas Arnold and 7 privates wounded, and 4 privates missing. Colonel Durkee was wounded in both Hands; I had my Horse slightly wounded, and a Button shot from the Knee of my Breeches. The Enemy did not pursue us far in our Retreat; observing our Army formed on the Heights in our Rear, they [the British Grenadier Battalions] halted on a Height, and began a brisk Cannonade, which lasted upwards of an Hour …[5]

Colonel Christopher Greene's segregated 1st Regiment (including, as of the end of July 1778, Arnold's former company, now commanded by Captain Jonathan Wallen) served in Rhode Island from its inception in 1778 until the end of 1780. The first summer of their formation Greene's Regiment (with 129 privates present, and 17 sick, present or absent) participated, alongside the 2nd Regiment, in the 29 August 1778 Battle of Rhode Island, the result of Major General John Sullivan's decision to abandon the siege of British-held Newport. The action was at times hard-fought and the 1st Rhode Island was in the thick of it; the regiment, however, did not do as well as some historians have claimed, which, consisting largely of inexperienced soldiers, is not surprising. Daniel Popek made a comprehensive survey of primary sources for the battle and found no mention of the 1st Rhode Island repelling three Hessian assaults, as claimed by 19th century and some modern accounts. Private Reuben Gulliver of Wade's Massachusetts State Regiment recalled in his pension deposition, that 'between Butts Hill and Quaker Hill … [we] had a bloody engagement with the enemy, Colonel Green's regiment of blacks being literally cut to pieces …'. An examination of the extant muster rolls

---

4   Popek, *They fought bravely*, p.208.
5   Popek, *They fought bravely*, p.209

for casualties reveals Gulliver's claim as a bit of old-age hyperbole. Major Ward gave an accurate synopsis in an 30 August 1778 letter, for which see below. Drummer Winthrop Robinson of Peabody's New Hampshire State Regiment noted, 'Colonel Green had a regiment of negroes who were in the same engagement, fought bravely, but were unfortunate'.[6] The acting 1st Rhode Island commander, Major Samuel Ward, wrote his wife on 30 August,

> early yesterday morning the Enemy moved out after us … and took possession of the Heights in our Front they sent out parties to their Front and we made detachments to drive them back. After a skirmish of three or four hours with various successes, in which each party gave way three or four times and were reinforced we drove them quite back to the ground they first took in the morning, and they have continued there ever since … I am so happy as to have had only one Capt. slightly wounded in the hand. I believe a couple of the blacks were killed and four or five wounded but none badly …[7]

Major General John Sullivan's 30 August after orders noted of the 1st Rhode Island during the battle:

> It having been represented by some persons that the conduct of Colonel Commandant Greene's Regiment was not, in the action yesterday, equal to what might have been expected, and also that Major [Samuel] Ward, who commanded the regiment, was much dissatisfied with their Conduct, the General assures the officers and soldiers of that regiment that no person has undertaken to censure their conduct to them, and that upon inquiry from Major Ward and sundry other officers who were with them in action, there was not the least foundation for censure. Doubtless in the heat of action Major Ward might have said something to hurry the troops on to action which, being misinterpreted, gave rise to the report, but from the best information the commander-in-chief [Major General Sullivan] thinks that regiment entitled to a proper share of the honor of the day.[8]

In spite of Sullivan's dissembling it is obvious some mis-step occurred on the battlefield, possibly because the men of the 1st Regiment misunderstood orders or due to their fundamental lack of experience.

Several units *were* mentioned in a variety of accounts for their bravery, Angell's, Jackson's, and Webb's Regiments among them, but Greene's 1st Rhode Island was not similarly spoken of. Given the concept of honor at the time, if the unit was deserving but neglected when others were singled out their officers would certainly have made their objections known. Still, one company, most likely Captain Wallen's veterans, did receive some notice that day. During an advance by Brigadier General Solomon Lovell's Massachusetts militia brigade, Major Samuel Lawrence was caught between the battle lines

6   Popek, *They fought bravely*, pp.178–195, 220, 224–237.
7   Popek, *They fought bravely*, p.232.
8   Popek, *They fought bravely*, p.235.

and saved by a 1st Rhode Island company, which moved forward and stood firm long enough for the major to escape.[9]

On 6 September 1779, the 1st Rhode Island Regiment contained 147 black soldiers.[10] In the ensuing two years Greene's Regiment remained understrength, until in June 1780, with only 124 private soldiers, the unit was formed into two large companies. In July a battalion of Rhode Island Six Month Levies was formed, supposed to consist of 600 men, in fact garnering only 400, both black and white. These men were intended to reinforce the 2nd Rhode Island, then serving with the main army in New Jersey, but were instead formed into eight companies. These were paraded with the two 1st Rhode Island companies to form a single temporary battalion commanded by Colonel Christopher Greene. As one white levy soldier, Abner Simmons, recalled, 'Capt. [Elijah] Lewis commanded the Black Company [actually two companies] which took post on the right of the regiment', the place of honor. In the meantime, Colonel Henry Sherburne's Additional Regiment was disbanded and 32 Rhode Islanders from the unit, including a few black soldiers, were transferred to the 2nd Rhode Island, thus ending its existence as a segregated organization.[11]

In February 1781 the first detachment from the former 1st Rhode Island joined the 2nd Regiment at 'Rhode Island Village' in the Hudson highlands, thus forming the conjoined Rhode Island Regiment. When all the 1st Regiment private soldiers arrived they were formed into two segregated companies, the 6th and 8th. At the same time the Rhode Island Regiment was seeking new recruits, with Lieutenant Colonel Jeremiah Olney supervising. Olney noted, 'Negroes will not be received, nor any but able-bodied effective men'. When looking for recruits in March 1782, Olney again stipulated in a newspaper advertisement, 'It has been found, from long and fatal Experience, that Indians, Negroes and Mulattoes (and from a total Want of Perserverance, and Fortitude to bear the various Fatigues incident to an Army) cannot answer the public Service; they will therefore not on any Account be received ...'. The service of African Americans throughout the war showed this to be untrue, but Olney's disallowance was likely due to the inordinately high number of black Rhode Island soldiers who died from smallpox and other diseases during the 1781–82 winter. It must be noted that Olney also barred 'Foreigners' from service partly due to their being unable to withstand 'uncommon Fatigues in the Field ...'.[12]

In April 1781 a small Rhode Island detachment was posted at Pines Bridge guarding a crossing over the Croton River. On 14 May, De Lancey's Loyalist militia attacked, killing Colonel Greene, Major Ebenezer Flagg, and six enlisted men. In addition, five enlisted men were wounded, and three subalterns, one surgeon, and 34 men missing. Many historians and others

---

9   Popek, *They fought bravely*, p.233.
10 NA (US), Revolutionary War Rolls, Miscellaneous, Returns of Brigades, Divisions, Armies, etc., folder 9, frame 55, 'Return of the Brigade of Foot Commanded by Brigadier General Stark ... Sept. 6 1779'.
11 Popek, *They fought bravely*, pp.270–284, 317, 318, 347.
12 Popek, *They fought bravely*, pp.356, 421–432, 442–453, 532–536, 552.

have written of this incident as if the entire Continental enlisted contingent involved in the action, and all those wounded or killed, were African American Rhode Islanders. In truth, one of the dead was a Massachusetts enlisted soldier and seven New Hampshire enlisted men were among the missing. Add to that, the Rhode Island force comprised both white and black rank and file. Four of the six dead enlisted Rhode Islanders were black. Two other black Rhode Islanders were mortally wounded and one of the other two wounded men was black, while ten of the 27 men missing or captured were soldiers of color. Daniel Popek concludes, 'Of these 36 total casualties from the Rhode Island Regiment, only twelve were men of color', though more black than white Rhode Islanders died in the affair. This historical rectification does nothing to detract from the courage of any and all who fought that day.[13]

The Rhode Island Regiment marched to Virginia with the combined Franco-American army at summer's end to confront Cornwallis at Yorktown. On 4 September 1781 the Rhode Island Regiment contained 116 black soldiers.[14] Also present were three Rhode Island soldiers (two black) selected to join the Corps of Sappers and Miners, and one lieutenant, two non-commissioned officers, and 19 privates (including seven black soldiers) detached from the Rhode Island Regiment to serve with Colonel Alexander Scammell's Light Infantry Battalion, formed in late May 1781. Following the British capitulation at Yorktown, the Rhode Islanders endured several months of rampaging illness while forming part of the Philadelphia garrison. In June 1782 the regiment joined the grand army at West Point and took part in the encampment and field maneuvers at Verplank's Point that autumn. Ordered to join the Northern Department, the Rhode Islanders spent the winter at Saratoga, and in February 1783 portions of five Rhode Island companies, with both black and white soldiers, took part in an ill-fated expedition against British-held Fort Oswego.[15] Sergeant Immanuel Doke of Colonel Marinus Willett's (New York) Regiment recalled the march to and from Oswego:

> Declarant believes there were five companys of Colonel Willets regiment that started for Oswego, he cannot recollect how many there were of the Rhode Island reinforcement … [he] well recollects that this was in the dead of winter. There were Indian guides employed … They travelled several days through the snow, as they supposed, towards Oswego. A great number … went ahead on snowshoes …

13 Popek, *They fought bravely*, pp.490–496.
14 Rhode Island Historical Society, Negative RHi X17 3696, John Rogers Returns Book, p.28A. Wilmington, DE, 'Return of Officers, NCommissd. Officers & Soldiers, Waggoners, Teamsters & Women, present in the Rhode Island Regiment', 4 September 1781. Ink on paper. Manuscript, Mss 673 SG2 B1 F60. The return shows 27 sergeants, 16 musicians, and 338 rank and file present. One sergeant and 20 rank and file absent with Scammell's Light Infantry were not listed. The ninth (light infantry) company, with 5 sergeants, 2 musicians, and 51 rank and file (2 of those were black), was absent serving with Lieutenant Colonl Jean–Joseph Sourbader de Gimat's Light Battalion, the Marquis de Lafayette's corps. Total for the entire regiment was 33 sergeants, 18 musicians, and 409 rank and file; Popek, *They fought bravely*, pp.362–372, 472.
15 Popek, *They fought bravely*, pp.497–498, 513–554, 590– 604.

instead of leading the army to Oswego, the guides lead us into a swamp, about nine miles … from Oswego. After it was found out that we were misled fires were built to warm us, when it was ascertained a great number were frozen considerably … when we started on our return to [the nearest shelter, the ruins of] Fort Stanwix our provisions were nearly all exhausted & the last five days before we arrived … we had no provision, except dead horse flesh, or something of that kind …[16]

Two Rhode Island veterans suffered long-lasting effects. John Cole testified in 1818, 'he is well acquainted with Reuben Roberts … a man of Colour & formerly a soldier in the Revolutionary army … Reuben has been crippled by having his feet very badly frozen while he belonged to the army … he has never had the entire use of his feet since …'.[17] Prince Vaughan noted:

he enlisted in the Black Regiment commanded by Colonel Greene, in the company commanded by Captain Elijah Lewis as a private in … March 1778 … for and during the War … was in the battle of New Port, White Plains [possibly confused with Kingsbridge in 1781], and at the Siege of Little York in Virginia at the time Lord Cornwallis surrendered – was in the Oswego expedition under the command of Colonel Willet [formerly a Continental officer, after his January 1781 retirement from that service, a commander of New York Levies and militia] when he had all his toes frozen on his right foot, and his left foot partially frozen … he was honorably discharged by Captain William Allen at Albany in the year 1783.[18]

In February 1783 the regiment was reorganized into a six-company Rhode Island Battalion. Four of the companies consisted of white soldiers, a fifth company had only African American musicians and privates, while the sixth was integrated. In June all but the 1781 three-years men were discharged and the battalion reformed with two companies. The Rhode Island Battalion was dissolved and the soldiers discharged at Saratoga, New York on 25 December 1783.[19]

Rhode Island Soldier Narratives

The Rhode Island black veterans' old-age depositions provide few compelling narratives, but some details shine through. One man who surely experienced the Valley Forge winter camp, as well as the battles of Red Bank, Monmouth, Rhode Island, and Yorktown, merely noted, 'I Prosper Gorten (a man of colour) … say that in the Month of June … 1777 I enlisted as a private soldier in Capt Flaggs Company in Colonel Christopher Greens regiment … in the Rhode Island line In which service I continued untill the 15 June 1783 when

16 Popek, *They fought bravely*, pp.599–600.
17 NA (US), Pension, reel 2059, Reuben Roberts (S39834), deposition of John Cole.
18 NA (US), Pension, reel 2455, Prince Vaughan (S42603).
19 Popek, *They fought bravely*, pp.603, 606–607.

I recivd a regular discharge signed by George Washington which discharge is hereto annexed …'[20]

Prince Bent was more expansive, stating he was:

a man of Colour (being Born in Africa his age cannot be ascertained) … enlisted (in March 1778) in Hopkinton … under Lieut David Johnson joined the Company Commanded by Capt Elijah Lewis in Colo Green's Regiment … then at East Greenwich … he was discharged from service in Albany (at the hospital) in the State of New York …he Served Five years Three Months and some Days … he Carried his [final] Furlow in his Pocket Got it wet and it come to Peaces … he was in the Battle of Rhode Island in Sulivans Expedition … he was after words taken Prisoner by the Enemy on Gard at Quitnent [Quidnesset] Neck he was Carried to Newport where he was a prisoner about Eight Months then carried to Holmeses hole [modern Vineyard Haven] Martha's Vineyard where he & fore others in the Night Stole a boat and made their escape to New Bedford and joined the army again at East Greenwich … he was in the Battle at York Town at the Taking of Corn Wallace … he wintered in Philadelphia was at Planks [Verplank's] Point Saratoga Swago [Oswego] &c.[21]

Richard Rhodes related 'that he is a Mariner & has followed the sea ever since the war, but is unable to follow that business in consequence of age – that he is very much crippled in one arm in consequence of a wound received in the battle of Monmouth … he was born in Africa brought to this country and sold as a slave and enlisted in the black Regiment so called to obtain his freedom …'. In another account Rhodes provided additional information: 'In the battle of Monmouth I received a severe wound in my arm from a musket ball. I was born in Africa – was a slave to Nehemiah Rhodes when I entered the army …'. Ichabod Northup 'enlisted as a private soldier in the company commanded by Captn [Elijah] Lewis in Colo. Christopher Greenes Regiment … in the spring of the year [1778] … he continued a soldier in said Regiment … until the time of the death of Colonel Greene [14 May 1781], when the Deponent was taken prisoner by the Enemy and carried to New York where he remained a prisoner until after the army was disbanded …'. His friend Wanton Casey added, 'I am Eighty one years of age … I was well acquainted with Ichabod Northup … [who told him] when Colonel Greene was taken prisoner Ichabod himself was also taken, and they put a rope around his neck and threatened to hang him to make him divulge some secrets about the positions of the troops, which he would not tell …'.[22]

The smallpox epidemic that overtook the Rhode Island Regiment during the winter of 1781–82 hit both black and white soldiers, but the former suffered out of proportion to their numbers. Daniel Popek calculated that 'men of color in the … Regiment clearly suffered a higher death rate, approximately

---

20 NA (US), Pension, reel 1099, Prosper Gorten (S38741).
21 NA (US), Pension, reel 222, Prince Bent (S38541).
22 NA (US), Pension, reel 2030, Richard Rhodes (W22060); *Ibid.*, reel 1828, Ichabod Northup (W20279), deposition of Wanton Casey.

58 percent of the total deaths for November and December 1781'.[23] Numbers do not tell the whole story. Private Asa Redington, Scammell's Light Infantry, was sick during the same period and tells of smallpox infection and treatment:

> On the 4th of November [1781], the skeleton of the Regiment to which I belonged, was embarked on board a French Frigate of 32 guns to be transported by the Chesapeake Bay to Annapolis, and sailed out of York river, and proceeded up the Bay … during 8 or 10 days they made but little progress, and provisions becoming scarce on board, and the small pox breaking out among the Americans, orders were given for all those not having that disorder to go on shore. Accordingly about 70 men were landed by the boats from the ship (I being one of the number) on the Virginia shore, under the command of an Officer – the ship then lying at anchor some 5 or 6 miles from the shore.
>
> We then took up our line of march for the North, procuring provisions from the inhabitants on the route, and at night taking shelter in their houses.
>
> Our party became very sickly, a number being daily taken down with the small pox, and were left behind, very few recovered and I saw them no more.
>
> We travelled on, crossing a number of rivers, and at length arrived at Annapolis … After resting there for one day, we again resumed our march, passing through Baltimore, and on to Wilmington, (State of Delaware) where three of us tarried one night at the house of an Apothecary, or Physician. He treated us with much kindness, I then being quite unwell, and felt myself unable to continue the route on foot. This physician invited me to stop and remain at his house until I should get recruited, … but I did not like to leave my party, and be left alone among strangers. I therefore thanked him for his kindness, and proceeded on next morning towards Philadelphia, and arrived there about the 15th of December. I was then very sick, and I think went to the hospital the same evening, after we arrived, with two others of my company, Turner and Lord, both fine young men. The former died of the dysentery and the latter of small pox at this place. Small sacks of straw were thrown on the floor for our beds. Lord lay next to me on my left hand, and Turner on the right. In this position they both perished.
>
> The Hospital was a large and extensive brick building of three stories high with a large cellar under the whole building, and had been built and formerly occupied for a poor house.
>
> I found a great many soldiers groaning and perishing under that fatal disease, the small-pox. I suffered exceedingly the first night with burning fever, and had it not been for a pail of cold water, to which I had free access, it seems as if I could not have lived through the night, during which I think I must have drank at least a gallon of that beverage. Soon after this the small-pox began its attack, and handled me very severely. We had a narrow bed sack filled with straw and thrown on the floor for each of us and a small blanket – these, with the addition of an old one which we always carried with us in a knapsack, constituted our bedding. I remained at this sick house till about the 10th of February, being unable to leave before that time.

---

23 Popek, *They fought bravely*, p.536.

This dreadful disorder made fatal ravages among the men, many of whom died daily and hundreds fell victims … I have seen soldiers apparently in good health and vigorous, come into the room I occupied, early in the morning, having some appearance of the small-pox about them, and by nine o'clock in the evening would be dead men.

About the 18th of February, 1782, several who had been left sick on the road arrived at the [Philadelphia] Barracks (where I quartered a few days after leaving the hospital) … We mustered 5 in number, and began our march to join our Regiment … Of about 40 men who had been drafted from the New Hampshire line and incorporated into Scammell's Regiment of light infantry, as before mentioned, I think no more than 12 or 15 joined their original regiments, the rest perished by disease, or by the sword of war.[24]

24 Redington, Asa, 'Short Sketch of [the] Life of Asa Redington' (January 1838), Stanford University Libraries, Department of Special Collections, Misc. 383.

9

New York: 'The Enemy made a stand and threw up a b[r]east work'

As with most Continental contingents the New York regiments changed identities, while generally retaining the same officer corps and many of the same enlisted men. The four 1775 regiments were authorized in May, but did not begin recruiting and organizing until June. Alexander McDougall commanded the 1st New York, Goose Van Schaik, James Clinton, and James Holmes (with Philip Van Cortlandt as lieutenant colonel) the 2nd, 3rd, and 4th Regiments. These organizations served in the Northern and Canadian Departments, from the Mohawk Valley to Quebec. In 1776 McDougall's 1st Regiment retained that numeric, but was reassigned to the main army operating in and around New York city. With McDougall's promotion to brigadier general in August and the lieutenant colonel imprisoned, the unit's major had command until his resignation in early October. The 1775 3rd and 4th Regiments were respectively renumbered the 2nd and 3rd New York (the latter commanded by Philip Van Cortlandt). A new one-year 4th Regiment (Cornelius Wynkoop) formed in January 1776, was assigned to the Northern department and the remnants absorbed by Van Schaik's 1777 1st New York. The old 2nd New York was now called Van Schaik's Regiment and two new named Continental regiments authorized, John Nicholson's (January 1776) and Lewis Dubois's (June 1776). The 1st and 3rd Regiments joined the main army, while the 2nd New York and all three named regiments were assigned to the Canadian and Northern departments.[1]

With the 1777 army reorganization, in late January the 1775–76 the 1st Regiment, lacking any field officers and a ghost of its former self, was dissolved. Van Schaik's Regiment was combined with the remnants of the 1776 4th New York and designated the 1st New York Regiment with Colonel

---

1   Wright, *Continental Army*, pp.60, 247–251; T.W. Egly, *History of the First New York Regiment, 1775–1783* (Hampton, N.H.: Peter E. Randall, Publisher, 1981), pp.16, 30–31, 34. 'List of Continental Army units (1776)', https://en.wikipedia.org/wiki/List_of_Continental_Army_units_(1776).

Van Schaik in command. Dubois's Regiment and the 2nd and 3rd Regiments of 1776 were renumbered in 1777 as the 3rd (Peter Gansevoort), 4th (Henry Beekman Livingston), and 2nd (Van Cortlandt) New York Regiments. The 5th Regiment was first authorized for service in 1777, with Colonel Dubois as commander, succeeded by Marinus Willett in July 1780.[2]

Another readjustment occurred in January 1781, when the New York line was reduced to two regiments. The 4th New York was disbanded and the enlisted men transferred to the 1st New York, while the 2nd New York was augmented with personnel from the dissolved 3rd and 5th Regiments. These two units served until June 1783, when their men were discharged.[3]

New York Soldier Narratives

Several New York African American would-be pensioners left lengthy service narratives, but let us begin with a more matter-of-fact deposition. John Patterson (aka Peterson) was brief: 'he enlisted in the Month of March 1777 for the term of three Years, in Colo Van Cortlandt's Regiment … was at the Battle in which Genl. Burgoyne and his Army was taken, he was also in the Battle of Monmouth … [and] a Battle at Newtown, with the Indians …'. When someone applied for a pension, Revolutionary military documents, most often muster rolls or nineteenth century compilations thereof, were consulted, but it did not hurt to have your former commander's support. 'This is to Certify that the bearer hereof John Peterson served under my Command in the Continental Establishment … in the years 1777–1778 and 1779 and was discharged from Captain S[amuel]. Pells Company near Morris Town in the beginning of the Year 1780 – given under my hand the 4.th day of April in the Year 1818 Ph V.Cortlandt late Colo 2. N.Y Regt'.[4]

For some black veterans one obstacle to confirming military service was determining the name they served under. Slave-soldiers, or those formerly enslaved, had particular problems. Charles Mason wrote the Federal War Office in 1834 concerning veteran Marlin Brown:

> I have made out the enclosed application for a pension … With regard to his name he was the greater part of his life a slave & was frequently called by the surname of his master At the time he was in the army he says he was frequently called Marlin Roorback but whether his name was so entered on the muster roll he does not remember He is now sometimes called Marlin Brown from the name of his last master but he is generally known by the simple name of Marlin & therefore I have so styled him in the application.[5]

Mr Brown's 1832 personal deposition is a bit more enlightening:

2   Wright, *Continental Army*, pp.110, 247–251.
3   Wright, *Continental Army*, pp.247–251.
4   NA (US), Pension, reel 1887, John Patterson/Peterson, 'a Man of Colour', (S43783).
5   NA (US), Pension, reel 1629, Marlin Brown (R6978), Charles Mason (letter).

He enlisted in the army of the United States in the year [1776] … & remained in the service until the last of May or first of June in the year [1778] …. He was as he believes enrolled among the regular Continental troops Colonels John Fisher [lieutenant colonel of Nicholson's New York Regiment] & Barney Teneyck [possibly Barent, captain 2nd New York, 1776 to 1778] were the highest officers of the regiment in which he was enrolled … Applicant served all the time of his enlistment as a waiter or servant of Colonel Fisher, but his name was on the muster roll of the regiment & he drew the pay of a soldier of the line. Once too on muster day he took his station in the ranks with his musket & answered to his name but never afterwards.

He was present in attendance on Colonel Fisher at the battle of Stillwater where Burgoyne was taken prisoner General Gates commanded & General Arnold was wounded either in or just before the battle. The main battle was fought on Friday beginning about noon & continuing till near midnight … When he first entered the service he was stationed at Albany for a short time. He then went to Ticonderoga where he remained till the Spring of 1777 when the army retreated before Burgoyne. In one of the skirmishes on the retreat [New York militia] Colonel Hendrick or Henry Rensselaer was severely wounded in the thigh by a musket or grape shot [at Fort Ann, 8 July 1777]—after the surrender of Burgoyne Applicant came to Albany where he remained through the winter & until his discharge. The greater part of the army went to the south in the fall after the surrender.

Applicant was the slave of John Roorback of Wallkill, then Ulster now Orange County & state of New York at the time he entered the service About the beginning of June 1778 he was to be transferred to Frederick Roorback the brother of his former master. He enlisted with the permission of his master John Roorback during all the time he was to have remained in his service & he served out all the time of his enlistment. He was in the service in all at least one year & five months. He never received any written discharge & he knows of no person now alive who can testify as to his service.[6]

Former private Benjamin Latimore submitted an extensive and accurate service narrative. At one point he noted his 'officers were Colonel Dubois, Lieut. Colonel Brown [Lieutenant Colonel Jacobus Bruyn] Major James Logan Capt Hutchinson and Lieutenant John Furman …'.[7] Here are a few more excerpts:

In the month of September [1776] … enlisted … as a private in Captain Amos Hutchens company of the 5th New York Regiment then under the command of Colonel Lewis Dubois … a few days after his enlistment he went with his Regiment by water from New Malbury to New York. On their arrival the American Army commanded by Genl Washington & which had been fighting with the enemy was retreating from Long Island. Some days afterwards the American Army retired from New York … A very few days afterwards a skirmish was had between a part of our troops and the Enemy [likely Harlem Heights, 16 September 1776] and a

6   NA (US), Pension, reel 1629, Marlin Brown (R6978).
7   NA (US), Pension, reel 1529, Benjamin Latimore, African American (S13683).

truce was declared for the purpose of burying the dead … after this skirmish our troops marched back to Kings Bridge and after remaining there a considerable time they … went to White Plains. … [two months following the 28 October 1776 battle] … it was time to go into winter quarters when they passed through a place then called Cumpon [Crum Pond] and Peekskill at this latter place they halted a number of days [then] … went by water to New Windsor.[8]

At this point Latimore became sick and was furloughed home, staying there until April 1777. He continues with a description of the capture of Fort Montgomery on the Hudson River:

[W]ent by water to Fort Montgomery at the High Lands Genl Geo Clinton had command of the Fort … In the Early part of [October] some vessels belonging to the Enemy came in sight and when within five miles of the Fort the wind having slackened they disembarked at place called Dunkerbarach [Dunderberg] or Thunder Hill and marched from thence to the fort. Before they arrived at the fort Gov [George] Clinton sent out different detachments of men to meet them and a fire was kept up between them and the Enemy until our men returned to the Fort. Shortly after orders were given by Gov Clinton to stop firing as the Enemy had sent a flag by [Lieutenant] Col [Mungo] Campbell [52nd Regiment]. The Col approached near to me as the gates of the Fort and was met on the outside of the … Fort by Gov Clinton & Dr. [Samuel] Cook [5th New York] After the usual salutations had passed between them and Col Campbell the Colonel was asked by Gov Clinton the nature of his Business who replied that he came to demand a surrender of the Fort which if done within one hour and our troops grounded their Arms they would be permitted to go as it was not wished to take them prisoners because they (the Enemy) had more men with them than could be accommodated in the fort. Gov Clinton replied that the Fort would not be surrendered as long as he had a man able to fire a gun. Col Campbell then said he would Eat his supper or would sleep … in the fort that night or in hell. They then parted. An Attack was made on the fort by the Enemy and was defended until six or seven oClock [sic] P.M. when it was taken. Gov Clinton, Gen James Clinton Col Dubois, Dr Cook and others escaped. Col … [Jacobus] Brown, Stephen Lush aid to Clinton And others and this declarant were made prisoners. In taking the fort Col Campbell was killed, he was stabbed on the walls of the fort by Capt [James] Rosecranse [5th New York] of Fishkill. The enemy and the prisoners of whom this declarant was one remained until the latter part of October when the Fort was destroyed by the Enemy and they all went by Water to New York.[9]

By his testimony, in March 1778 Benjamin Latimore was forced to become a British officer's servant and was recaptured by American forces. Taken to Major General Israel Putnam, who discovered his identity, he was ordered back to his unit, then at New Windsor. Dubois's Regiment soon joined the main army at White Plains and late that autumn returned northwards to spend the winter at Schoharie, New York, 25 miles west of Albany. Lattimore's

---

8   NA (US), Pension, reel 1529, Benjamin Latimore (S13683).
9   NA (US), Pension, reel 1529, Benjamin Latimore (S13683).

narrative concludes with the New York brigade's participation (minus the 1st Regiment at Fort Schuyler and Albany) in Major General Sullivan's 1779 expedition against the British-allied Iroquois tribes:

> In the month of April Col Dubois with his regiment left Schoharie and went to Johnstown, shortly after their arrival at this place a detachment of 40 or 50 men of whom declarant was one was sent by Colonel Dubois under the command of Capt Henry Van den bugh and stationed as an outside guard at a block house near the fishing place of Sir William Johnson about Eight Miles from Johnstown. They continued here for two Months and were not during the time engaged in any skirmish or affair with the foe. From Johnstown they returned to Schenectady and were there a few days and left there some in battoes [bateaux] on the Mohawk [river] and some on foot for Canajoharie where they found Col Livingston's regiment ... [which] was then forming a circle around a gallows on which was hung a Canada Spy. These two Regiments after the lapse of a few days left Canajoharie from Otsego Lake where they found Colonel Gansevoort ... and Courtland['s] Regiments. While here they damed up the end of the lake so as to raise it and enable them to carry their stores and baggage by water to the Susquehannah River. On daming up the lake and the waters being raised they proceeded as far as Tioga Point where they found Genl Sullivan & stayed a short time. While here they receivd the news of the Capture of Stony Point by [Major] Genl [Anthony] Wayne and the Regiment had a general rejoicing. From this place they proceeded through the woods to Niagara and halted within hearing of the Enemys Guns. On their way they passed through and destroyed a number of Indian settlements friendly to the Enemy but had no battle with them except at a place called Newtown about two days March from Tioga Point. Here the Enemy made a stand and threw up a b[r]east work and after resisting about an hour they gave way and fled. At Niagara they remained a short time possibly a fortnight when they All left and returned nearly by the same route they had gone until they reached Tioga Point which was in October. Here the declarant received his discharge he having served the period of his Enlistment it being three years when he together with Sergeant James Pride Samuel Langdon Daniel Robison and Abraham Oakie who were privates & had also been discharged returned home.[10]

Joseph Johnson, sometimes called Thomas Rosekrans, also left an extensive and interesting narrative. He began by noting,

> he enlisted ... at a place called Continental Village in the State of New York in the fall of 1778, as a substitute for Thomas Johnson to serve during the war with or under [his master's son] Captain James Rondecrants [Rosekrans], afterwards Major... in a Regiment of Infantry [5th New York] commanded by Colonel Lewis Debois or Deboze, in the New York line Genl. James Clintons Brigade ... [Lieutenant] Henry or Harry Dodge I think was for a time adjutant ... Captain [John] Hamtrammick Captain Devier and Captain [James] Steward or Stewart belonged to ... the Regiment ... I served as a Waiter to Major James Rondecrants

---

10 NA (US), Pension, reel 1529, Benjamin Latimore (S13683).

… At the time I enlisted I recollect that an officer took hold of my hand and made me write my name that I would serve during the War that I would be true to my country & that when I had enlisted the said Thomas Johnson whose substitute I was, was then discharged, And I was then called Joseph Johnson on account (as I suppose) of my having taken Thomas Johnsons place, and I think that I was entered upon the roll Joseph Johnson, I know that I was so called during the time I was in the service.

Soon after my enlistment I went with the regiment to which I belonged to Albany and remained a short time at that place & while there I recollect that a soldier was shot on the hill near the Barracks, for Desertion, we then went to Schoharrie about thirty miles from Albany at which place we remained through the winter, Major James Rondecrants remained with the troops through the winter & took Quarters in a house belonging to George Mann who was a tory & at that time confined in Albany Goal.[11]

Johnson also recounted the events of Sullivan's campaign, but only a few details are repetitive:

[A]t a place … called Newtown a few miles from Chemung we had a battle with the Indians Genl Sullivan commanded, Genl Clinton, [and] Genl Poor … was in the Battle, The Indians were commanded by Colonel Butler [likely loyalist Walter Butler]. The Battle continued a considerable … time at length the Indians discovering that they were liken to be surrounded by our troops fled & were Defeated, Major James Rondecrants was engaged in the battle, he gave me orders to stay with the pack horses, I did so a short time, but becoming uneasy I left the horses, took my Gun and engaged in the battle for which I was censured by Major Rondecrants, we pursued the Indians through the country to the Genesee River, burnt their Towns, Destroyed their cornfields, gardens & fruit trees wherever we found them, we burnt an Indian Town or settlement at the Genesee river containing I should think two or three hundred Indians huts or houses, called Genesee Town When we arrived at the Genesee river we were told that we were to go to Niagara, General Sullivan soon concluded not to go to Niagara & we then marched back & went to Easton in Pennsylvania & soon Joined the Army, we then went to New Jersey and spent the winter [of 1780] at or near MorrisTown, several of the officers took quarters at a place called Westfield near Morris Town, Major Rondecrants, with whom I lived put up at Captain Meckers, I remained with Majr Rondecrants & others at Westfield until sometime in the winter I should think in the month of January 1780, I then went with Major Rondecrants & others on to Staten Island [American Major General William Alexander, Lord Stirling's 15 January cross-ice raid] after we got on to the Island Majr Rondecrants sent me back to our Quarters & the next Day he & others with him returned to Westfield & brought with them many valuable articles which they had taken from the inhabitants who had submitted to the British Government.[12]

11 NA (US), Pension, reel 1426, Joseph Johnson aka Thomas Rosekrans, 'coloured' (R5636).
12 NA (US), Pension, reel 1426, Joseph Johnson aka Thomas Rosekrans (R5636).

Joseph Johnson's service narrative continues, but is problematic given that he was listed as having deserted on 15 January 1780, which coincides with the Staten Island expedition. Because of that his application was rejected.[13]

Two acquaintances provided depositions with interesting stories. Eighty-year-old Rom Adnance stated:

> I have been acquainted with the late Major James Rosekrans & his former man Joseph from my boyhood … He [Joseph] was said to have been engaged in the battle which took place between the American Army & the Indians, & I well remember an anecdote which was told of sd Joseph immediately after his return from the army … that during that battle [he] … loaded his piece with the ball at the bottom … [so] that the piece could not be discharged but that Joseph would snap his piece & seeing the priming flash thought his gun was discharged, & put in other charges upon the first … the Serjeant of the Company discovered the difficulty & removed it by taking out the breechpin [breech plug] of the gun. … Joseph labored on my farm for me after his return from the service & he used frequently to speak of his service while in the army & relate the circumstances & events which took place there'. Mary Dewitt, sister of James Rosekrans, related, 'I well remember … Joseph left Fishkill on Sunday morning to join the army & that I furnished him with some food to put in his knapsack to eat by the way. … My … Brother used frequently to write home from the army & in his Letters often mentioned Joseph, speaking of his health or in some other way attending to him. … I understood that my Brother selected sd Joseph from the company as a waiter … Joseph remained in the service so long as my Brother did & returned from the army at the same time as my Brother did.[14]

Major Rosekrans retired from the service in January 1781.

One last New York prospective pensioner served in a military support roll. Charles Stourman,

> a molatto man … In the spring or early in the summer of … (1776) I enlisted a private under Colonel [Hugh] Hughes who was then acting as Commissary of [Military] Stores at Fishkill … N. York. I entered immediately in the Hospital service situate[d] about three fourths of a mile from Fishkill. I acted as assistant or waiter to Doctr. McKnight [probably Pennsylvanian Charles McKnight] who was the surgeon of the Hospital / During the summer & fall I attend[ed] on the sick / The hospital & barracks were full of sick & dying I continued there during the winter cutting and preparing wood for the hospital &c. some time in the next summer [1777] I went to Fort Montgomery & was there at the taking of said Fort. When the British besieged the fort so closely we found we could not Keep it – Genl. George Clinton was in Command told every man to make his escape that could & he himself plunged into the river & swam across [to] safety [Clinton actually crossed the river by boat]. I took a team and baggage wagon & drove

---

13 NA (US), Pension, reel 1426, Joseph Johnson (R5636), War Department to George Woodruff (letter).
14 NA (US), Pension, reel 1426, Joseph Johnson (R5636), depositions of Rom Adnance and Mary Dewitt.

it up the river & saved it from the British I went back to Fishkill & staid there that winter and attended to the same duties I had formerly … to wit tending the Hospital. The next spring [1778] I was sent by Colonel Hughes with a team to get Provision & forage & followed that business during that summer & fall. I staid there during the next winter & spring, when I was discharged having served at least three years. After that I went to Virginia & was at the taking of Cornwallis at York Town, at this time I was acting as waiter to Capt or Colonel Hopkins [possibly Assistant Deputy Quartermaster General John Hopkins] – I was in service at this Time about six or eight months.[15]

15   NA (US), Pension, reel 2308, Charles Stourman (R10240); LOC, Washington Papers, series 4, George Clinton to George Washington, 9 October 1777.

10

New Jersey: 'Enlisted ... for nine months ... was in the Battles of Crosswick & [M]onmouth'

New Jersey first raised regiments for Continental service in late 1775. The state's initial contingent consisted of two units, the 1st and 2nd Regiments commanded by colonels William Alexander, Lord Stirling, and William Maxwell; William Winds succeeded Alexander after his promotion to brigadier general. Both units served in Canada before retreating back into New York under pressure from Crown forces, forming part of the Fort Ticonderoga garrison from early summer to November 1776. Early in 1776 a 3rd Regiment (Colonel Elias Dayton) was added. Leaving its home colony in early May, that unit spent from mid-May to October in the Mohawk Valley before joining its sister regiments at Ticonderoga in early November. A few days after the arrival of the 3rd Regiment the 1st and 2nd Regiments headed for home, their one-year enlistments having expired. The 3rd New Jersey Regiment remained at Ticonderoga until January 1776, when they, too, marched south.[1]

All three units were reconstituted in 1777, with most men signing on for the war. Matthias Ogden, Israel Shreve, and Elias Dayton commanded the 1st, 2nd, and 3rd Regiments. At the same time a 4th was added, with Ephraim Martin as colonel. All four New Jersey regiments were combined into a single brigade for the first time that year, with William Maxwell as brigadier. The New Jersey brigade served with the main army for most of the war, the only exception being 1779 when they joined Sullivan's campaign in Indian country. The New Jersey contingent was reduced several times. In January 1779 the 4th Regiment was disbanded and the enlisted men dispersed

---

1   William Stryker, *Official Register of the Officers and Men of New Jersey in the Revolutionary War* (Trenton: William T. Nicholson & Co., Printers, 1872), pp.13–27. See also Doyen Salsig (ed.), *Parole: Quebec; Countersign: Ticonderoga, Second New Jersey Regiment Orderly Book of 1776* (Rutherford, N.J.: Fairleigh Dickinson University Press, 1980).

among the remaining regiments; the 3rd Regiment was similarly dissolved in January 1781. The two remaining New Jersey regiments were commanded by Matthias Ogden and Elias Dayton until the end of 1782. In January 1783 the New Jersey contingent was reduced to a regiment, commanded by Elias Dayton, and a smaller battalion, under John Noble Cumming. These units were furloughed in June 1783.[2]

The exact number of African American New Jersey Continental soldiers is not known, likely not more than 40, perhaps as low as 20 to 25. In his booklet *Men of Color at the Battle of Monmouth*, Richard Walling lists nineteen known New Jersey veterans. Using available muster rolls and service records the presence of three of the men cannot be verified. One man, William Cuffey, was an Indian according to wartime records, another veteran may have been mixed Caucasian-Indian and three served with the militia only. That leaves only eleven or twelve black New Jersey Continentals remaining from that roster. To these can be added four 2nd New Jersey soldiers discovered during research for this book: James Aray, Thomas Case, Samuel Peterson, and Adam Pearce.[3] The current roster of known black Continentals with New Jersey regiments is as follows:

James Aray/Arey, mulatto, 2nd New Jersey, Captain Francis Luse's company, nine-month levy, enlisted 5 June 1778.

Pompey Black (a.k.a., Block), 2nd New Jersey, Lieutenant Colonel's Company, enlisted for the war in March 1779.

James Casar, 1st New Jersey, Captain Joseph Anderson's company, enlisted for the war, January 1781.

John Casar, 1st New Jersey, Captain Joseph Anderson's company, enlisted for the war, January 1781.

Thomas Case, mulatto, 2nd New Jersey, Captain Jonathan Phillips' company, nine-month levy, enlisted 28 May 1778.

John Cato, 4th New Jersey, enlisted for the war, May 1777, served to February 1779, discharged March 1779.

2   Stryker, *Officers and Men of New Jersey*, pp.28–58; Wright, *Continental Army*, pp.255–257. See also John U. Rees, "'One of the best in the army.': An Overview of Brigadier General William Maxwell's Jersey Brigade', *The Continental Soldier*, vol. XI, no. 2 (Spring 1998), pp.45–53, http://revwar75.com/library/rees/njbrigade.htm; Rees, "'We … wheeled to the Right to form the Line of Battle": Colonel Israel Shreve's Journal, 23 November 1776 to 14 August 1777 (Including Accounts of the Action at the Short Hills)', https://tinyurl.com/ShrevesJournal. Rees, and Bob McDonald, "'The Action was renew.d with a very warm Canonade": A New Jersey Officer's Diary, June 1777 to August 1778', https://tinyurl.com/NJOfficer; Rees, "'Their presence Here … Has Saved this State …": Continental Provisional Battalions with Lafayette in Virginia, 1781', Part I., "'This Detachement is Extremely Good …": The Light Battalions Move South', http://revwar75.com/library/rees/pdfs/light.pdf. Rees, Barber's Light Battalion, 1781 (New Jersey Light Company Personnel), http://revwar75.com/library/rees/pdfs/Barber.pdf.
3   Richard S. Walling, *Men of Color*, p.19; John U. Rees, "'I Expect to be stationed in Jersey sometime…": An Account of the Services of the Second New Jersey Regiment': Part I., 'December 1777 to June 1778' (1994, unpublished, copy held in the collections of the David Library of the American Revolution, Washington Crossing, Pa.), appendix, 'A Listing of Non-Commissioned Officers and Privates of the 2nd N.J. of 1778'.

John Caesar, 1st New Jersey, Captain Joseph Anderson's company, April 1782, enlisted for nine months, September 1781.

Negro Cuff (a.k.a. Cuff Warner), 3rd New Jersey, Captain Thomas Patterson's company, enlisted January 1778, deserted September 1778.

Oliver Cromwell (described in 1852 as a 'colored man', military records describe him as Indian; elsewhere he is described as a mulatto, possibly mixed Indian-African heritage), 2nd New Jersey, Captain Nathaniel Bowman's company, enlisted for the war, May 1777.

Dick Negro, 1st New Jersey, Captain Daniel Baldwin's company, enlisted 18 February 1777, captured 25 April 1777 (a skirmish at Amboy, N.J. occurred that day; American losses, 4 killed, 26 captured).

Adam Pearce/Pierce/Percey, mulatto, 2nd New Jersey, Captain John N. Cummings' company, nine-month levy, enlisted 24 May 1778.

Samuel Peterson, mulatto, 2nd New Jersey, Captain Henry Luse's company, nine-month levy, enlisted 5 June 1778.

Negro Sambo, 4th New Jersey, Captain John Anderson's company, nine-month levy, enlisted 20 May 1778.

Negro Titus, 1st New Jersey, enlisted 10 February 1777, deserted before first muster.

Amos Tomson, mulatto, 2nd New Jersey, Captain John Hollinshead's company, nine-month levy, enlisted 26 May 1778, deserted 20 September 1778.

Peter Williams, 1st New Jersey, Captain Jonathan Dayton's company, enlisted for the war, August 1781 (captain's waiter to late February 1782).[4]

New Jersey Soldier Narratives

The New Jersey soldiers of color who applied for pensions stinted on their narratives. Adam Pearce was typical: 'Adam Pierce labourer … aged sixty four … enlisted in the Spring of 1778 for nine months in Captain J.N.

---

4   Soldier records verified via Fold3.com searches in Revolutionary War Rolls (National Archives), and Compiled Service Records (National Archives). New Jersey State Archives, Revolutionary War Manuscripts (Numbered), Military Records, reel 5798831908; Document #3587. 'A List of Recruits rais'd for the Jersey Brigade in the first Regiment of the Militia of Burlington County, New Jersey, who have inlisted for 9 Months, agreeable to a late Act of the Legislature of said State'.; lists Amos Thompson as a mulatto. Document #3614. 'A List of Recruits from the 1st Regt of Militia in Hunterdon County State of N Jersey Commanded by Colonel Joseph Phillips who are to Serve Nine months from the Day of their Joining any of the four Regts raisd by said State in service of the United States May 28 1778'; lists Thomas Case as a mulatto. Document #3592. 'List of recruits from the 2nd: Battalion of Militia in the County of Cumberland, raised agreeable to an Act of Assembly of this State passed the 3rd: day of April ADom 1778, intitled an Act for the speedy & effectual recruiting the four New Jersey Regiments in the service of the United States Delivered to my Care to be Conducted to Camp May 25th 1778 Witness my hand{Jon: Beesley Captn'; lists James Delap and William Holmes as Indians; Document #3608. '… Coll. Taylor's Battalion of Hunterdon Militia …'. [4th Regiment]; lists James Array and Samuel Peterson as mulattoes; Document #3634. '… Colonel Samuel Forman's Regt. of Mon[mou]th Militia …'.; lists William Cuffey as an Indian.

Cummings Company of the second New Jersey Rigement Commanded by Colonel Israel Shreve … he was in the Battles of Crosswick [23 June 1778] & monmouth …'. Pearce (also Percey) was a nine-month levy drafted from the militia to provide a temporary manpower boost for the state's Continental regiments. Enlisting in May 1778, he was discharged the following March after an eventful year that included the June Monmouth campaign, a large-scale British foraging operation in northern New Jersey that autumn, and an enemy raid on the Jersey brigade's winter post at Elizabethtown just a few days before the levies were due to be discharged.[5]

Perhaps the best-known black New Jersey Continental may not have had African heritage after all. At 25 years of age, Oliver Cromwell enlisted for the duration of the war in May 1777 and served to June 1783. His discharge certificate, on file with his pension papers, states, 'Oliver Cromwell Private has been honored with the Badge of Merit for Six Years Faithful Service'. By his own account he 'was in the Battle of the Short Hills where Captn [James] Laurie was wounded and taken prisoner …'. In an 1852 newspaper article the interviewer noted Mr Cromwell claimed to have been in the actions at 'Trenton, Princeton, Brandywine, Monmouth and Yorktown, at the latter place, he told us, he saw the last man killed … he was also at the battle of Springfield, and says that he saw the house burning in which Mrs. [Hannah] Caldwell was shot, at Connecticut Farms [7 June 1780]'. The first two cited events occurred before his 1777 enlistment, so those claims are suspect, but Cromwell certainly was present at the other battles. The old soldier also recalled quite accurately the 1782–83 organizational change: in 1777 'he enlisted… in the second Jersey Regiment commanded by Colonel Shreve … [after Captain Laurie's death in captivity] the deponent was put under the Command of Captain [Nathaniel] Bowman - that not long before the discharge of the Deponent from service - the regiment to which he belonged was reduced to a Battallion - when he thinks he was commanded by Captain Dayton …'. Cromwell did indeed serve in Bowman's light infantry company from July 1777 to December 1783; he was then transferred to the Captain Absolum Martin's (4th) company, Colonel Cumming's New Jersey Battalion.[6]

The question of Oliver Cromwell's heritage is interesting. In 1852 he was called 'an old colored man' and then 'half-white'; Eric Grundset's work, *Forgotten Patriots*, notes that in some records he was termed a 'Mulatto', in others Indian. The question will likely never be settled but does bring to mind a related matter. What were the terms used to denote persons of color of mixed blood? Mulatto seems to be reserved for people with black and white parentage; some people so-termed were described as having 'black hair, [and] yellow skin', but yellow was not then used as a synonym for mulatto. Mustee, and less often 'mustezoes' or 'Mestizoes', was used to denote African and Native American forebears, at least in Rhode Island and the Carolinas.[7]

5 NA (US), Pension, reel 1933, Adam Pearce (Pierce/Percey), mulatto (S34468).
6 NA (US), Pension, reel 695, Oliver Cromwell, 'colored man' (S34613), including copy of clipping from the *Burlington Gazette*, New Jersey, 1852.
7 NA (US), Pension, reel 695, Oliver Cromwell (S34613), including copy of clipping from the *Burlington Gazette*, New Jersey, 1852; Grundset, *Forgotten Patriots*, p.383; Joseph Lee

Lacking any distinctive narratives from Jersey veterans we turn to a worthy alternative, a Massachusetts Continental born in New Jersey. Jacob Francis enlisted in the Bay State while residing there and was discharged in New Jersey, where he remained and served in the militia for the remainder of the war.[8] With remarkable recall, in 1832 he recounted his odyssey to New England.

> I was born in the township of Amwell in the County of Hunterdon on the 15 January 1754 … [when] I was of age, as I always understood I was bound [as an indentured servant] by my mother a colored woman … [to] one Henry Wambough, (or Wambock) in Amwell, he parted with me to one Michael Hatt, he sold my time to one Minner Gulick (called Hulick) a farmer in Amwell he sold my time when I was a little over 13 years of age to one Joseph Saxton, he went in the spring of the year 1768 and took me with him as his servant to New York from thence to Long Island where we took shipping in May 1768 and went to the Island of St. Johns [possibly the island of Montserrat, in the Caribbean] we visited different parts of that Island and spent the summer there towards fall we came to the town of St. Peters where we took shipping and returned to Salem Massachusetts … in Salem Mr Saxton sold my time to one Benjamin Deacon with whom I was to serve 6 years & until I was 21 years of age, with him I lived and served in Salem until my time was out which was in January 1775.[9]

Francis was soon caught by the early-war *rage militaire*:

> I lived in Salem & worked for different persons til the fall of 1775 in the spring of that year the war had commenced … about the last of October I enlisted as a soldier … I was told they were enlisting men to serve one year from the 1st. of January 1775 but I should receive pay from the time I enlisted … I enlisted at Cambridge about 4 miles from Boston under Captain John [Wiley] Wooley or Worley or Whorley in Col Paul Dudley Sergeants [16th Continental (Massachusetts)] Regement … When I left New Jersey and went with Mr. Saxton to St. Johns I did not know any family name but called myself Jacob Gulick (or Hulic) after the Mr. Gulick I had lived with And was enlisted by that name but after I returned to New Jersey was informed by my mother that my family name was Francis & after that time I went by the name of Jacob Francis – Captn. Wooley …was Captain, his brother [Aldrich Wiley] was Lieutenant … and he had two

Boyle, *'He loves a good deal of rum … '.: Military Desertions during the American Revolution, 1775–1783*, Vol.2 (30 June 1777–1783) (Baltimore, Md.: Genealogical Publishing Co., 2009), mustee, 257; yellow, pp.294–295, 298–299; Patrick Neal Minges, 'all my Slaves, whether Negroes, Indians, Mustees, Or Molattoes': Towards a Thick Description of 'Slave Religion' (1999), http://are.as.wvu.edu/minges.htm; Philip D. Morgan, *Slave Counterpoint: Black Culture in the Eighteenth Century Chesapeake & Lowcountry* (Chapel Hill, N.C.: The University of North Carolina Press, 1998), pp.240, 330, 479, 482; Warren Eugene Milteer, Jr., 'The Complications of Liberty: Free People of Color in North Carolina from the Colonial Period through Reconstruction' (PhD dissertation: University of North Carolina at Chapel Hill), pp.82 (page note), 84, 86, 88.

8   NA (US), Pension, reel 1015, Jacob Francis, 'a colored man' (W459). See also, Dann, *Revolution Remembered*, pp.390–99.
9   NA (US), Pension, reel 1015, Jacob Francis (W459).

sons one a sergeant & the other a Drummer in the company in which I enlisted – the Majors name was Ashton or Aston [Jonathan Austin] the Lieutenant Colonels name was [Michael] Jackson … I remember there was in the Regement Captain's [Frederick] Pope, Scott [Lieutenant William Scott], [Asa] Barnes, Ferrington [Thomas Farrington] … [10]

Participating in the Boston siege, the fledgling soldier soon found himself plying a pick and shovel more often than a musket, but that work exposed him to an early-American hero and the making of a myth.

General [Israel] Putnam was the General … At the time I enlisted the British Army lay in Boston, after that I remained with the Regement at Cambridge and in the neighbourhood of Boston until the British were driven out … I recollect General Putnam more particularly from a circumstance that occurred when the Troops were engaged in throwing up a breastwork at Leachmon's-point across the river opposite Boston between that & Cambridge, the men were at work digging, about 500 men on the fatigue at once, I was at work among them, they were divided into small squads of 8 or 10 together, & a non commissioned officer to oversee them, General Putnam came Riding along in uniform … to look at the work / they had dug up a pretty large stone which lay on the side of the ditch. The General spoke to the corporal who was standing looking at the men at work & said to him 'my lad throw that stone up on the middle of the breast work', the Corporal touching his hat with his hand said to the General 'Sir I am a Corporal'. – 'Oh (said the General) – I ask your pardon sir' and then immediately got off his horse and took up the stone and threw it up on the breastwork himself & then mounted his horse & rode on, giving directions &c.[11]

This story was embellished and published in the Philadelphia *North American* in October 1839, one major difference being that George Washington had replaced Putnam as the protagonist.[12]

Following the British evacuation of Boston, Jacob Francis with his regiment garrisoned Castle William in Boston harbor until mid-August, then marched and sailed to New York, eventually being ordered on to Long Island: 'marched on to the Island … but did not get to join the Army til after the battle had commenced & … [they] was on the retreat. We had to cross a creek to get to our Army who had engaged the enemy on the other side but before we got to that creek our Army was repulsed and retreating & many of them were [down?] into the creek & some drowned. The British came in [pursuit?] & the balls flew round us & our officers finding we could do no good, ordered us to retreat which we did under the fire of the enemy …' Leaving the island, they shortly after, 'marched to West Chester by way of Kings bridge – we lay there some time and every night we had a Guard stationed out 2 or 3 Miles from where the Regement lay at a place called

10 NA (US), Pension, reel 1015, Jacob Francis (W459).
11 NA (US), Pension, reel 1015, Jacob Francis (W459).
12 John L. Bell, 'Boston 1775', 11 January 2018, http://boston1775.blogspot.com/2018/01/i-will-come-and-help-you-second-time.html

Morrisania I mounted Guard there every time it came to my turn / there was an Island near there the tide made up round it. The British had a station on the Island & a British ship lay there (in an attack on the Island one night Col Jackson was wounded).[13]

Colonel Sergeant's Regiment soon after marched to White Plains, was involved only on the periphery of the 28 October battle there, and afterwards was positioned to observe British forces in the area. A short time after the fall of Fort Lee above the Palisades cliffs on the New Jersey side of the Hudson (North) River, Francis and his comrades,

> received orders & Marched to Peeks kiln [Peekskill] on the North river – we halted a day & night a little distance from the river and then crossed at Peeks kiln to the West side of the river from there we marched on … we got to Morris town New Jersey. We lay there one night then marched down near to Baskin ridge & lay there the next night / that night [13 December 1776] General [Charles] Lee was taken in or about Baskin ridge I heard the Guns firing – the next morning we continued our march across Jersey to the Delaware and crossed over to Eastown from thence we marched down the Pennsylvania side into Bucks County, it was then cold Weather and we were billeted about in houses our company lay off from the river a few Miles below Coryells ferry [present-day New Hope] & above Howiles [Howell's] ferry we lay there a Week or two.[14]

At this point the quest for an independent America seemed fated to fail. Barring successes at Boston in March and in repulsing the British attempt to take Charleston, South Carolina, in June, the year 1776 was a disaster. American forces were pushed out of Canada, and Benedict Arnold's Lake Champlain fleet suffered defeat in October (though that action did stave off a British northern invasion until 1777); the defense of New York, with the losses of Forts Washington and Lee and the ensuing retreat across New Jersey was, to put it bluntly, a debacle. Sergeant's 16th Continental Regiment had marched south with Major General Charles Lee, who seemed to be taking his time in moving to join Washington's depleted forces on the Pennsylvania side of the Delaware River. Major General John Sullivan replaced Lee as division commander after Lee's mid-December capture and hastened on to form a juncture with Washington.[15] Jacob Francis continues with his description of the 26 December 1776 attack on the Hessian garrison of Trenton, New Jersey:

> [W]e received orders to march & Christmas night crossed at the [Delaware] river, down to Trenton early in the morning. Our Regement crossed at Howells ferry four Miles above Trenton & marched down the river Road & entered the West end of the town – General Washington with the rest of the Army crossed

13 NA (US), Pension, reel 1015, Jacob Francis (W459).
14 NA (US), Pension, reel 1015, Jacob Francis (W459).
15 Christopher Ward (ed. John Richard Alden), *War of the Revolution* (New York: The MacMillan Company, 1952), Vol.1, pp.188–305, 384–397; vol. 2, pp.665–678; William M. Dwyer, *The Day is Ours! – November 1776–January 1777: An Inside View of the Battles of Trenton and Princeton* (New York: The Viking Press, 1983), pp.139–149, 194–213.

Two of four Continental soldiers drawn in 1781 by French *Sous-Lieutenant* Jean-Baptiste-Antoine de Verger, Royal Deux-Ponts Regiment. The soldier on the left is from the Rhode Island Regiment of 1781, wearing a leather cap bearing the state's anchor symbol and what seems to be a linen hunting shirt with red cuffs. On the right is a private of Hazen's Canadian Regiment clad in a wool regimental coat. Both men wear belted waistcoats and linen or wool overalls (gaitered trousers). Howard C. Rice and Anne S.K. Brown (eds. and trans.), *The American Campaigns of Rochambeau's Army 1780, 1781, 1782, 1783*, vol. I (Princeton, N.J. and Providence, R.I.: Princeton University Press, 1972), between pages 142-143 (description on page xxi). (Anne S.K. Brown Military Collection)

A soldier of Bradford's (Massachusetts) Regiment, October 1778. (Image courtesy of Nick Johnson)

Private soldier, 6th Connecticut Regiment, Autumn 1780. This regiment contained a number of African Americans, integrated with their white comrades. In 1782 Captain David Humphrey's company of Colonel Zebulon Butler's 4th Connecticut Regiment (formerly the 6th Regiment), was composed of solely black private soldiers, with white non-commissioned officers. Jeffrey Brace was a 6th Connecticut private, and in 1781 may have been in Captain Humphrey's 4th Connecticut company. One man stated in support of Brace's pension application, 'he then well understood that Jeffery … enlisted in the army to obtain his freedom … [he] remembers that he saw Jeffery a number of times after his enlistment in a soldiers Uniform with a Leather Cap he further recollects that some time in the War … does not recollect but thinks it must be in the year 1780 he was in the State of New York near West Point – met a Seargeants Guard all in Uniform – among the Guard was Jeffery & conversed with him – I am now acquainted with a Colored man calling himself Jeffery Brace & know him to be the same person then known by Jeffery Stiles – Jeffery sometimes was necked named [i.e., nicknamed] Pomp London'. (Artwork by Don Troiani courtesy of the artist, www. historicalimagebank.com)

Captain Thomas Arnold's veteran 1st Rhode Island detachment at the Battle of Monmouth, 28 June 1778.
In winter 1778 the 1st Rhode Island Regiment command staff returned to their home state to recruit a new unit with enlisted men consisting of freed black and Indian slaves. Meanwhile, at Valley Forge most men of the old 1st Regiment were transferred to the 2nd Rhode Island. The African American soldiers of both regiments would eventually join the re-formed 1st Rhode Island in July 1778, but were initially formed into a single detached company under Captain Thomas Arnold and continued to serve with Washington's main army. Arnold's detachment, commanded by white commissioned and non-commissioned officers, marched from Valley Forge in mid-June 1778 with Brigadier General James Varnum's brigade of Major General Charles Lee's division. Temporarily attached to the 2nd Rhode Island Regiment, Arnold's company participated in the June 1778 Monmouth campaign, and during the culminating battle took part in a hard-fought midday defensive stand. On the morning of the 28 June battle, Lee's force of picked regiments advanced on the British rear at Monmouth Courthouse, but was soon forced to retreat in the face of a numerous and aggressive enemy. Nearing the van of the main army Lee encountered Washington, who first questioned the withdrawal and then placed Lee in charge of an ad hoc holding action. Varnum's brigade was positioned behind a hedgerow and fence line, where they were almost immediately attacked.

Second Regiment Lieutenant Colonel Jeremiah Olney recounted, 'Gen. Varnum's brigade was ordered to halt, and form by a cross Fence, to cover two pieces of artillery [under Lt. Col. Eleazar Oswald], which were in Danger of being lost. We there exchanged about ten Rounds, and were then obliged to retire with considerable Loss, but not until the Enemy had out-flanked us, and advanced with charged Bayonets to the Fence by which we had formed. Our Brigade suffered more than any that was engaged: The Loss in our Regiment was Lieutenant [Nathan] Wicks, a Sergeant and 8 Privates killed; Captain Thomas Arnold and 7 privates wounded, and 4 privates missing. Col. Durkee was wounded in both Hands; I had my Horse slightly wounded, and a Button shot from the Knee of my Breeches. The Enemy did not pursue us far in our Retreat; observing our Army formed on the Heights in our Rear …'

Daniel M. Popek, *They '... fought bravely, but were unfortunate:': The True Story of Rhode Island's 'Black Regiment' and the Failure of Segregation in Rhode Island's Continental Line, 1777-1783* (Authorhouse, 2015), 209. National Archives (US), Revolutionary War Rolls (Microfilm Publication M246), Record Group 93, Capt. Thomas Arnold's 1st Rhode Island detachment (company), May, June, July 1778, Rhode Island, 1st Regiment (1777-80), folder 2, pp. 20, 23; folder 11, p.26. (Original artwork by Peter Dennis, © Helion & Co.)

'Battle of Cowpens,' William Ranney (South Carolina State House collection)

This 1845 painting shows Col. William Washington, 3rd Continental Light Dragoons, being saved at the Battle of Cowpens by one of his men, here pictured as a bugler. Two 19th century accounts refer to him as a 'boy' or waiter. In actuality none of the descriptions note the trooper as being black, though later accounts say he was an African-American named William Collins or Ball. Maryland Colonel John Eager Howard witnessed the incident and recounted it to William Johnson in 1822: 'The three [British troopers] advanced a breast and one of them aimed a blow the effect of which was prevented by Sergeant Perry who coming up at the instant disabled this officer. On the other side another had his sword raised when the boy came up and with a discharge of his pistol disabled him. The one in center who it is believed was Tarleton himself made a lunge which Washington parried & perhaps broke his sword. Two of the three being thus disabled the third then wheeled off and retreated ten or twelve paces when he again wheeled, about & fired his pistol which wounded Washington's horse - By this time Washington's men had got up and & Tarleton's horse moved off at a quick step. Thus, the affair ended. Washington had given orders not to fire a pistol and when the boy was questioned for disobeying the order he said he was obliged to do it to save the life of his Colonel. The excuse was admitted'. John Marshall, an officer in the Virginia Continental line from 1776 to early 1781, and later Chief Justice of the Supreme of the United States, in his account noted that, 'a waiter, too small to wield a sword, saved him [Colonel Washington] by wounding the officer with a ball from a pistol.' See Bobby G. Moss and Michael C Scoggins, *African-American Patriots in the Southern Campaign of the American Revolution* (Blacksburg, S.C.: Scotia-Hibernia Press, 2004), 62-63. (Quoted letter from, Daniel Murphy, 'The Cavalry at Cowpens: Thinking Inside the Box,' http://www.schistory. net/3CLD/Articles/insidethebox.pdf. John Eager Howard to William Johnson, 1822 (courtesy of Dr. Lawrence Babits and Sam Fore). See also John Eager Howard, Letters to John Marshall, 1804, excerpts held at the Cowpens National Battlefield, courtesy of the Army Command and General Staff College. Original held in the Bayard collection, Maryland Historical Society.) John Marshall, *Life of George Washington*, vol 3, chapter 9 (five volumes–Fredericksburg, Va.: The Citizens' Guild of Washington's Boyhood Home, 1926), pp. 307-308; for the Cowpens cavalry fight see Note 58. See also, 'Unsung Patriots: African-Americans at the Battle of Cowpens,' http://www.nps.gov/cowp/forteachers/unit-7-the-battle-the-human-element.htm.

A soldier of Lieutenant Colonel Thomas Gaskin's Virginia Battalion, during the unit's summer and autumn 1781 service with the Marquis de Lafayette against Lieutenant General Charles Cornwallis's forces. Like the two Virginia Continental regiments commanded by Colonels John Green and Samuel Hawes, and fighting under Major General Nathanael Greene, Gaskins' unit contained a number of African Americans. Five black veterans' pension narratives show service under Gaskin in 1781, Francis Bundy, John Chavers, William Jackson, Bennett McKey, and William Wedgbare. (Artwork by Don Troiani Courtesy of the artist, www.historicalimagebank.com)

Rachel (previously called Sarah) and her son Bob, were with the 1st Maryland Regiment in 1778. Image based on a 28 October 1778 *New Jersey Gazette* runaway advertisement. (Artwork by Bryant White, courtesy of the artist, https://whitehistoricart.com/)

at McConkeys ferry four miles above Howells & marched down the Scotch road & came into the North End of the town – We marched down the street from the river road into the town to the Corner where it crosses the street running out towards the scotch road & turned up that street & General Washington was at the head of that street coming down towards us & some of the hessians between us & there we had the fight & the principal firing was. After about half an hour the firing ceased & some officers among whom I recollect was General Lord Stirling Rode up to Col: Sergeant & conversed with him then we were ordered to follow him And with these officers & Col Sergeant at our head. We marched down thro the town toward Assanpink [Assunpink Creek] & cross the Assanpe[nk] on the North side of it & to the East of the Town where we were formed in line and in View of the Hessians who were paraded on the south side of the Assanpink & grounded their Arms & left them there & marched down to the Old ferry below the Assanpenk between Trenton & Lamberdon [Lumberton], soon after that a number of Men from our Regement were detailed to go down & ferry the Hessians Across to Pennsylvania I went as one & about noon it began to rain & rained Very hard we were engaged all the afternoon ferrying them across til it was quite dark when we quit, I slept that night in an Old Mill hous above the ferry on [the] Pennsylvania side / the next morning I joined my Regement where I had left them the Day before up the Assanpenk East of Trenton … [16]

Private Francis soon ended his Continental Army career, recalling:

We lay there a day or two & then the time of the Years men was out and our Regement received part of their pay & were permitted to Return home. I did not get a discharge at that time / I had 7 1/2 months pay due to me & I believe Others had the same & we were ordered after a certain time to come to Peeks kiln on the North river and there we should receive our pay & get our discharge. I was with the Regement & in service … about 14 Months & never left it until I had recd. the three months pay & had permission to return to the place of my nativity in Amwell about 15 miles above Trenton – I immediately returned from Trenton to Amwell & found My Mother living, but in ill health; I remained with her and when the time came to go to Peeks kiln for my pay and discharge I gave up going and never received either my pay or a discharge in Writing …[17]

The remainder of Francis's lengthy deposition recounts his militia career, but only portions in detail.

After I came home I was enrolled in the Militia in Captain Philip Snooks company … the next spring I was called out in the Militia in the Months service / the Militia took turns one part went one month & then the other part went out a month & relieved them & then those that were out the full month went again so that one half [of] the Militia in this part of Jersey was out at a time & this continued several years. I always went out when it came to my turn to the end of the war … & went out once as a substitute for a person who … could not and gave me $45

16 NA (US), Pension, reel 1015, Jacob Francis (W459).
17 NA (US), Pension, reel 1015, Jacob Francis (W459).

continental money to take his place … In the spring of 1777 the first month I went out was under Captain Phillet or Captain Charles Reading … [After recounting several militia stints Francis related] I was out another month under Captain Philip Snook / we marched … to New Ark & staid a month we lay in a building in New Ark called an Academy or schoolhouse / at that time the British & hessians lay on staten Island – An alarm came that there was an Attack on the militia at Elizabeth Town & our company marched out toward Elizabeth Two Miles or more along the road til we came to a piece of rising ground when the British came in sight, when we saw their numbers We fired on them and then retreated, a piece of low ground covered with bushes lay in the West of the road We turned into that. The Hessians I think came fore most there was 3 Columns blue Coats, Green Coats, & red coats & when they got on the rising ground fired on us after we gott off some distance. Some of us concluded to creep back toward the road and get a shot at them. One Joseph Johnson belonging to the company & myself went. He and I crept along among the bushes til I got almost within Gun shot when I heard a noise behind me and looked round & there was three hessians near me that belonged to a flanking party and had got between me and the company. They took me prisoner – Johnson was some distance from me And was taken prisoner by Another party [than the one] I was taken by. The Hessians that took me, out to the road, to the British Army & [I] marched with them under Guard through New Ark And was carried some distance up the river called second river / night came on and some time in the night we came to a creek that ran down into the river – some of our Militia … expecting the british, had placed themselves in some bushes on the left of the road near the creek & fired on the British as we came up. This created some confusion & broke the ranks & most of them left the road & turned off to the right toward the river. There was four men had me under Guard they turned in the Alarm & left me / I stood near a steep bank that came down into some bushes toward the creek / finding the men a little way from me I stepped down the bank into the bushes and laid down / the Militia that had fired retreated & I saw Nothing of them. The British staid a few Minutes, one of the Captains was wounded, then they formed in the road again & marched on … I lay in the bushes some time til they were all gone then came out & pushed back to New Ark & joined Captain Snooks company there about 2 oClock in the Morning …[18]

Jacob Francis's service in the cause of liberty is profound when set against his own experience. He served in the military as a free man, but had been sold into indentured servitude when 'of age', and at just over 13 years old had passed to his fourth master. He returned home to Amwell, New Jersey where friends and acquaintances were still enslaved and would be for many years. When married in 1789 he struck another small blow for freedom, as testified by former slave Philis Duncan; she

was present and saw … Mary Francis married to … Jacob Francis by Cato Finley … at the time of said marriage deponent & Mary Francis & Cato Finley all lived

---

18 NA (US), Pension, reel 1015, Jacob Francis (W459).

with and were the slaves of Nathaniel Hunt where the marriage took place …
Jacob Francis immediately after his marriage to … Mary bought … Mary of her
… Master Nathaniel Hunt … Mary in a few days left the employ of … Hunt &
went with her husband … [and] have ever since that time lived together as man &
wife up until the death of Jacob … and raised a family of Children.[19]

19 NA (US), Pension, reel 1015, Jacob Francis (W459), deposition of Philis Duncan,

11

Pennsylvania: 'Wounded in the right thigh, at Brandywine …'

The first Pennsylvanians to join the fledgling Continental Army were nine companies of riflemen in Colonel William Thompson's Rifle Battalion. They reached Cambridge at the end of August, joining four Maryland and Virginia rifle companies already arrived. Thompson's men served a one-year enlistment, ending 1 July 1776; in January of that year their unit was redesignated the 1st Continental Regiment. During the 1781 Pennsylvania line mutiny it came to light that many men who served in the 1775 rifle battalion in fact never formally enlisted, and since their first service had 'continu[ed] ever since upon that voluntary plan'.[1]

In autumn 1775 the state authorized the formation of the 1st through 6th Pennsylvania Battalions. The 1st, 2nd, 4th, and 6th Battalions were sent to reinforce the army in Canada, while the 3rd and 5th Battalions served with the main army at New York. A seventh Continental unit commanded by Colonel Aneas Mackay was organized to protect western Pennsylvania from enemy incursions. The 1777 army reorganization led to a shift in unit designations; the 1st Continental Regiment of 1776 was officially added to the state's complement, becoming the 1st Pennsylvania Regiment in 1777. Thus, the reformed and reenlisted 1st through 6th Battalions were renumbered as the 2nd through 7th Pennsylvania Regiments. Five new units were added that year. The 8th Regiment was formed from Mackay's 1776 corps, while the 9th, 10th, 11th, and 12th Regiments were newly-organized. Pennsylvania fielded two state units in 1776, both of which in early 1777 were consolidated into the Pennsylvania State Regiment. In June 1777 that unit was transferred to the Continental contingent as the 13th Pennsylvania Regiment. All these

---

1   Wright, *Continental Army*, pp.16, 24–25; Aaron Wright, 'Revolutionary Journal of Aaron Wright, 1775', *The Historical Magazine of America* (New York: Charles B. Richardson & Co., 1862), Vol. VI p.209; John B.B. Trussell, Jr., *The Pennsylvania Line: Regimental Organization and Operations, 1776–1783* (Harrisburg: Pennsylvania Museum and Historical Commission, 1977), pp.21–25, 102–106. LOC, Washington Papers, series 4, James Potter and Joseph Reed to George Washington, 19 February 1781.

organizations served with General George Washington's main army in New Jersey and Pennsylvania in 1777, and all wintered at Valley Forge.[2]

From 1778 to 1781, with several exceptions, the Pennsylvania troops remained in the Middle department under General Washington. In May 1778 the 8th Regiment was detached to Fort Pitt in western Pennsylvania, where it was to stay for the remainder of the war. By 1778 combat losses, illness, and desertion had whittled down all the units. In July several amalgamations occurred, reducing the number of regiments allotted the state, with senior units absorbing their juniors. The 2nd Pennsylvania merged with the 13th Pennsylvania, the 3rd Regiment absorbed the 12th Regiment, and the 10th Pennsylvania was consolidated with the 11th. To make matters more confusing in January 1779 a 'new' 11th Pennsylvania was formed from the remnants of Hartley's and Patton's Additional Regiments. The new unit was assigned that year to Major General Sullivan's Iroquois expedition, after which it joined the main army in New Jersey. In January 1781 the Pennsylvania line underwent its own internal revolution. Outside Morristown, New Jersey, the rank and file mutinied over pay and breach of enlistment terms. As a result, most of the men were discharged and the number of regiments reduced to six. In truth, these organizations would only be used for recruiting purposes and personnel depots. When the Pennsylvania line was reformed that spring, slated for southern service, it was formed into three provisional battalions, the 1st, 2nd, and 3rd. Fighting under Lafayette against Cornwallis in Virginia, they were mauled at the 6 July 1781 Battle of Green Spring. Reconsolidated into two battalions, the officers of the 3rd Battalion returned north to recruit anew. Increased to three battalions that winter for service in South Carolina, that complement was continued almost to the end of 1782. In January 1783 the troops remaining in South Carolina were reformed into a new 1st Pennsylvania Regiment and served as such until the final discharge that autumn.[3]

2   Trussell, *The Pennsylvania Line*, pp.21–137, 153–163, 164–187; Wright, *Continental Army*, pp.109–110, 259–268.

3   Trussell, *The Pennsylvania Line*, pp.21–137, 164–187; Wright, *Continental Army*, pp.259–268; John U. Rees, "'Their presence Here ... Has Saved this State ...": Continental Provisional Battalions with Lafayette in Virginia, 1781'; Parts 2–4. "'Almost all old soldiers, and well disciplined ...": Brigadier General Anthony Wayne's 1781 Pennsylvania Provisional Battalions', A. "'I fear it is now too late ...": The Pennsylvania Line Mutiny, January 1781', http://revwar75.com/library/rees/pdfs/PA-A.pdf; B. "'Our Regiments are yet but very small ... ': Settling with the Troops and Rebuilding the Line http://revwar75.com/library/rees/pdfs/PA-B.pdf; C. "'The whole Line ... behaved in a most orderly manner": Reorganizing the Pennsylvania Provisional Battalions and Service in the 1781 Campaign' http://revwar75.com/library/rees/pdfs/PA-C.pdf; *The Brigade Dispatch*, Vol. XXXVII, no. 2 (Summer 2007), pp.2–19; vol. XXXVII, no. 4 (Winter 2007), pp.2–15; vol. XXXVIII, no. 1 (Spring 2008), pp.2–21; Appendix, "'A Smart firing commenc'd from from both parties ...": Brig. Gen. Anthony Wayne's Pennsylvania Battalions in Virginia, June to November 1781'; A. "'We will be much inferior to the enemy ...": May 31 to July 5 1781'; B. "'A charge ... under a heavy fire of Grape shot ...": Battle of Green Springs, 6 July 1781'; C. "'Cornwallis ... threatens every Devastation that fire & sword can produce ...": Marching and Countermarching, 9 July to 25 August'; D. "'The batteries were opened and fired with great success ...": September to November 1781'; E. "'The Cloathing was drawn near twelve month ago ...": 1780–1781 Pennsylvania Clothing, Letters and Returns', https://tinyurl.com/smartfiring.

Drummer, 2nd Battalion, Philadelphia Associators. Artwork by Bryant White (Image courtesy of the artist, https://whitehistoricart.com/). In 1775 Polydore Redman was forcibly purchased from his owner Dr. John Redman, by members of the Philadelphia Associators (Pennsylvania's early-war voluntary military association, in lieu of a state militia.). Doctor Redman (Dr. Benjamin Rush's former teacher) was a non-Associator, and seems to have been suspected of Loyalist proclivities. The purchasers freed Polydore who became a drummer with the Associators; he served until 1776 when he joined the 5th Pennsylvania (Continental) Battalion. During the latter enlistment he was known as Polydore 'a negro drummer'.[5]

Of the American states with large troop contingents, Pennsylvania had the fewest African Americans in Continental service. This was true even before the first Pennsylvania militia law in 1777 which allowed only white males to serve, though there does seem to have been more blacks in the state's regiments before the law than afterwards. Whatever the cause, the 1778 'Return of Negroes' shows that Pennsylvania's two brigades had only two black soldiers in one, none in the other. John Hannigan contends that ineligibility for service in a state's militia did not necessarily prohibit men of color from enlisting in a Continental regiment. Mr Hannigan provides several instances where such a ban was overridden in Massachusetts, but, in actuality, eligibility for state militia service usually led to acceptance for Continental enlistment. Furthermore, the absence of African Americans on the militia rolls meant they could not be drafted into Continental regiments when a short-term levy was enacted. There also may have been an ingrained aversion among Pennsylvania officers, many of whom possibly agreed with Captain Alexander Graydon, who, in complimenting Glover's Massachusetts troops, added the caveat, 'even in this regiment there were a number of negroes, which, to persons unaccustomed to such associations, had a disagreeable, degrading effect'. Captain Persifor Frazer was not as politic, writing his wife from Fort Ticonderoga in July 1776, 'The miserable appearance, and, what is worse the miserable behavior of the Yankees, is sufficient to make one sick of the service. They are by no means fit to endure hardships. Among them is the strangest mixture of Negroes, Indians, and Whites, with old men and mere children, which together with a nasty, lousy appearance make a most shocking spectacle. No man was ever more disappointed than I have been in respect to them' (Frazer's comments are curious, considering he was among the men responsible for an early-war draft of what later became the state's 1780 abolition law). Whatever the reason, the dearth of Pennsylvania soldiers of color is striking.[4]

That said, there was a small number of black Pennsylvanians who did serve. The best roster comes from Eric Grundset's *Forgotten Patriots*, but

---

4   Arthur J. Alexander, 'Pennsylvania's Revolutionary Militia', *Pennsylvania Magazine of History and Biography*, vol. 69, no. 1 (January 1945), p.18; Hannigan, 'Massachusetts laws', pp.1–3; Graydon, *Memoirs of His Own Times*, pp.148–149; 'Some Extracts from the Papers of General Persifor Frazer', *Pennsylvania Magazine of History and Biography*, Vol. 31, no. 2 (1907), p.134.

even that has inaccuracies.[5] Tallying only those listed specifically as soldiers or marines, that resource contains 40 claimed soldiers of color. Removing suspect entries, including those with inadequate documentation and duplicates, leaves us with a roster of 22 soldiers, Continentals and militia:

Pitt Adams, 'colored', private, September 1778 to April 1779, Colonel Lewis Nicola's Invalid Regiment.

Negro Bob, fifer, Captain William Semple's company, Colonel Joseph Dean's 4th Regiment, Philadelphia militia.

John Bristol, 'negro', marine, muster roll 3 December 1776, armed boat *Franklin*, Pennsylvania State Navy.

Levi Burns, 'negro', waiter, enlisted for the war, muster roll September 10 1778, Lieutenant Colonel's company, 10th Pennsylvania Regiment.

Caesar, 'negro boy', drummer, enlisted 1 March 1776, armed boat *Warren*, Pennsylvania State Navy.

Cezar/Cizar Negroe, pay arrearage certificates January 1782 to November 1783, 4th Regiment Continental Light Dragoons.

Sebastian Day, 'negro', seven months levy, enlisted 1 August 1780, unknown Pennsylvania Continental regiment.

John Francis, 'a negro', private, Captain Henry Epple's company, 3rd Pennsylvania Regiment; abstract of state pension application, 'Had both legs much shattered by grape shot at Battle of Brandywine on 11th. of Sept. 1777'.

Edward Hector, 'a colored man', bombardier and wagoner, Captain Hercules Courtenay's company, Colonel Proctor's Battalion State Artillery, March 1777, Pennsylvania State Artillery Regiment and 4th Continental Artillery Regiment.

Cato Freeman, private, muster roll at discharge April 1783, Colonel Lewis Nicola's Invalid Regiment.

John 'the negro', seven months levy, private, muster roll 17 January 1781, Captain George Tudor's company, 4th Pennsylvania Regiment.

John Leoman, 'black', private, muster roll 20 April 1778, Captain Thomas Robinson' company, Lancaster County militia.

William Lukens, 'negro', waiter, captured at Fort Washington 16 November 1776, Captain Stake's company, Colonel Michael Swope's Pennsylvania Battalion of Flying Camp militia.

Abraham Moore, 'a free man of colour', private, four tours 1781–1783, Captains Fox's, Stewart's, Sharp's, and Giddes' companies, Colonel Thomas Giddes' Regiment Pennsylvania militia.

Orange, 'negro', marine, enlisted 1 October 1776, pay roll Captain Robert Mullan's Company of Marines to 1 December 1776. The pay roll was written in a book containing the minutes of a Masonic Lodge that met at Tun Tavern, on Water Street in Philadelphia. Robert Mullan was tavern's proprietor and likely a member of the lodge.

Peter Negro, private, York County militia,

---

5   Grundset, *Forgotten Patriots*, pp.412–414.

Francis Pomenay, color uncertain, slave or indentured servant noted as 'discharged, taken by his Master, May 22, 1776', marine, enlisted 19 May 1776, armed boat *Congress*, Pennsylvania State Navy.

Ferdnand Ponsley, color uncertain, slave or indentured servant noted as 'discharged, taken by his Master, May 22, 1776', marine, enlisted 5 May 1776, armed boat *Congress*, Pennsylvania State Navy.

Polydore or Polydore Redman/Rodman, 'a negro drummer', 1776, company unknown, 5th Pennsylvania Battalion.

Isaac Walker, 'negro', marine, enlisted 27 August 1776, pay roll Captain Robert Mullan's Company of Marines to 1 December 1776. The pay roll was written in a book containing the minutes of a Masonic Lodge that met at Tun Tavern, on Water Street in Philadelphia. Robert Mullan was tavern's proprietor and likely a member of the lodge.

Cuff Warner/Warren, fifer, enlisted 5 May 1776, armed boats *Dickinson* (1776) and *Bulldog* (1776–1778), Pennsylvania State Navy.

Stacey Williams, 'a negro', private, enlisted 15 April 1777, served to 1783, Captain Jacob Humphrey's company, 6th Pennsylvania Regiment; wounded at Brandywine, 11 September 1777.[6]

The revised list shows five soldiers of color serving in the Pennsylvania militia, seven as marines with the State Navy, and ten in Continental regiments, as follows; two in Nicola's Invalid Regiment, and one each in the 5th Regiment 1776, 3rd Regiment 1777, 10th Regiment 1778, 4th Regiment 1780, 6th Regiment 1777–1783, 4th Continental Light Dragoons 1782–1783, 4th Continental Artillery 1777, and a levy in an unknown 1780 regiment. Undoubtedly, this is not a comprehensive roster.

Pennsylvania Soldier Narratives

Only two black Pennsylvania soldiers applied for Federal pensions, one in the militia and the other a Continental. Both accounts are given below. Their service, plus the men listed above who were soldiers after the 1777 militia law, shows that some African Americans continued to serve despite the ban. In 1833 Abraham Moore detailed his military career,

> In the year 1781 ... Augustine Moore was drafted in the militia ... to go on an expedition to the west against the Indians ... this declarant went out as a substitute of said Augustine Moore, in the company of militia commanded by Captain George (or William) Fox, in the Regiment commanded by Colonel Thomas Giddes, in the Brigade of General Broadhead [Daniel Brodhead, former colonel of the 8th Pennsylvania, transferred to the 1st Regiment in January 1781]

6 Grundset, *Forgotten Patriots*, pp.412–414. Pennsylvania State Archives, Revolutionary War Military Abstract Card File, Cezar/Cizar Negroe and Peter Negro. http://www.digitalarchives. state.pa.us/archive.asp; John B. Linn, and William H. Egle, (eds.), *Pennsylvania Archives* (Harrisburg: Lane S. Hart, State Printer, 1880), Series 2, Vol.10, p.606.

… he marched with said Company from … Uniontown, and crossed the Ohio river, at the Mingo Bottom (now in … Jefferson County) where there was then a Block House – from thence he marched through the wilderness to Wapatamika [Wakatomika, variously spelled, name for a series of Shawnee towns], in … Ohio, where they arrived in the month of June … 1781. Here the American troops attacked the Indians, and defeated them – Several Indians were killed and several taken prisoner in this engagement … this declarant was wounded by a ball passing through his arm – Captain Fox was wounded in the breast – Shortly after this engagement, the Company returned to Uniontown – their return was in July … 1781 … [he] was on this expedition two months … in the fall of the same year (1781) the Indians again became troublesome on the frontier settlements, and … Augustine Moore was again drafted, in the Pennsylvania militia, on an expedition against the Indians, and the deponent again entered the service as a substitute … He was under … Captain Edward Stewart, in this expedition … Colonel Giddes still commanding the regiment – He was marched from Uniontown to what is now called Hollidays Cove [now a section of Weirton, West Virginia], on the Ohio River, and crossing the … Ohio at that place, the troops proceeded through the wilderness to the Muskingum river, where they met and engaged with a body of Indians, departed there, and returned again to Uniontown … about the last of October [Moore noted they were gone 'six weeks'] … The following spring (1782) the Indians committed the same murders and depredations on short Creek, Virginia, and another draft was made from the Pennsylvania Militia, to go out against the Indians … [he] again entered the service as a substitute … in the Company … commanded by Captain – Sharp – there was but this company called out at this time … [the] company … crossed the Ohio river at the mouth of short Creek, and proceeded on to stlll Water (somewhere in what is now Harrison County, Ohio) where they went and had an engagement with a body of Indians who were defeated and routed – and then returned … was absent … but two weeks.

In the spring of 1783 … [he] again went out, as [Augustine Moore's] substitute … in the Company … commanded by Captain John Giddes … [and] Colonel Thomas Giddes … said company acted in the capacity of scouts, and was stationed at a Block house, at what is now called Beach Bottom, in Brook County, Virginia … was out, and in service … five months … During the several terms of his service … [his company and regiment] never were in company with any regular or continental troops, as the defence of the frontier was committed solely to the Militia … [7]

Stacey Williams was the single African American Pennsylvania Continental to leave a pension narrative, however brief.

[H]e served in the Revolutionary War … In the 6th. Regiment commanded by Colonel [Henry] Bicker and afterwards by Colonel [Josiah] Harmar Pennsylvania Line and in the Company commanded by Captain [Jacob] Humphries … [in an

---

7 NA (US), Pension, reel 1753, Abraham Moore, 'free man of colour' (S2855).

earlier deposition Williams noted, 'he was in many engagements during the war one of which was the battle of Monmouth'.][8]

One detail the old soldier did not tell was recorded in a compendium on the Pennsylvania regiments: 'wounded in the right thigh, at Brandywine …'.[9]

Despite his brevity, Private Williams is an excellent representative for the entirety of Pennsylvania common soldiers. He enlisted in April 1777 and served until autumn 1783. During that time he was very likely present at all the actions his regiment fought in: Short Hills, 26 June 26 1777; Brandywine, 11 September 1777; Germantown, 4 October 1777; the Darby Expedition, 22–28 December 1777; Monmouth, 28 June 1778; Bull's Ferry Block House, 20–21 July 1780; Green Spring, 6 July 1781; Yorktown, 28 September to 18 October 1781. His military travels took him from West Point, New York, in the north, to Charleston, South Carolina, on foot the entire way.

Two 6th Regiment officers, former lieutenants James Glentworth and John Markland, submitted testimonials supporting Williams. Markland wrote, 'I do certify that Stacy Williams, the bearer hereof, was a soldier in Captain Jacob Humphreys company 6th Pennsylvania Regiment, in April 1777, enlisted for the war; and that he served faithfully, until he was discharged at the barracks in Philadelphia, November, 1783, soon after our return from South Carolina, under Colonel Harmar'.[10]

In March 1777 Edward Hector, a 'colored man', was listed as a bombardier in Colonel Thomas Proctor's Pennsylvania State Artillery Regiment. It was a rank that engendered some skill and responsibility, as bombardiers were 'those employed about mortars [and other types of artillery]; they drive the fuse, fix the shell, and load and fire the mortar; they work with the fire-workmen, and are the third rank of a private man in a company of artillery' (note that examined muster roll extracts seem to use the terms bombardier and gunner interchangeably: the 'fire-workmen' or 'fire-workers' were 'the youngest commissioned Officers in a company of artillery'). By autumn 1777, perhaps due to the ban on black participation in the newly-enacted militia law or that a black bombardier was superior in rank to a white matross (the least-skilled position on a gun crew), Hector was relegated to being a wagoner in Proctor's Regiment.[11]

Mr Hector never applied for a federal pension, and when he petitioned for a state pension was denied. The year prior to his death he was awarded a

8 NA (US), Pension, reel 2265, William Stacey, 'negro' (40688).
9 Linn and Egle, *Pennsylvania Archives*, Series 2, Vol.10, p.606.
10 NA (US), Pension, reel 2265, William Stacey (40688), deposition of John Markland.
11 Thomas Lynch Montgomery, (ed.), *Pennsylvania Archives*, (Harrisburg: Harrisburg Publishing Co., State Printer, 1906) Series 5, Vol.3, p.1056; Thomas Simes, *The Military Medley: Containing the most necessary Rules and Directions for attaining a Competent Knowledge of the Art: To which is added an Explanation of Military Terms*, second edition (London: Publisher Unknown, 1768), 'Military Dictionary' following page 302; gunner, 'one appointed for the service of the cannon, and is the second in rank of private men in the artillery'; matross, 'is a soldier in the train of artillery, properly an apprentice of a gunner, and hath the least pay of any soldier in the artillery'.

one-time 40-dollar gratuity in recognition of his service.[12] His death notice, published in the January 1834 Norristown *Free Press*, noted:

> During the war of the revolution, his conduct on one memorable occasion, exhibited an example of patriotism and bravery which deserves to be recorded. At the battle of Brandywine he had charge of an ammunition wagon attached to Colonel Proctor's regiment, and when the American army was obliged to retreat, an order was given by the proper officers to those having charge of the wagons, to abandon them to the enemy, and save themselves by flight. The heroic reply of the deceased was uttered in the true spirit of the Revolution: 'The enemy shall not have my team; I will save my horses and myself!' He instantly started on his way, and as he proceeded, amid the confusion of the surrounding scene, he calmly gathered up a few stands of arms which had been left on the field by the retreating soldiers, and safely retired with his wagon, team and all, in face of the victorious foe.[13]

Private Stacy Williams enlisted in the 6th Pennsylvania Regiment in April 1777 and 'was discharged at the barracks in Philadelphia, November, 1783'. Thousands of Continental soldiers, black and white, at various times were housed in this large complex. The barracks were built 1757; the commandant's house is the large three-story building at the center of the far row of barracks buildings. This view is towards the west. See John F. Watson and Willis P. Hazard, *Annals of Philadelphia and Pennsylvania, in the olden time: being a collection of memoirs, anecdotes, and incidents of the city and its inhabitants, and of the earliest settlements of the inland part of Pennsylvania, from the days of the founders. Intended to preserve the recollections of olden time, and to exhibit society in its changes of manners and customs, and the city and country in their local changes and improvements,* (Philadelphia: Edwin S. Stuart, 1884), Vol.I, image opposite page 112.

---

12 'Report of the committee on claims, on the claim of Edward Hector, a revolutionary soldier', *The Journal of the (Pennsylvania) House of Representatives*, 1826–1827, Report No. 218, pp.493–494; William Summers, 'Obituary Notices of Pennsylvania Soldiers of the Revolution', *Pennsylvania Magazine of History and Biography*, vol. 38 (1914), pp.443–444.
13 Summers, 'Obituary Notices of Pennsylvania Soldiers', pp.443–444.

12

Georgia: 'He served as a drummer in this company'

With one notable exception the regiments of the two southernmost states never served with Washington's main army or, indeed, much beyond their own borders. Authorized to form one regiment and four battalions beginning in 1776 (commanded, in order, by Colonels Lachlan McIntosh – succeeded by Joseph Habersham – Samuel Ebert, James Screven, and John White), due largely to sparse population Georgia's recruiting efforts were lackluster at best. Able only to raise a single regiment, the state stipulated the 2nd, 3rd, and 4th Georgia Battalions be recruited in Virginia and the Carolinas, a decision that caused some friction.[1]

In late May 1777 Congressman George Walton wrote General Washington, noting that while the 4th Battalion had enlisted some men in the south many more were needed. Walton asked that Colonel John White, who delivered the letter personally, be allowed to 'recruit a few companies' in the north. By 4 July 1777 Colonel White and his understrength battalion were in Philadelphia where they added to the day's festivities with a few celebratory *feux de joie*. With or without official permission, the 4th Georgia enlisted a number of British deserters; ensuing disciplinary problems soon caused them to be moved out of the city. They were first quartered six miles west in Lower Merion township. The battalion's common soldiers soon began robbing, abusing, and threatening the locals and in late August again were moved west, this time to the town of Lancaster, some 70 miles away. There they continued their depredations. Finally, in October White was ordered to immediately join his battalion and to begin the journey back to Georgia. Another Georgia officer, 3rd Battalion Captain John Lucas, was also

---

1   E.M. Sanchez-Saavedra, *A Guide to Virginia Military Organizations in the American Revolution, 1774–1787* (Richmond: Virginia State Library, 1978), pp.83–85 (2nd, 3rd, and 4th Georgia Battalions); Berg, *Encyclopedia of Continental Army Units*, pp.45–46; Wright, *Continental Army*, 107–109, 146–148.

recruiting in Pennsylvania and was convicted at a court martial in August 1777 for enlisting soldiers already belonging to other regiments.[2]

From 1776 through 1777 Georgia Continentals and militia contended with British and Loyalist incursions into the state from the south, and retaliated with their own operations into northern Florida. Two ambitious expeditions against British-held St. Augustine ended in failure, after which state Continental forces were spread among small forts and defensive garrisons from the coast into the hinterland. In late 1779 the four existing understrength units were combined into a single battalion of under 200 men. The British easily captured Savannah in December 1778 and the Georgia Continentals took part in the unsuccessful siege of that city the next autumn. With the capture of the state's six remaining Continental officers at Charleston in May 1780, the Georgia line ceased to exist. In 1782 a single Georgia Battalion was raised, with only 150 men enlisted by year's end. They were furloughed home in November 1783.[3]

Georgia Soldier Narratives

A small number of black Georgians are known to have been in Continental service as soldiers, but we have only their names and brief details, as follows:

Wallace Dunstan, 'a free Mullato', deserted in autumn 1777 with ten other men from Captain Shem Cook's company, 2nd Georgia Battalion.

David Monday, enslaved Georgian, enlisted 5 January 1783, still on payroll as of 4 November 1783, Captain William McIntosh's company, Georgia Battalion; emancipated in recognition of his service, with his master being paid 100 guineas in compensation for his loss.

Joseph Scipio/Scepio, served 1 June to 1 July 1779, 4th Georgia Battalion.

James Smith, 'free Mullato', deserted in autumn 1777 with ten other men from Captain Shem Cook's company, 2nd Georgia Battalion.[4]

One Georgia soldier with a varied career was also among those found.

---

2   LOC, Washington Papers, series 4, George Walton to Washington, 27 May 1777; Thomas J. McGuire, *The Philadelphia Campaign: Brandywine and the Fall of Philadelphia* (Mechanicsburg, Pa.: Stackpole Books, 2006), Vol.1 pp.63–64, 118–119. Mike Malsbary 'The Fourth Continental Battalion from Georgia 1777: A footnote from the dusty records of the American Revolution', http://lowermerionhistory.org/wp-content/uploads/2012/07/2The-Fourth-Continental-Battalion-from-Georgia-1777-FINAL2.pdf; Sanchez-Saavedra, *Virginia Military Organizations*, pp.83–85; Berg, *Encyclopedia of Continental Army Units*, pp.45–46; Wright, *Continental Army*, pp.107–109, 146–148; General orders, 13 August 1777, Fitzpatrick, *Writings of George Washington*, Vol.8 (1933), pp.63–64.

3   Kenneth Coleman, *American Revolution in Georgia, 1763–1789* (Athens: University of Georgia Press, 1958), pp.95–129; Sanchez-Saavedra, *Virginia Military Organizations*, pp.83–85; Berg, *Encyclopedia of Continental Army Units*, pp.45–46; Wright, *Continental Army*, p.313.

4   Bobby Gilmer Moss, and Michael C. Scoggins, *African-American Patriots in the Southern Campaign of the American Revolution* (Blacksburg, S.C.: Scotia-Hibernia Press, 2004), pp.81, 162–163, 209, 215.

> Nathan Fry a colored man ... enlisted in the town of Savannah in the year 1775 for the war in the company commanded by Captain Mosby [John or Littlebury Mosby] and Colonel [Samuel] Elbert's [2nd Georgia] Regiment] ... He served as a drummer in this company until he was taken out of that to wait on Major Duval [probably Maj. Peter De Veaux] who was aid-de-camp or Brigade Major to [Brigadier]General [Lachlan] McIntosh. He attended the Major Duval in the capacity of a waiter until he accompanied General McIntosh to the Army under General Washington [McIntosh joined the army at Valley Forge in December 1777, and took command of the North Carolina brigade] and remained with him until he was taken into the service of the Baron Steuben with whom he remained as a waiter or Batman until after the siege of York in Virginia. He was then transferred to General [Arthur] St. Clair by whom he was discharged in the course of the winter [1781–1782]. His discharge is lost. He says that during the whole of this service he remained a soldier under his first enlistment in 1775 and that he continued a soldier and was uninterruptedly in service from the time of his enlistment to the time of his discharge ...[5]

An earlier account provided several more details:

> Nathan Fry, a man of Color, and native of Virginia ... was born free in the County of Westmorland – enlisted in the minute Service under Dennis Duval of Henrico County in the year 1775 – went to Savannah in Georgia and served under Colonel Elbert against the Creek Indians in the capacity of a Drummer ...[6]

Fry's service with Major General Friedrich Wilhelm de Steuben was corroborated by a supporting deposition.

> I do hereby certify that I was well acquainted, and had the honor to be very intimate with the Late Baron Steuben, and his several aids, Major [William] North, Major Fairby [James Fairlie], and Colonel Benjamin Walker, for several years; and, particularly from January 1781 ... to the close of the War; and am certain that Nathan Fry, the Black man in question was the greater part, if not the whole of that time in the service of the Family aforesaid: I am positive that Nathan Fry was attached to the family more than 9 months, and that on the Continental establishment. Given under my hand this 31st of October 1827 D. M. Randolph[7]

Austin Dabney is perhaps the best-known Georgia Revolutionary soldier, though not a Continental. Unfortunately, many inaccuracies were passed down from the first accounts in an 1855 work by George R. Gilmer, *Sketches of Some of the First Settlers of Upper Georgia*, and two earlier pamphlets. Dabney was supposedly a falsely enslaved man, whose mother was discovered to be white, which legally entitled him to freedom. As the original story goes, thus emancipated, he served in the militia and fought at the 1779 Battle of Kettle Creek, where he was severely wounded and saved by one William Harris.

---

5   Graves and Harris, Southern Campaign Pension, Nathan Fry (S39545).
6   Graves and Harris, Southern Campaign Pension, Nathan Fry (S39545).
7   Graves and Harris, Southern Campaign Pension, Nathan Fry (S39545).

New research shows that he was in fact a slave and remained so through the war. In his Georgia pension no mention is made of the Kettle Creek action, but that he received his crippling wounds in May 1782, still ten years before his supposed savior Mr Harris settled in Georgia. No such action occurred in 1782, but on 23 May 1781 Georgia militia under Colonel Elijah Clarke and Lieutenant Colonel Henry Lee's Legion took Loyalist-held Fort Grierson in Augusta. It is possible Dabney was wounded there, but other than the death of North Carolina Major Pinketham Eaton, little is known of American casualties. This dovetails with information given in the 1786 act granting Austin Dabney a state pension.[8]

> An Act to Emancipate and set free … Austin a Mulatto Man at present the property of the Estate of Richard Aycock, esquire, during the late revolution instead of advantaging himself of the times to withdraw himself from the American lines and enter with the majority of his Colour and fellow Slaves in the service of his Brittanick Majesty and his Officers and Vassels, did voluntarily enroll himself in some one of the Corps under the command of Colo Elijah Clark, and in several actions and engagements, behaved against the common Enemy with a bravery and fortitude which would have honored a freedman and in one of which engagements he was severely wounded, and rendered incapable of hard servitude, and policy as well as gratitude demand a return for such service and behavior from the Commonwealth.
>
> Be it Enacted that said Austin be, and he is hereby emancipated and made free and he is and shall be hereby entitled to all the liberties, privileges and immunities of a free Citizen of the State so far as free Negroes and Mulattos are allowed, and is and shall be entitled to annuity allowed by this State to wounded and disabled soldiers.[9]

The proclamation also granted Dabney's former master's estate compensation not to 'exceed the sum of seventy pounds….'[10]

8   Robert Scott Davis, 'Austin Dabney: Georgia's African American Hero of the Revolution', *Journal of the American Revolution*, 5 July 2013, https://allthingsliberty.com/2013/07/austin-dabney-georgias-african-american-hero-of-the-revolution/; Andrew F Smith, (ed.), *Oxford Encyclopedia of Food and Drink in America*, (New York and London: Oxford University Press, 2004), Vol.1 p.45.

9   Georgia Archives, Vol. D, Enrolled Acts and Resolutions, House and Senate Legislature RG37–1–15, 'An Act to Emancipate and set free Austin a Mulatto, also Harry a Negro Fellow', 10 August 1786, http://vauLieutenantgeorgiaarchives.org/cdm/ref/collection/adhoc/id/582.

10   Georgia Archives, 'An Act to Emancipate and set free Austin a Mulatto, also Harry a Negro Fellow', 10 August 1786.

13

South Carolina: 'A Ball … passed through his left side, killing the Drummer immediately behind'

The colony authorized the formation of three units in June 1775, the 1st, commanded by Christopher Gadsden, later Charles Pinckney, and 2nd South Carolina, under William Moultrie, then Isaac Motte, as foot regiments, and the 3rd, under William Thomson, as mounted infantry assigned to the western region to counter Indian incursions. That winter Colonel Owen Roberts 4th (artillery) Regiment was formed, as well as two small rifle regiments, the 5th and 6th South Carolina, the former commanded by Isaac Huger and Alexander McIntosh; the latter by Thomas Sumter. All but the rifle regiments were taken into the Continental establishment in June 1776. In the war's first two years South Carolina may have been considered a backwater, but its soldiers were busy, from their first strike in the fight for independence at the capture of Fort Charlotte, to operations against Loyalist forces and the Cherokee Nation, actions in Georgia and Florida, and the successful defense of Charleston against a British fleet and land forces. The years 1777 and 1778 were relatively quiet in the south, though the capture of Savannah, Georgia, in December 1778 was a precursor of increased British focus. With that new base of operations, in 1779 Crown forces activity increased and the year ended with the unsuccessful Allied attempt to retake Savannah.[1]

By the time of the May 1780 Charleston siege South Carolina's original Continental contingent had been reduced to three foot battalions, plus the artillery battalion. The 1780 1st and 2nd South Carolina (led by Colonels Pinckney and Motte) were amalgamations of the old 1st and 5th Regiments, and the old 2nd and 6th Regiments. The 3rd Battalion (commander unknown) was merely retained and reorganized. All were captured and interned when the city fell. No serious attempt was made by the state afterwards to form

---

1 Berg, *Encyclopedia of Continental Army Units*, pp.109–112 (South Carolina); Wright, *Continental Army*, pp.107–109, 146–148.

new Continental regiments, though mention is made in several sources. More likely any referred-to late-war South Carolina regiments were state units organized after Charleston by state Brigadier Generals Francis Marion, Andrew Pickens, and Thomas Sumter.[2]

South Carolina Soldier Narratives

Pension files for a small number of South Carolina veterans have been found, several with interesting narratives. Jim Capers stated:

> that he entered as a Volunteer and was Regularly Mustered into service, according to the best of his recollection about the 15th day of June AD 1775. and served in the 4th Regiment of the South Carolina line State …as Regular Drum Major under Gen'l [Francis] Marion [possibly served with Marion's Partisan Brigade later in the war], with the following named officers to wit, Col John Brown [possibly Lieutenant John Brown, 3rd Regiment, killed at Stono Ferry, 20 June 1779] in the Company of Capt John White. (The Declarant here being very deaf and an Illiterate [sic] man, is unable to distinguish the Rank of a Coln. from that of Lieutenant Coln. or Major) (But says) that he was with Major John Pearcey and Lieutenant John Jeffry Also mentions the names of Major Wm Sabb, and Colo. Wm. Capers [lieutenant, 2nd South Carolina Regiment, 1777–1781; promoted captain in 1781] as Two of his Officers. When he entered the service he resided in Christ Church Parish Oposite Bull's Island in the State of South Carolina and served until the 1st day of October AD 1782, a Period of seven years 5 months and about 15 days; Declarant further states that he … was engaged with the Enemy in the following places, at Savanah Ga, St. Helena, Port Royal, Camden, Biggins Church, was garrisoned at Charleston some time, (does not know how long) … he was in the Battle of Eutaw Springs, at [that] … Battle he received four Wounds, Two cuts upon the face, one on the head with a sword & one with a Ball which passed through his left side, killing the Drummer immediately behind him, whose name was Paul Ram Lee; after the Battle of the Eutaw Springs, Declarant marched to State of Virginia, and was present at the Surrender of Lord Corn Wallace & was one of the principle Drummers when the Captive Army surrendered and that Gen'l. OHarry, or OHara [Brig. Gen. Charles O'Hara] Represented the British Commander Cornwallace on that occasion. After said surrender, he took shipping for Philadelphia, does not recollect how long he remained there. But from thence he sailed to Charleston, South Carolina and in six months thereafter was discharged. These were the only Engagements and placed he was in, and the only Country through which he marched. During his service in the Army, Drum Major was the only Rank he held, and that he held all the time.[3]

---

2   Wright, *Continental Army*, pp.305–309. Michael C. Scoggins provided important insights and information on the late-war South Carolina Continental contingent (Scoggins to John Rees, email, 18 April 2011). Salley, Alexander S., *Records of the Regiments of the South Carolina Line in the Revolutionary War* (Baltimore: Genealogical Publishing Company, 1977); McCrady, Edward, *History of South Carolina in the Revolution 1775–1780* (New York: Macmillan, 1902); Moultrie, William, *Memoirs of the American Revolution* (New York: D. Longworth, 1802).
3   Graves and Harris, Southern Campaign Pension, Jim Capers, 'man of Color' (R1669).

The only dubious portion of Mr Capers' account is his presence at the Yorktown siege; as far as is presently known no South Carolina troops took part in those operations.

Free black South Carolinian Allen Jeffers detailed his military experience in an October 1832 deposition:

> He enlisted May the twelfth 1778 under Captain Brown [probably John or Richard, lieutenants in the 3rd Regiment] in Colonel [William] Thomson's … third Regiment Continentals … he enlisted for three years. They went down to Charleston immediately upon being enlisted and joined the corps and lay in Charleston nearly a year. They were stationed in the barracks out upon the green. The Regiment then marched out of Charleston to Savannah, at Savannah he was in a brush before the first Battle, and afterward was in the first Battle of Savannah when the French came in to assist there and often saw [Count Casimir] Pulaski, who was wounded at this battle and his thigh cut off he died & was carried to Charleston afterward & was buried there [actually buried at sea]. Before this battle he was placed under the command of Captain Geo. Little who commanded the company for a while & there it was put under the command of Captain Felix Worley [Warley]. They were then marched up Savannah River to Purisburgh [Purysburgh South Carolina]. Does not remember the date of the Battle of Savannah, but it was some time before the Fall of Charleston. Gen. Isaac Huger commanded the attacking forces on Savannah. Lay at Purisburgh awhile & marched on from there to Charleston & was stationed there until the Fall of the city. He was there taken prisoner & parolled. Charleston was taken in 1780, he believes it was in May, but it has been so long. It was any how in the Spring of the year. He rec'd a discharge, but it has been worn out or lost long ago. The applicant was born in North Carolina, but brought to South Carolina when a child … He was living … on the Fork of Congaree & Wateree, where he has lived ever since the war & where he now resides. He was drafted in '78 … His discharge was given to him by Colonel [William] Henderson [3rd South Carolina].[4]

At least seven other African Americans served in the 3rd South Carolina Regiment; their pension accounts and supporting depositions evidence the difficulty in evaluating the accuracy of applicants' statements. Even those men whose veracity and service were unquestioned made mistakes in their retelling, and often portions must be taken at taken at face-value. The depositions in the files of Gideon and Morgan Griffin, and Edward Harris, all have claims that, at first glance, seem preposterous. As with Allen Jeffers, it seems they were all captured with the 3rd Regiment when Charleston fell on 12 May 1780. Morgan Griffin's daughter stated in 1849 that among the actions her father participated in were 'Savannah, Georgia [autumn 1779], Stono [Stono Ferry, 20 June 1779], Monk's Corner [Monck's Corner, 14 April 1780 or 27 November 1781], Cowpens [17 January 1781], and Eutaw Springs [8 September 1781] in South Carolina'. Gideon Griffin's son repeated that verbatim. In 1850 Edward Harris's son reiterated the list and added

4   Graves and Harris, Southern Campaign Pension, Allen Jeffers, 'free colored' (S1770).

Hanging Rock (6 August 1780) and Camden (16 August 1780), both in South Carolina. If in fact all these men had surrendered at Charleston, they would have been held by the British until, at the earliest, the first prisoner cartel arranged in the first half of 1781. That discounts any claims for actions between May 1780 and summer the following year. Still, only Jeffers noted his capture at Charleston, while Gideon Griffin merely mentioned his being discharged in the city. Given that the Charleston garrison retained an open line of communications across the Cooper River until 27 April 1780, it is possible the Griffin brothers and other discharged soldiers may have left the city before that date.[5]

Berry Jeffers, like Edward Harris, did not live to submit his own deposition. His daughter testified,

> about the years 1775 or 1776 [Berry Jeffers] enlisted as a private soldier in the third South Carolina Continental Regiment Commanded by Colonel William Thomson and in the company of Captain Rich'd Brown, That in said capacity he served out his full period of enlistment to wit three years and as such was a fellow soldier of Gideon and Morgan Griffin, Allen and Osborne Jeffers … a brother of Declarant's father was killed in battle … in Charleston South Carolina [probably the Charleston siege] … afterwards he served under General Thomas Sumter Captain William Smith's Company in what was called Sumter's Brigade … after serving as aforesaid he came back to his old neighborhood and on Twenty third Day of August AD. 1782 he married Joannis, or as she was often called by the family, Hannah Griffin …[6]

Neighbor James Rawlinson added more details and emphasized the sizable group of men from the same vicinity who all served together.

> he is Eighty Eight years of age and has with the exception of two years ever lived in Richland District … he was living in said District during the Revolutionary War and was a near neighbor of and well acquainted with Berry Jeffers who to this deponent's distinct knowledge & recollection was a regular enlisted soldier in Captain Richard Brown's Company in the Regiment commanded by Colonel William Thomson, commonly called the Rangers and … served out three years … from the same neighborhood were Morgan & Gideon Griffin, Allen Jeffers, Orsburn Jeffers & five of this Deponents brothers one of whom did not survive the war. … of the battles in which this Deponent recollects of hearing said Berry Jeffers speak of having been in were those of Savannah [24 September to October 1779], Charleston [siege], Brier Creek [3 March 1779], Eutaw [Springs,

---

5   Graves and Harris, Southern Campaign Pension, Gideon Griffin, 'free colored' (W8877), Morgan Griffin, 'free colored' (S18844), Edward Harris, 'Free Person of Color' (R4649); Michael C. Scoggins, '"Voluntarily Enlisted as a Soldier in the Revolution": A Case Study of Free African-Americans in the South Carolina Continental and State Troops during the Revolutionary War' (Unpublished research paper), Southern Revolutionary War Institute, York, SC, February 2015; Carl P. Bobrick, *A Gallant Defense: The Siege of Charleston, 1780* (Columbia: University of South Carolina Press, 2003), pp.187–189.

6   Graves and Harris, Southern Campaign Pension, Berry Jeffers, 'other free' (W10145), deposition of Harriet Jeffers.

8 September 1781] and King's Mountain [7 October 1780] … he spoke frequently of being in the Eutaw Battle, and the spring after said Battle he came home in Richland District and soon after so coming home said Berry Jeffers engaged with this Deponent's father in the blacksmith trade and continued with him seven years during which time this Deponent worked in the said shop with him and during the summer after said Berry Jeffers came home from the war he married Joannis Griffin living in the same neighborhood …[7]

Drury Harris, a light-complexioned mulatto, applied for and received a state pension. His 3rd Regiment comrade John Davis stated, 'in the fight at Savannah [9 October 1779], I saw no man, officer nor private, more Activer nor braver, than Drury Harris was, also Seeing and knowing him, to receive two wounds, a shot wound in the thigh, and a bayonet in the arm, in trying to scale the walls of his Inamy …'. Harris also fought at Stono Ferry in June 1779. It is uncertain if he was captured at Charleston, but in April 1781 he enlisted for 10 months as a light dragoon in Lieutenant Colonel Wade Hampton's State Regiment, Sumter's Brigade, and fought at Eutaw Springs that September.[8]

Drury Harris was eligible for 'Sumter's bounty', a policy that awarded late-war state troops 'one grown negro' for their service. For some reason Harris seems not to have received this reward, but his neighbors and fellow-soldiers Gideon Griffin, the Jeffers brothers, and cousin Edward, all mulattoes, did. Brigadier General Thomas Sumter in early 1781 took it upon himself to make this offer in an effort to gain troops for state service. In February 1782 the South Carolina government enacted this program as a state statute, with the codicil that for every 25 men enlisted one slave would be awarded the individual who recruited them. The required slaves were confiscated from Loyalist owners, thus the program imposed no financial burden on the state. Georgia enacted a similar plan and also used slaves as legal tender to pay debts or purchase needed goods. The Virginia legislature passed a like measure in January 1781, giving men who voluntarily enlisted in a Continental regiment a substantial cash bonus, plus the choice of a 'healthy sound negro' between 10 and 30 years of age or 60 pounds in gold or silver. The slaves and cash bounties were to be paid for via a general tax. This effort was derailed by a British invasion that same month, increases in men called out for militia service, and protests and resistance against the new act and associated tax. As Michael McDonnell notes, 'few recruits actually stepped forward, and many counites refused to implement the recruiting law in sympathy with their militia, or in fear of what might happen if they did'.[9]

---

7   Graves and Harris, Southern Campaign Pension, Berry Jeffers (W10145), deposition of James Rawlinson.
8   Scoggins, 'Voluntarily Enlisted as a Soldier'.
9   Scoggins, 'Voluntarily Enlisted as a Soldier'; Michael Lee Lanning, *Defenders of Liberty: African Americans in the Revolutionary War* (New York: Citadel Press, 2000), pp.71–72; 'Sumter's Law and the 'Black Currency'' from 'Jubilo! The Emancipation Century', https://jubiloemancipationcentury.wordpress.com/2012/03/08/trivia-sumters-law-and-the-black-currency/; McDonnell, ''Fit for Common Service?', Resch and Sargent, *War & Society in the American Revolution*, pp.119–121; L. Scott Philyaw, 'A Slave for Every Soldier: The Strange

Many black soldiers never applied for a pension or received any other recognition for their service. Appended are a few discovered in the service records compiled from various military documents and held by the United States National Archives:

- Negro Bob, drummer, 3rd South Carolina Regiment, enlisted 24 July 1776.
- Negro Isaac, 3rd South Carolina Regiment, enlisted 24 July 1776.
- Negro Adam, 3rd South Carolina Regiment, enlisted 1 January 1778.
- Neptune, drummer, 6th South Carolina Regiment, enlisted 30 July 1776.
- Tom Negro, drummer, 6th South Carolina Regiment, enlisted 27 August 1776.
- Ned Negro, drummer, 6th South Carolina Regiment, enlisted 25 August 1777.
- Bram Negro, 6th South Carolina Regiment, enlisted 7 October 1777.
- Peter Negro, 6th South Carolina Regiment, enlisted 14 December 1777.[10]

History of Virginia's Forgotten Recruitment Act of 1 January 1781', *Virginia Magazine of History and Biography*, vol. 109, no. 4 (2001), pp.367–386.

10 NA (US), Compiled Service Records (South Carolina), Negro Bob, Negro Isaac, Negro Adam, Neptune, Tom Negro, drummer, Ned Negro, Bram Negro, Peter Negro.

14

Maryland: 'He will never forget the roaring of Cannon …'

In July 1775 two Maryland rifle companies under Captains Michael Cresap and Thomas Price marched north to join the Army of Observation investing Boston. They were the state's first contribution to the fledgling Continental forces. Following the successful culmination of the siege, and the movement of Washington's forces to New York, in July 1776 the two Maryland companies joined Colonel Hugh Stephenson's Maryland and Virginia Rifle Regiment (which contained four Maryland companies). Meanwhile, in January 1776 the state legislature authorized the formation of Colonel William Smallwood's Regiment, enlisted to serve for one year. That regiment joined the Continental forces in and around New York City, and was decimated at Long Island; the remnants went on to assist in reviving the cause for independence at Trenton and Princeton. Seven Maryland independent companies were also formed that year, a number of which eventually served with the 1776 Flying Camp (comprising mostly militia) or joined the main army. The German Regiment, raised in late summer of the year, was filled with men enlisted for three years and contained four Maryland and four Pennsylvania companies.[1]

In 1777 the state's contribution increased to seven Continental regiments, commanded by colonels John Stone, Thomas Price, Mordecai Gist, Josias Hall, William Richardson, Otho Holland Williams, and John Gunby. By July 1780 losses in personnel led to those units, plus the Delaware regiment, being consolidated into four (under Otho Williams, John Gunby, Peter Adams, and Thomas Woolford). Major General Horatio Gates reversed that decision soon after and it was under the old organization the Maryland and Delaware troops fought at the Battle of Camden in August. In the meantime, an additional Maryland unit, called the Regiment Extra, was authorized in spring 1780

---

1   Clayton C. Hall, Henry Stockbridge, and Bernard C. Steiner (eds.), *Muster Rolls and Other Records of Service of Maryland Troops in the American Revolution, 1775–1783: Archives of Maryland*, Maryland Historical Society (Baltimore: The Lord Baltimore Press, The Friedenwald Company, 1900), p.4; Berg, *Encyclopedia of Continental Army Units*, pp.47, 67–68, 120; Wright, *Continental Army*, pp.107–109 (overview of southern states' contribution of Continental regiments to 1777), pp.146–148.

and raised during the summer under a new contingent of officers. Following the Battle of Camden, the remnants of the Maryland line, plus the company-size Delaware Regiment, were formed into a single Maryland Regiment, with two battalions of four companies each (first battalion, 1st, 3rd, 5th, and 7th Maryland; second battalion, 2nd, 4th, and 6th Maryland, and the Delaware Regiment). While the Regiment Extra headed for Hillsborough, North Carolina, Major General Nathanael Greene led his small army into South Carolina. Due to a squabble among the supernumerary veteran Maryland officers, settled by their replacing the new officers who raised and trained the unit, the Regiment Extra did not immediately join Greene's forces. Re-officered and renamed the 2nd Maryland Regiment on or about 10 March 1781, its men fought their first battle at Guilford Courthouse less than a week later. The 3rd and 4th Maryland were present at the Yorktown Siege, brigaded under Brigadier General Mordecai Gist. Expiring enlistments led to the demise of the 3rd and 4th Regiments, with all remaining men sent south to the 1st and 2nd Regiments. In October 1782 a re-formed, but severely undermanned, 3rd Maryland, marching to join Washington's army, was ordered to halt and take post at Pompton, New Jersey. The 3rd Maryland, now known as the Maryland Detachment under Major Thomas Lansdale, continued in service until June 1783. The contingent serving with General Greene in South Carolina was reduced a single regiment, and seems also to have been disbanded the same month as Landale's Detachment.[2]

Maryland Soldier Narratives

Several Maryland black veterans related their varied experiences, though, to date, none are known to have served in Colonel Smallwood's 1776 Regiment, or any other Maryland units that year. Despite that, by 1777 numbers of African Americans were recruited by Maryland regiments, with some serving to the war's end.

Abednego Jackson's Continental service was brief, but again highlights the contribution of short-term levy soldiers. Jackson noted in 1833,

---

2   Wright, *Continental Army*, pp.146–148 (1778 reduction and reorganization of states' regiments); Babits, Lawrence E., 'The "Fifth" Maryland at Guilford Courthouse: An Exercise in Historical Accuracy', *Maryland Historical Magazine*, vol. 84 (Winter 1989), pp.370–378. Babits and Howard, *Long, Obstinate, and Bloody*, pp.72–76; George Washington to William Smallwood, 24 August 1781; General orders, 24 September 1781; Washington, Memorandum for Lieutenant Colonel Lewis Morris, Jr., 6 October 1781; Washington to William Smallwood, 6 October 1781; Washington, Instructions to Captain William Dent Beall, 4 November 1781, 25 October 1781, Fitzpatrick, *WGW*, vol. 23 (1937), pp.44–45, 134–135, 193–194, 196, 263–264, 330–331. Washington to Benjamin Lincoln, Secretary at War, 1 April 1782; Washington to William Smallwood, 15 April 1782, ibid., vol. 24 (1938), pp.98–99, 120–121. Washington to Benjamin Lincoln, 1 September 1782; Washington to Maj. Thomas Lansdale or officer commanding the 3rd Maryland Regt., 21 October 1782, ibid., vol. 25 (1938), pp.98–99, 283–284. General orders, 3 June 1783, ibid., vol. 26 (1938), pp.467–468. Library of Congress, George Washington Papers, series 3, Varick Transcripts, 1775–1785, Subseries 3A, Continental and State Military Personnel, 1775–1783, Letterbook 7: 3 January 1783 to 23 December 1783, George Washington to Assistant Secretary at War, 5 February 1783, https://www.loc.gov/item/mgw3a.007/.

In the spring of 1777 [actually 1778], he thinks, in the month of April, being a resident of St Marys County, in the State of Maryland, and Subject to Militia duty, which he was frequently called on to perform, on account of the very exposed situation of that County to depredations from the British Cruisers, by which they were much infested, he determined with many of his acquaintances in that Country, to the number of about 50 or 60, to enroll themselves as Volunteers, to join the Army of Genl. Washington in the Jerseys [which] at that time, as he understood, was in great need of men; and being enrolled by Colonel Barnes of that County, they set out from Leonard town under the Command of Captain [Mullehorn?] for Annapolis, where they remained for sometime [waiting] for recruits – From Annapolis they proceeded to the Head of Elk, from whence they marched to Brunswick [New Jersey], where they joined the Army and where they were placed in the Company of Capt: Davis [unidentified] in [Major John] Stewart's [2nd] Regiment, to which Regiment belonged a Capt: Anderson [unidentified], who was Adjutant … After going into Winter quarters, his term of service from the time he left home expired, & being prevailed on to serve three months longer, he remained with the Army until twelve months expired. … The names of many of the men who volunteered with him, he well remembers, viz: Richard Sweaney [private 2nd Maryland], Francis Wheatley, Sylvester Wheatley [private 2nd Maryland], James Barrett [private 2nd Maryland], Joseph Reswick, William Chatley, Joseph Fields [private 3rd Maryland], Robert Greenwell [private 3rd Maryland], James Winsett [private 2nd Maryland], Barton Godred, and some others.[3]

Mr Jackson also wrote he had 'been in the employment of the Catholic College [Georgetown University] for a great number of years …'.[4] Among his papers was this testimonial:

District of Columbia County of Washington viz: On this day of June, 1833 before me … appears the Reverend Mr. Thoms F. Mulledy President of the Catholic College of George Town … deposeth, that he was educated at this College, and entered it at an early period of his life, when he first became acquainted with Abednigo Jackson, who has been in the College employment ever since – That he has often heard, many years ago, and at various times since, the said Abednego talk of his Service as a Soldier in the Revolutionary War, and that he did so serve, he believes to be the general opinion of his acquaintances, and that no doubt ever existed on the subject.[5]

Abednego Jackson did indeed serve, and, as he said, his enlistment was extended beyond nine months. However, his memory was faulty with respect to part of his experience, as evidenced by his claim that from the time he

3 Graves and Harris, Southern Campaign Pension, Abednego Jackson, 'free Negro' (S10909). NA (US), Compiled Service Records (Maryland), Joseph Fields, Robert Greenwell, Richard Sweeney, Salvester Wheatley, James Winsitt.
4 Graves and Harris, Southern Campaign Pension, Abednego Jackson (S10909).
5 Graves and Harris, Southern Campaign Pension, Abednego Jackson (S10909) Thomas Mulledy testimonial.

joined the army in 1778, 'they were employed in the various movements of the Army, until they moved towards Trenton. He was with the Army during the Cannonade of that place at the Battle of Princeton. He will never forget the roaring of Cannon at that time, which remained in his Ears for a long time afterward'.[6] Without addressing the other inaccuracies of this statement, the only battle that occurred during Jackson's service was at Monmouth Courthouse in June 1778. That action did indeed have a two to three hour cannonade, which is likely what the veteran recalled. While some Maryland levies were present at Monmouth, others did not arrive in time. Former levy George Dent recalled,

> I lived in St. Mary's County, Maryland … [and] volunteered to relieve a Class out of the Charlotte Hall company in Saint Mary's County … it was in the year 1778 the year in which the battle of Monmouth was fought, we tried to get there in time, but could not, we heard the fireing. I was marched with I think seventy one others, some of whom were Volunteers & some drafts under the Command of Captn [Henry] Carberry as far as Annapolis … from Annapolis … by water to the head of Elk, there we remained some seven or eight days and Lieutenant [John] James [3rd Maryland] came from Baltimore and Marched us to head quarters in New Jersey, where we arrived the day after the battle of Monmouth, we were there dispersed to fill up the Vacancies in the deficient companies … [7]

George Brewer of the Annapolis Land Office confirmed Mr Jackson's wartime stint: 'I hereby Certify that it appears by the muster rolls remaining in this Office, that Abednego Jackson enlisted as a private, in the 2nd. Maryland Regiment, for the term of nine months, on the 25th. day of May 1778, and was discharged on the 3rd. day of April 1779'.[8]

Second Maryland levy veteran Francis Freeman enlisted 25 May 1778. In a June 1818 deposition 'Genl. Hezekiah Foard', former 2nd Regiment lieutenant, noted that Freeman was a 'Coloured Man … belonged to the Second Regt of [the Maryland] line in the Spring of 1780 Marched With the same to South Carolina and I believe he Continued in the Service untill the Close of the War'. Ninety-three-year-old Freeman testified the same year that,

> in the year one thousand seven hundred and seventy six [in actuality 1778], he inlisted in the second company, then under the command of John Hardman, in the Second Regiment of the Maryland Line, in the Continental Service; that at the expiration of the term for which he inlisted, which was about nine months after he entered the said service, he re-inlisted in the said Company and Regiment, for and during the Revolutionary war, and that he continued in the said service until

---

6   Graves and Harris, Southern Campaign Pension, Abednego Jackson (S10909).

7   NA (US), Pension, reel 798, George Dent (S12755).

8   Graves and Harris, Southern Campaign Pension, Abednego Jackson (S10909), George Brewer (letter).

the termination of the said war, at which time he received his discharge, which he lost a few years ago …[9]

Two years later he added that, 'he served … in the Company commanded first by Captain John Hardman and after his death [from wounds incurred at Camden 16 August 1780] by Captain Hezekiah Forde in the Second Maryland Regiment commanded by Colonel [Thomas] Woolford … my occupation is that of a Labourer, that I am disabled from pursuing it by reason of my being afflicted with severe pain occasioned by the wounds I received in the service of my Country'.[10]

Lazarus Harman enlisted as a long-term soldier and participated in several hard-fought actions in Greene's Southern army. He was,

enlisted in Snowhill in Worcester County and State of Maryland, in 1780 by lieutenant Co. Joseph Dashiell, and after being transferred to Annapolis entered the Company commanded by Captain [George] Armstrong [1st Maryland Regiment], who was killed at the Battle of 96 S. Carolina [Siege of Ninety Six, 18 June 1781]; and whose place was supplied by Captain Bell [Lloyd Beall, 1st Maryland] … he continued to serve in said corps or in the service of the U. States untill the close of the War, when he was Discharged from service at Annapolis & State of Maryland, by Colonel [John] Gunby who was Colonel of his Regiment … he was in the Battles of Guilford [Guilford Courthouse, 15 March 1781], at Cambden S. Carolina [Hobkirk Hill near Camden, 25 April 1781] (where he was badly wounded & by which he is still disabled) [in another testimonial Harman noted that after his wounding 'he remained in the Hospittle] … he is in reduced circumstances and stands in need of his Country's assistance for a support.[11]

Edward Chambers' narrative shows the difficulty of old-age recollections regarding the organizations a veteran served in. In 1818 Chambers recalled, 'he served three years and a half in … the third Maryland Regiment [actually 5th Maryland] Captain Grays [possibly James Woolford Gray's] company and was regularly discharged at the peace in the year seventeen Hundred and eighty three …'.[12] In 1820 he provided more details, but muddied the waters further:

Edward Chambers aged about fifty six years resident in Anne Arundel County State of Maryland … doth on his oath declare that he … enlisted in new Town Chester in said County in or about July 1777 under Major [John] Deane in the 3. Md. Reg't. in the Maryland line commanded by Colo. [Peter] Adams and served in s'd. Reg't. three years & six months during which time he was in the battles of the high hills of Santee [likely Camden, 16 August 1780, and Hobkirk's Hill, 25

9   Graves and Harris, Southern Campaign Pension, Francis Freeman, 'a person of colour' (S35951).

10 Graves and Harris, Southern Campaign Pension, Francis Freeman (S35951).

11 Graves and Harris, Southern Campaign Pension, Lazarus Harman, 'Free Colored Person' (S34911).

12 Graves and Harris, Southern Campaign Pension, Edward Chambers, 'a man of color' (S34684).

April 1781, to the north; Eutaw Springs, 8 September 1781, to the south], and during the Siege of Cornwallis [1781] and at Charleston [1782], and was with Gen'l. Washington as one of his body guard & that he was discharged in Frederick Town Maryland in 1780 ... [13]

According to the Federal service records Edward Chambers was with the 1st Maryland Regiment in January 1783 and likely served to the war's end. If he in fact served three and a half years, his enlistment began in 1779, not 1777. Furthermore, he probably was not at Yorktown, especially if he was in the 1781 South Carolina battles he alludes to. The regiments he served with prior to 1781 are also in question. Chambers mentions John Dean as a 3rd Maryland officer; in actuality, Dean was a British prisoner from November 1776 to sometime in 1778; that year he was appointed major in the 4th Maryland, and transferred to the 2nd Regiment in January 1781. Colonel Peter Adams was a captain in Smallwood's 1776 regiment, major and then lieutenant colonel of the 7th Maryland from 1777 to summer 1779; in August that year he moved to the 1st Regiment, and in January 1781 to the 3rd Regiment.[14]

Some veterans purposely lied about their military record. Former private Frederick Hall was one. Hall recalled in 1832,

he enlisted on the eighth day of May in the year 1777 in the 3rd Regiment of the Maryland line commanded by [Lieutenant] Colonel [Nathaniel] Ramsay and in the Company of Captain [Joseph] Marbury on the Continental establishment for three years ... after the battle of Germantown [4 October 1777] while on a scouting party near the Rising Sun within a mile of the Philadelphia market he was taken prisoner by a reconnoitering party of British Soldiers, when he was sent to Philadelphia, from thence he was sent to New York, and placed on board the prison ship Jersey, & from thence he was sent to London (first to Newcastle & then to London where he thinks he remained near a twelve month awaiting an exchange of prisoners, with a number of men as follows all prisoners with him – Henry Meed [unknown], Richard Coons [unknown], Robert Hackenson [unknown], John Hope [unknown], Samuel Henson [unknown], Henry Hines [3rd Maryland], and John Adams [1st Maryland, deserted 6 March 1778] – he undermined his way out of prison, and went to Holland from whence he came to Philadelphia and re-joined his Regiment in which he continued to serve until the summer of 1783 at which time he was (conditionally) discharged from service at Charleston, South Carolina. – That, including the time he was a prisoner of war he served from the 8th May 1777 until the summer 1783 – a period of six years ... he was engaged in the battles of Germantown, Brandywine [11 September 1777] & Whiteplain [Whitemarsh, December 1777] was never wounded ... he marched from Port Tobacco to Annapolis and from thence to Baltimore where

13 Graves and Harris, Southern Campaign Pension, Edward Chambers (S34684).
14 NA (US), Compiled Service Records (Maryland), Edward Chambers; Francis B. Heitman, *Historical Register of Officers of the Continental Army During the War of the Revolution – April, 1775, to December, 1783*, New, Revised, and Enlarged Edition (Washington, D.C.: The Rare Book Publishing Company, Inc., 1914), pp.64, 190.

he with a number of others were inoculated by Dr. Lavington & from thence to Philadelphia.... he was living in Borge's hole in Virginia when he enlisted – he has lived principally in Fairfax County, Virginia, since the Revolutionary war and ... now lives in Washington City, in the District of Columbia ... he does not remember of any of the regular officers excepting Colonel Forest [Uriah Forrest; major 3rd Maryland; lieutenant colonel, 1st Maryland, April 1777, wounded and lost a leg at Germantown], Colonel Ramsay & Captain Marbury ... he received a written discharge, purporting that should peace not be ratified, he was still to consider himself in service, but that he has since lost it ...[15]

His mention of being imprisoned in England makes Hall's account immediately suspect; as Todd Braisted notes, captured Continental Army personnel were held in British-occupied American territory. Mr Braisted also provided information that Frederick Hall deserted not once, but twice. Published Maryland records indicate he 'deserted 10 Jan 78, joined 25 March 79 and was on the Rolls to April 80'. An appended note states, 'Captain [Henry] Baldwin [3rd Regiment] say[s] he [Hall] deserted on ye way to S. ward'. Desertion barred an applicant from receiving a pension so it is understandable, though not laudable, that Mr Hall prevaricated in his deposition.[16]

Henry Dorton served with one of the two Maryland levy regiments sent to reinforce the troops surrounding Cornwallis's forces at Yorktown in autumn 1781. Dorton had seen some early and harrowing service with the Virginia militia:

[H]e was drafted in the fall of the year 1777 at Red-stone [Redstone] settlement near Brownsville, Pennsylvania [Fayette County, then claimed by Virginia], in a company of militia commanded by Captain Foard, and immediately marched to Fort Pitt, where Foard's company was placed under the command of Colonel John Gibson of Virginia, who he believes was a Regular officer ... while at Fort Pitt, he was transfered to a company ... from the South Branch of the Potomac river, commanded by Captain Foreman ... Foreman was soon ordered to a fort at Grave creek, on the Ohio river, twelve miles below Wheeling — upon arriving there we found the fort burnt, and ... commenced a march back to Wheeling along the bank of the river — in the narrows of Grave creek, we were attackted by about seventy indians, and Captain Foreman and twenty of his men were killed, twenty two were saved ... he made good his escape back to Wheeling, and in ten days after, he went with others to bury the dead, putting fourteen in one hole and seven in another ... he then returned to Fort Pitt, where at the end of a month, the term for which he was drafted, he was discharged by Captain Foard, which discharge he has preserved, and is hereto annexed.[17]

15 Graves and Harris, Southern Campaign Pension, Frederick Hall, 'Free Colored Person' (R7569).
16 Hall, Stockbridge, and Steiner, *Muster Rolls and Other Records of Service of Maryland Troops*, pp.78, 120, 122.
17 Graves and Harris, Southern Campaign Pension, Henry Dorton, 'free colored person' (S5362).

The action at Grave Creek, Virginia (now West Virginia) was fought on 27 September 1777. Virginia militia Captain William Foreman and 46 men were ambushed, with 21 killed and four wounded.[18]

He went on for another six months tour in 1778, helping to build Forts McIntosh and Laurens. Dorton recalled:

> from the western country, he removed back to the place of his birth, and in the month of May 1781 he was again drafted near Bladensburg in Maryland in Capt Cross['s] company [probably Joseph Cross, lieutenant, 2nd Maryland, served also in the 1783 Maryland Battalion] … in June we marched to Annapolis where we were reviewed and remained a week … we had seventy five men in our company, marched to Falmouth — other troops were marching the same direction, but taking different roads on account of provisions — from Falmouth we continued our march thro' Virginia to a place called the Savannah below Yorktown, and was there stationed with five other companies under Gen'l. [William] Smallwood, to keep the enemy from retreating from York town … after the surrender of Lord Cornwallis [19 October 1781] we were all discharged …[19]

Another Maryland Continental, Philip Savoy, had a varied career but missed the hard-fought southern battles:

> He enlisted at the Rising Sun tavern [Anne Arundel County] … in Captain James Peale's Company first Maryland Regiment on the 20th of May 1778 and served in said Company until he was taken prisoner at Elizabeth Town … he was in the battles of Monmouth, White Plains and Elizabeth Town where he was taken prisoner and sent to New York. On his return to Annapolis he was then drafted into Captain Ball's Company [probably Lieutenant Samuel Beall, 4th Maryland, 1781], and was at the taking of Cornwallis and on his return to Annapolis was honorably discharged after peace was declared.[20]

Savoy's capture is confirmed by a 'List of Rebel Prisoners taken at Eliza. Town 25th Jany. 1780', which gives the names and regiments of 46 men captured in the 14–15 January attack on British-held Staten Island. Phillip Savoy is listed as a 'Negro' private in the 1st Maryland Regiment.[21]

One black soldier is known to have served with the German Regiment, though his enlistment date and company affiliation are unknown. Henry J. Retzer notes in his book on the unit, Abraham 'Veach … deserted, disch[arged] 22 November 1780'. British Lieutenant General Sir Henry Clinton's 1780–81 manuscript 'Information of Deserters and Others' provides additional information: '25th November 1780 Wm. Mansell of the German Battalion left West Point last Monday on command to Dobbs's

18 Howard H. Peckham (ed.), *The Toll of Independence: Engagements & Battle Casualties of the American Revolution* (Chicago and London: The University of Chicago Press, 1974), p.41.
19 Graves and Harris, Southern Campaign Pension, Henry Dorton (S5362).
20 Graves and Harris, Southern Campaign Pension, Philip Savoy (S35057).
21 William L. Clements Library, University of Michigan, Frederick Mackenzie Papers, 'List of Rebel Prisoners taken at Eliza. Town 25th Jany. 1780'.

ferry left that place last night … [also deserted was] Abraham Veetch a Negroe of the same Regt'. Veach (or Veatch) is also mentioned in a list of eight men who received the regimental coats promised as part of their enlistment bounty at Baltimore on 5 April 1780. Private Veach and the other recruits would have first joined their regiment at Fort Augusta, Pennsylvania, on the Susquehanna River, before that corps marched east to New Jersey in early August 1780.[22]

---

22 Henry J. Retzer, *The German Regiment of Maryland and Pennsylvania in the Continental Army, 1776–1781* (Westminster, Md.: Family Line Publications, 1991), p.117. New York Public Library, Thomas Addis Emmett Collection, Miscellaneous Manuscripts (microfilm reel 11), Sir Henry Clinton, 'Information of Deserters and Others, Not Included in Private Intelligence, From October 1780 to 26 March, 1781 (Under the date 15 August 1780)'. Maryland Archives, Maryland State Papers (Revolutionary Papers), MSA No. S997, Account of clothing, MdHR 19, 970–3–12–14[–] 1–7–3–9, SL 99–9539, George P. Keeports' report, 'Account of Cloathing Delivered The German Regmt. at Baltimore Town to the 1st of June 1780 –', clothing return entitled, 'An Account of Clothing Deliver'd The German Regiment at Baltimore Town the 5th of April 1780 By order of His Excellency The Governor and Council'; document courtesy of Thaddeus Weaver who notes, 'Abraham Veatch was no. 5 of 8 men each issued one bounty coat on 5 April, 1780 (the coat was delivered to Captain Michael Bayer)'. Weaver to John Rees (email), 25 January 2019.

15

Delaware: 'Discharged … 1782, being a slave for life & claimed'

Delaware, the smallest colony and state, contributed a single regiment to the Continental Army. Colonel John Haslet's 1776 Delaware Regiment was enlisted for one year; re-formed and re-manned in 1777, the unit was first commanded by Colonel David Hall, who was wounded at the Battle of Germantown that October. Hall never re-joined the regiment up to his May 1782 retirement and two lieutenant colonels led the unit in the field, first Charles Pope until December 1779, then Joseph Vaughan to the war's end. The Delaware Regiment served in all of Washington's major campaigns and battles in the north. It was sent south in late May 1780, with a division commanded by Major General Johann von Robais, Baron de Kalb. The regiment was shattered at the 16 August 1780 Camden battle, after which the two remaining Delaware companies were consolidated with the Maryland troops. One Delaware company served in the post-Camden Maryland 2nd Battalion, the other was attached to a combined Delaware-Maryland-Virginia Light Infantry Battalion. Captain Robert Kirkwood's company fought under Brigadier General Daniel Morgan at the small but stunning victory at Cowpens, and both Delaware companies were with Major General Nathanael Greene from Guilford Courthouse onwards. Later augmented by recruits to four companies, the Delaware Continentals were furloughed home from South Carolina at the end of 1782.[1]

Delaware Soldier Narratives

A single Delaware African American soldier applied for a pension, leaving a matter-of-fact narrative:

---

1   Christopher L. Ward, *The Delaware Continentals, 1776–1783* (Wilmington: The Historical Society of Delaware, 1941), pp.3–10, 158–163, 350–351, 354, 356–358, 482; Heitman, *Historical Register of Officers of the Continental Army*, p.267; Lawrence E. Babits, *A Devil of a Whipping: The Battle of Cowpens* (Chapel Hill and London: The University of North Carolina Press, 1998), p.27; Babits and Howard, *Long, Obstinate, and Bloody*, pp.62–63.

Be it remembered that on this twentieth day of April in the year of our Lord one thousand eight hundred and eighteen, Edward Harmon a soldier of the revolution, aged about sixty ... did depose and say that in the year seventeen hundred and seventy seven he enlisted under Captain [Robert] Kirkwood of the first Company of the Delaware Regiment, and continued in the service from that time as a common soldier until the conclusion of the war, when he was discharged by general proclamation, and that from the time of his enlistment to his discharge he served in the southern states in the Army under the command of Generals Gates and Green. And the said Edward Harmon did further depose and say that from his reduced circumstances in life he needs the assistance of his country. Edward his X mark Harmon.[2]

Harmon's application was supported by Delaware militia Colonel Mitchell Kershaw, who stated:

that he knows Edward Harmon ... an inhabitant of Sussex County, and has known him from the years seventeen hundred and seventy eight or nine ... he was at that time a soldier in the Delaware Regiment and continued in the said regiment to the knowledge of this deponent until the sixteenth of August seventeen hundred and eighty when this deponent [Kershaw] who belonged to the said Regiment was taken prisoner at Gates defeat [at Camden, South Carolina] and ... was taken on board the prison ship at Charleston.[3]

A local man, Hezekiah Lacey, testified:

Edward Harmon was a boy in the neighbourhood where he lived, that he worked much of his time before he inlisted with this Deponents Father, that about the year seventeen hundred and seventy seven ... Harmon inlisted under Captain Kirkwood, and marched off with the Delaware Regiment, that this Deponent never see said Harmon from the time he marched off aforesaid untill the year seventeen hundred and eighty three, when he see him with others of the Delaware Regiment, with uniforms and equipment just as they returned from the Army – at the same time he heard People say to Harmon he was a fool to spend so much time in the army without pay – that Harmon replied he was willing to go again and that he hoped he should get pay at some time.[4]

In an 1819 deposition supporting another Delaware veteran, Daniel Rodney noted, 'the only [other] applicant (that I know of) belonging to the Del Reg't within 20 miles of this place [Lewes] ... [is] one Edw'd Harman, a coloured man, who rec'd his certificate for a pension some time last year'. There is a discrepancy between these service claims and extant military records. Edward Harmon recorded as having enlisted on 26 May 1781, and is listed

---

2 Graves and Harris, Southern Campaign Pension, Edward Harmon, 'a coloured man' (S36000).
3 Graves and Harris, Southern Campaign Pension, Edward Harmon (S36000), deposition of Mitchell Kershaw.
4 Graves and Harris, Southern Campaign Pension, Edward Harmon (S36000), deposition of Hezekiah Lacey.

on a 20 June 1781 'Muster Roll of Recruits, and others, of the Delaware Regt under my Comman[d] at the Post of Christiana Bridge' signed 'W. McKennan Capt Comg Det DR'. This last document includes a list of 'Old soldiers' and Harmon is not on that list. So, in actuality, Mr Harmon seems only to have served during the war's final three years. Additionally, Charles Fithian notes that Harman may have been Native American as that surname is common in the local Nanticoke community.[5]

Several other black Delaware Regiment soldiers have been found. Three were listed in a 1782 deserter advertisement:

SIXTY-FOUR DOLLARS REWARD.
DESERTED from the DELAWARE REGIMENT, the following soldiers, viz. …

JAMES SONGO, a mulatto, born in Kent County, Delaware State, 25 years of age, 5 feet 6 inches high, has lost some of his toes.

EPHRAIM HENDRICKSON, born in Maryland, 20 years of age, 5 feet 5 inches high, fair hair, plays upon the violin, is supposed to be near Sassafras Church, Maryland. …

THOMAS CLARK, a mulatto, lives in Sussex County, Delaware State. …

JOHN WILSON, a very white mulatto, born in Maryland, 21 years of age, 5 feet 5 inches high, stout made, can weave and make shoes; he may pass by the name of John Green, or Bray; he rode off from Dover [on] a small bay horse …

JAMES MOORE, Captain D.R. New Castle, 30 August [1782][6]

James Songo enlisted for the war on 25 December 1781, was described as a 25-year-old Delaware-born farmer residing in Kent County, 5 feet 7 inches tall, with black hair and a yellow complexion. He was noted to have 'Deserted was taken & Deserted again July 28 1782'. John Wilson enlisted as a drummer for the war on 24 June 1782, 'a substitute for James Messix'. He, was, among other things, a weaver, but born in Maryland and residing in Sussex County, Delaware. Wilson deserted in July 1782 and was described as 22 years old, 5 feet 5 inches tall, with black hair and yellow complexion.[7] Another notice added more information:

5 Graves and Harris, Southern Campaign Pension, Whittenton Clifton (S35842), 'one Edw'd Harman, a coloured man'. Edward Harman/Harmond (Delaware), Compiled Service Records (National Archives). 'Muster Roll of Recruits, and others, of the Delaware Regt under my Comman[d] at the Post of Christiana Bridge', 20 June 1781, Delaware Regiment, Revolutionary War Rolls (National Archives), folder 11, frame 1; Charles Fithian to author (email), 21 November 2018.
6 *Pennsylvania Journal; and the Weekly Advertiser*, 14 September 1782, quoted in Boyle, *'He loves a good deal of rum'*, Vol.2, pp.298–299.
7 NA (US), Compiled Service Records (Delaware), James Songo, John Wilson.

Annapolis, September 10, 1782.

JACK BRAY, alias GREEN, [also known as John Wilson]
THE slave of Mrs. ANN STEWART, of Ann Arundel county, ran away from his mistress about the first of June, then on a visit near Queenstown on the Eastern shore of Maryland. Jack will pass very well as a whiteman, being a remarkable light mulattoe, with grey or blue eyes, brown curling hair, and some freckles; tho' by attending to his dialect it may be discovered he has been much with negroes; he is 22 years of age, of a low stature, stout and well set, his face is rather large for his size, his nose stubbed; he carried a variety of clothes with him, but as he offered some for sale before he went off, 'tis probable he has disposed of most of them; he is a tolerable good weaver, rough shoemaker, and occasionally rode as a postilion, in which character he was when he left his mistress. It appears from an advertisement of the first of July, under the signature of Captain James Moore, of the Delaware regiment, that Jack enlisted with a recruiting party at Dover, by the name of John Wilson, and had deserted and taken with him a small bay horse, old saddle and curb bridle ... CHARLES STEWART.[8]

Again, we turn to Grundset's *Forgotten Patriots* for a list of soldiers from the state. Though imperfect, it is the best we have for now. Of 10 possible Delaware African American Continental soldiers, only a few have some semblance of a military biography. Giles Bennett enlisted for the war on 12 July 1779 in Captain John Wilson's company; he died in service in January 1780. Cato Fagan served in Captain Thomas Kean's company, Colonel Samuel Patterson's Battalion, Delaware Flying Camp militia, enlisting on 14 August 1776. Born in Mill Creek Hundred, New Castle County, Delaware, Fagan was 22 years old, 5 feet 7 ¼ inches tall, with a dark complexion and black hair. He joined Captain John Learmonth's Delaware Regiment company on 5 June 1777 and deserted in June 1778.[9]

Two soldiers were re-enslaved after serving months or years with the regiment. As with Edward Harman, both men were enlisted late in the war and marched south from Delaware to participate in the Yorktown siege with two companies of recruits and ten veteran soldiers under Captain William McKennan. (All three men were on Captain McKennan's 20 June 1781, 'Roll of Recruits, and others ... under my Comman[d] at the Post of Christiana Bridge'). From there, they continued on to join the Delaware Regiment in South Carolina. George Laha (or Lehea) enlisted for the war on 9 March 1781 in Captain Paul Quenowault's company, Delaware Regiment. His service record relates, 'Discharged Feby 12 1782, being a slave for life & claimed'. It is unknown if he had joined with or without his master's permission. Lott Ford served about two and a half years in the same company, having joined in July 1780. According to Charles Fithian, Ford was manumitted to allow

---

8   *The Pennsylvania Gazette*, 6 November 1782, quoted in Boyle, *'He loves a good deal of rum'*, Vol.2, p.301.

9   Grundset, *Forgotten Patriots*, p.437; NA (US), Compiled Service Records (Delaware), Giles Bennett, Cato Fagan/Fagon/Fegan/Fegin. Both men are identified as African Americans via Grundset's work.

his enlistment, but was reclaimed by his owner in early 1783. As with the Maryland court decision to sell Rhode Island soldier Fortune Stoddard into slavery to pay legal costs, Privates Ford's and Laha's fates could not be visited on white soldiers.[10]

---

10 NA (US), Compiled Service Records (Delaware), Lott Ford and George Laha/Lehea. NA (US), Revolutionary War Rolls, folder 11, frame 1, Delaware Regiment, 'Muster Roll of Recruits, and others, of the Delaware Regt under my Comman[d] at the Post of Christiana Bridge', 20 June 1781; Ward, *Delaware Continentals*, pp.469–474; Charles Fithian to author (email), 21 November 2018.

16

Virginia: 'Served for two years ... in the light infantry commanded by Colo Harry Lee'

In early August 1775 two independent Virginia rifle companies commanded by Daniel Morgan and Hugh Stephenson joined the American army around Boston. That autumn Morgan's company took part in Colonel Benedict Arnold's expedition to Quebec through the Maine wilderness, while Stephenson's men remained behind. With Morgan and most of his company captured during an assault on Quebec City, Stephenson was promoted to colonel and tasked with raising the Maryland and Virginia Rifle Regiment (with five Virginia and four Maryland companies) in summer 1776. That November the Rifle Regiment, with Lieutenant Colonel Moses Rawlings commanding, was captured at Fort Washington.[1]

The 1st and 2nd Virginia Regiments, initially commanded by Colonels Patrick Henry and William Woodford, were first formed in mid-summer 1775. They began as provincial units and were accepted on the Continental contingent in February 1776. In December 1775 the Continental Congress decided that Virginia's defense force should be increased to eight regiments; accordingly, six more were raised, and those were transferred to the Continental establishment the following February. In early 1776 the sitting Virginia Convention dissolved the Eastern Shore minute battalion and organized an undersized seven-company 9th Regiment, which was increased to ten companies in June when adopted as a Continental unit. In October 1776 six more new regiments were authorized and over the ensuing winter

---

1 Danske Dandridge, *Historic Shepherdstown* (Charlottesville, Va.: The Michie Company, 1910), pp.77–82, 87–89; Henry Bedinger's Journal, 1775–1776, pp.97–162. Sanchez-Saavedra's *Virginia Military Organizations* is the best single source on the subject. That said, the connection between the pre-Charleston-surrender Virginia Continental regiments with their late-war successors is not clear in his work, and the author did not include the 1st and 2nd Virginia regiments of 1781.

and spring recruited and organized. The 10th, 11th, 14th, and 15th Regiments marched north to join Washington's army in New Jersey, while the 12th and 13th Regiments first served at and near Fort Pitt, then joined the main army in 1777.[2]

By 1777 Virginia had fifteen Continental regiments in the field. Manpower shortfalls due to campaign losses and battle casualties, plus expired enlistments, led to reductions in the state line in 1778 and again in 1779. In September 1778 the Virginia regiments were reorganized as follows: the 1st Virginia absorbed the remnants of the 9th Regiment, the 2nd Virginia was consolidated with the 6th Regiment, the 3rd Virginia was combined with the 5th Regiment, and the 4th Virginia absorbed the 8th Regiment.[3] With those amalgamations, the remaining units were renumbered:

7th Regiment renamed the 5th Virginia
10th Regiment renamed the 6th Virginia
11th Regiment renamed the 7th Virginia
12th Regiment renamed the 8th Virginia
13th Regiment renamed the 9th Virginia
14th Regiment renamed the 10th Virginia
15th Regiment renamed the 11th Virginia.[4]

In spring 1779 supernumerary officers had been sent south to recruit three Virginia detachments (formed from new levies and reenlisted veterans) under Brigadier General Charles Scott. The 1st Detachment commanded by Colonel Richard Parker marched into Georgia with Major General Benjamin Lincoln and took part in the siege of Savannah that September. The 2nd Detachment under Colonel William Heth marched in December 1779 to join Lincoln at Charleston, South Carolina. Both these units were in the Charleston garrison when the city was captured in May 1780. A third detachment, under Colonel Abraham Buford, was delayed and missed the city's capitulation. Buford's detachment was destroyed at the Waxhaws in late May.[5]

On 8 December 1779 Brigadier General William Woodford's Virginia Brigade, serving with Washington's army in New Jersey, marched towards its ultimate destination, Charleston, South Carolina. Bad weather and other difficulties impeded the movement; Woodford's troops finally entered the city on 7 April 1780. With him were three more Virginia Detachments,

2   Sanchez-Saavedra, *Virginia Military Organizations*, pp.27–72.
3   Sanchez-Saavedra, *Virginia Military Organizations*, pp.27–72
4   Sanchez-Saavedra, *Virginia Military Organizations*, pp.27–72.
5   Sanchez-Saavedra, *Virginia Military Organizations*, pp.177–181; George Washington to Charles Scott, 6 March 1779, 5 May 1779, Fitzpatrick, *Writings of George Washington*, Vol.14, pp.203–204, 498–499; George Washington to Colonel Richard Parker, 7 May 1779, Washington to Charles Scott, 25 May 1779, 28 June 1779, 8 July 1779, 27 July 1779, *ibid.*, Vol.15, pp.17–18, 150–151, 335–336, 384, 492–493; George Washington to Charles Scott, 17 August 1779, 19 October 1779, *ibid.*, Vol.16, pp.119–120, 490; LOC, Washington Papers, series 4, Charles Scott to George Washington, 22 March 1779, 24 April 1779, 28 April 1779, 12 May 1779, 18 May 1779, 10 June 1779, 20 July 1779.

Colonel Charles Russell's 1st (formed from the old 1st, 5th, 7th, 10th, and 11th Regiments), the 2nd commanded by Colonel John Neville (comprising companies of the 2nd, 3rd, and 4th Regiments), and the 3rd under Colonel Nathaniel Gist (from companies of the 6th, 8th, and Gist's Additional Regiments). Woodford's Brigade was also captured at Charleston.[6] The late-war Virginia regiments, and methods used to recruit them, are an interesting study. With the loss of Charleston, South Carolina, on 12 May 1780, and further disasters in the months following (Waxhaws, 29 May, and Camden, 16 August), Virginia's Continental contingent was decimated and the state desperate for men to fill new or reorganized units. In North Carolina and Virginia, the answer was to draft men from the state's militia serving 18 months to fill the 1781 regiments (drafted and volunteer levies had been used as early as 1777 by Virginia and other states to augment their Continental forces). Virginia funneled the men into three units. The earliest levy (autumn 1780) is generally known as the Chesterfield Supplement after the rendezvous point for the new men at Chesterfield Court House, twelve miles south of Richmond. These men were destined for the newly constituted 1st Virginia Regiment, commanded by Colonel John Green, and 2nd Virginia, Lieutenant Colonel Samuel Hawes. Those units served in Major General Nathanael Greene's army in the Carolinas, seeing action at Guilford Courthouse and later battles. A third organization, called in one instance by General Washington, the '2nd. Regmt. of Levies', eventually known as Lieutenant Colonel Thomas Gaskins' Virginia Battalion, served in their home state that summer and autumn, through the Yorktown Siege.[7] Major General Friedrich Wilhelm de Steuben described how the drafts were forwarded to the 1st and 2nd Regiments, as well as a second round of drafting slated to fill Gaskins' corps:

the state passed a Law to raise 3000 Men some for 8 Months some for 18 [months] – not more than one half of this number ever came into the field … The Enemy under General Leslie leaving the state the beginning of December, I immediately ordered the 900 Men, who had been employed against him to Petersburg in order if possible to equip & send them immediately to the Southward – But I found them so intirely destitute of every necessary that it was with the utmost difficulty I could fit out 400 which I sent off under Colonel Green about the middle of December [1780]. The remainder I ordered to the Barracks at Chesterfield Court house and exerted myself … to collect sufficient articles to fit them out – I had however hardly entered into the Business when the state was again invaded by the enemy under Arnold, the few articles that were collected, were then either taken or dispersed, & this caused such a delay that it was the 25th of March before I could equip the second detachment of 400 Men who marched that day under

---

6   Sanchez-Saavedra, *Virginia Military Organizations*, pp.177–181. See also, Lee Wallace (ed.), *The Orderly book of Captain Benjamin Taliaferro, 2nd Virginia Detachment, Charleston, South Carolina, 1780* (Richmond, Va.: Virginia State Library, 1980) and Bobrick, *A Gallant Defense: The Siege of Charleston*, pp.129–130.

7   Babits and Howard, *Long, Obstinate, and Bloody*, pp.72–76; Sanchez-Saavedra, *Virginia Military Organizations*, pp.91–93, 183–184.

Lieut. Colo. Campbell … By a Law of the state, while any part of the Militia of a County are in the field that County is not obliged to Draft and a large number of Militia being called out for this Expedition, the [second] Draft was put off till the 10th of April [1781] – the [British] reinforcement afterward brought by General Phillips, still obliging Government to keep those Militia in the field, it was agreed to relieve them by Counties in [order] that the Counties might Draft as they were relieved – in consequence of which only the upper counties on the north side James River, have sent in any Drafts and in the whole only 450 are yet assembled [all destined to serve in Gaskins' Battalion] … [8]

The 913 Chesterfield Supplement levies included (conservatively) 56 free African Americans (6.1 percent of the whole), and the two detachments from the Supplement sent to Greene's army in December 1780 and late March 1781 had some proportion of them. Similarly, the drafts that joined Gaskin also included African Americans; while full numbers are not known, five black veterans' pension narratives show service under Gaskin in 1781 (Francis Bundy, John Chavers, William Jackson, Bennett McKey, and William Wedgbare). After Yorktown, in 1782, a single Virginia regiment, commanded by Colonel Thomas Posey, was formed of veteran soldiers and levies. During the war's last two years Posey's men served under Brigadier General Anthony Wayne in South Carolina and Georgia.[9] (For further discussion of African Americans in the Chesterfield Supplement see Appendix 4.)

Virginia Soldier Narratives

As with other states, Virginia's soldiers of color saw extensive combat. In 1818 Shadrach Battles, 10th Regiment, recalled:

he … enlisted in Amherst County in the State of Virginia for the term of three years in the Company commanded by Capt James Franklin of the 10th Reg't of

---

8   Babits and Howard, *Long, Obstinate, and Bloody*, pp.72–76; Sanchez-Saavedra, *Virginia Military Organizations*, pp.91–93, 183–184.

9   Joseph A. Goldenberg, Eddie D Nelson, and Rita Y. Fletcher, 'Revolutionary Ranks: An Analysis of the Chesterfield Supplement', *The Virginia Magazine of History and Biography*, Vol.87, No.2 (April 1979), pp.182–189. Major General Friedrich Wilhelm de Steuben, commanding the Virginia Continental line, had established his headquarters at Chesterfield following the disastrous Battle of Camden, and called for the new recruits to join him there. 'The Chesterfield Size Roll: Soldiers who entered the Continental Line of Virginia at Chesterfield Courthouse after 1 September 1780' (Library of Virginia citation: Joseph Scott. Roll of troops who joined at Chesterfield Courthouse since 1780. State government records collection. Also, 'Size-Roll of Troops join'd at Chesterfield Ct. House since Sept. 1 1780 Capt'n. Joseph Scott' and, 'This book is a Supplement to "Papers concerning the Army of the Revolution" Vol 1, Executive Depart. …'. Note by C. Leon Harris, 'The history of the size roll after the Revolutionary War is somewhat obscure. A sheet inserted into the book has … two notes in different handwritings'. Transcribed from bound photocopies, accession 23816.), Transcribed and annotated by C. Leon Harris, http://southerncampaign.org/pen/b69.pdf. Transcription of the entire Chesterfield supplement list, with accompanying notes, provided by Joshua B. Howard and Lawrence E. Babits. Howard, Joshua to author, 15 September 2010 (email).

the Virg'a. line on Continental Establishment … Clough Shelton was his Lieut. who afterwards was advanced to a Captaincy … he continued to serve in the said corps or in the service of the United States untill the end of three years when he was honorably discharged from service in Augusta in the State of Georgia … he was in the Battles of Brandy Wine [11 September 1777] Monmouth [28 June1778], Germantown [4 October 1777], and at storming the fort at Savannah in Georgia [9 October 1779] …[10]

Isaac Brown was one of the 1780 levies who participated in the 1781 campaign in the Carolinas:

[He] enlisted for the term of eighteen months in the Fall of the year 1780, in the State of Virginia under Captain Wm. G Mumford at Charles City Courthouse … was from thence carried to Chesterfield Courthouse with other recruits by Captain Stith Hardyman and was there mustered in the Company Commanded by Captain Sandford[?] in the Regiment under the Command of Colo. [Richard] Campbell in the line of Virginia … he continued to serve … until the expiration of the said term of eighteen months, when he was discharged from … Service at the round O [in Colleton County, 45 miles west of Charleston], in the state of South Carolina … he was in the battles of Guilford Courthouse [15 March 1781], of 96 [Siege of Ninety-Six, 22 May to 19 June 1781], and of Eutaw [Springs, 8 September 1781], when the gallant Commander of the Regiment (Colo. Campbell) was Killed, and Colo. [William] Washington of the Cavalry was made prisoner.[11]

Of all the black Virginia Continentals found for this study, Andrew Pebbles had perhaps the most varied career.

[H]e enlisted … (the year precisely he does not recollect as being a poor unlearned Mulatto) under Captain George Lee Turberville [15th Virginia] of Westmoreland County who was a recruiting [officer] … he joined the Camp at Valley Forge and was placed under the Command of Captain Lewis Booker [likely Samuel Booker, with the 15th Virginia from November 1776 to September 1778, when that unit was incorporated with the 11th Regiment] … he belonged to the 15th [actually 11th] Virginia Regiment … under the command of Captain … Booker for two years … at Trenton he was detailed to serve in the artillery … he was commanded by a Capt Dandridge [1st Continental Artillery: John Dandridge was a captain from February 1777, captured at Charleston in 1780: Robert Dandridge was a lieutenant from October 1777] and served one year in the Artilory for a part of the … year he was under the command of a Captain Carler … a Captain [William] Miller commanded the gun with 12 men to which he belonged … he served for two years under Capt Michael Rudolph [of Maryland, captain as of November 1779] in the light infantry commanded by Colo Harry [Henry] Lee whose command was composed of infantry & Cavalry [Lee's Legion, authorized by Congress in April 1778, near full strength by November the same year] … he was in three general actions, at Monmouth, Gilford Courthouse & at Eutau Springs

---

10 Graves and Harris, Southern Campaign Pension, Shadrach Battles, 'a man of color' (S37713).
11 Graves and Harris, Southern Campaign Pension, Isaac Brown, 'free colored person' (S39214).

... at Eutau Springs he received three wounds he was wounded in the shoulder slightly lost the thumb of the left hand and was bayonetted in the belly ... he was discharged on Combahee River honorably ... the day before he was discharged he was in a battle in which Colo Lawrence [John Laurens] who commanded in the absence of Colo Lee was killed [27 August 1782] ... Colo Lee had gone home to be marryed [in April 1782, to Matilda Ludwell Lee] ... at Petersburg in Virginia he had his knee much injured by the wheel of a field piece.[12]

Pebbles provided additional details in an 1820 deposition: ' he served ... as follows, for a part of the time of service in the 15th Va Regiment in a Company commanded by Captain Booker a part of his time in the 5th Virginia Regiment under the same Captain and for one year he served in the Artilery commanded by Captain Dandridge and ... served two years in the light infantry under the command of Colo Henry Lee ... Michael ODolph [Rudolph] was then his Captain ... he served five years and some months altogether ...' His service records show he enlisted on 5 September 1777.[13]

Edward and Thomas Sorrell served with Lieutenant Colonel Charles Porterfield's Virginia State Regiment at the August 1780 Camden battle.[14] Porterfield had been a captain in the 7th Virginia (Continental) Regiment until his resignation in July 1779, and was wounded at Camden. Edward recalled,

he enlisted ... in the year 1779 with Capt Thomas Downing a militia officer and served in the 2nd Regt of the Virginia line, under the following named Officers Gen'l [Horatio] Gates. Colo [Charles] Porterfield, Capts [Thomas H.] Drew [formerly of Grayson's Additional Regiment, resigned July 1779] & [Charles] McGill [lieutenant in the 11th Virginia until resigning in April 1778] Lieutenant [David] Mann & Ensign Vaughan ... he lived in the County of Northumberland ... He marched from the County to Williamsburg Virginia in February or March of the following year ... he there joined the Regt of Colo Porterfield. after a few days stay at Williamsburg he marched with the Regt. of Colo Porterfield for Charleston South Carolina. The Regt marched through North Carolina by Sallsbury [Salisbury], Hillsborough & Guilford court house. the Regt. arrived in one or two days march of Charleston before it heard of its surrender. He was in frequent skirmishes with the british. He was at the battle of [Camden] where Genl [Horatio] Gates was defeated. he there received [a] musket ball in his right shoulder. Colo. Porterfield was there wounded. Seargent Booth t[w]o others & my self were carrying Colo Porterfield off after he was wounded but were so closely persued by the enemy that they had to leave him he was taken prisoner ... after the defeat of Gen'l. Gates he with others collected at Hillsborough & with Maj. Marzard [John Mazarett, Virginia State Artillery Regiment] marched to Richmond City Virginia, where he joined Capt Smith late in the fall & went with

12 Graves and Harris, Southern Campaign Pension, Andrew Pebbles, 'free Mulatto' (S38297).
13 Graves and Harris, Southern Campaign Pension, Andrew Pebbles (S38297). NA (US), Compiled Service Records, Andrew Pebbles.
14 Graves and Harris, Southern Campaign Pension, Edward Sorrel/Sorrell, 'free mulatto' (W26493) and Thomas Sorrell (S6137).

him to the western part of Virginia to obtain wagons & teams for the Army. they returned in the spring following. in a few days after their arrival at Richmond, he was ordered to Camden by Capt Smith for the purpose of attending Colo Porterfield to Virginia on parole. Colo Porterfield was confined a prisoner in Camden he went in company with Capt Singleton of the Maryland line to the neighbourhood of Camden he found Colo. Porterfield still a prisoner & being ill, he died [in January 1781] in four or five days after he arrived in Camden. he immediately brought Colo. Porterfields baggage to Richmond City Virginia & delivered it to Capt Smith it was then in the fall of 1781.[15]

James Nickens served at sea prior to his enlisting in the artillery:

> I enlisted in the Naval Service of the United States for the Term of three years and served the said Term in succession on Board the Ships, Tempest [a 20-gun Virginia Navy vessel], Revenge [possibly a Norfolk revenue vessel] and Hero [Virginia Navy galley], then in the Service of the said States … the Two latter were Commanded by Captains [George] Muter and [Wright] Westcott but I have forgotten the name of the Captain of the Tempest … after having Served the Term of Three years and Received a discharge which I have lost, I enlisted in the Land Service for the War at Lancaster Court House in Virginia and was marched from thence by a Captain Nicholas Correll [Cabell] to Join the Division of the Army under the Command of the Baron Steuben then stationed as well as I recollect at Cumberland Court House where I was placed under the Command of Captain Drury Ragsdale [1st Continental Artillery Regiment] subsequently thereto I was detached from the Command of the Baron Steuben to Join the Army of General [Nathanael] Greene in South Carolina and accompanied Captains Ragsdale and Flemming Gains of Colonel [Charles] Harrison's Regiment of Artillery to that State and was present at the Battle of the Eutaw Springs … I continued with the Southern Army until the close of the War … [16]

He stated in a later deposition, 'marched … to join the Southern Army under General Greene on the march Drury Ragsdale was taken sick and had to remain on the road. Flemming Gains continued to march with the men & joined the Army of General Greene previous to the battle of the Eutaw Springs, at which battle, he … James Nickens was stationed in the rear in charge of baggage belonging to … Flemming Gaines & John T. Brookes, officers he thinks in Harrison's Regiment of Artillery – soon after the battle of the Eutaw Springs Drury Ragsdale resumed his command …'. Again, we have a white former officer matter-of-factly supporting a black veteran's pension request: 'April 14, 1818 I do hereby certify that James Nickens a man of colour was a Soldier in the first Regiment of Artillery upon Continental

15 Graves and Harris, Southern Campaign Pension, Edward Sorrel/Sorrell (W26493). Maj. Guilford Dudley, North Carolina militia, wrote a detailed account of Porterfield's wounding and post-battle journey, for which see Jim Piecuch, *The Battle of Camden: A Documentary History* (Charleston, S.S.: The History Press, 2006), pp.72, 76–81.

16 Graves and Harris, Southern Campaign Pension, James Nickens/Nickins, 'a man of colour' (S38262).

establishment and commanded by Colonel Charles Harrison and that he served until the end of the War, signed John T. Brooke'. Nickins was awarded an eight-dollar monthly pension beginning in April 1818.[17]

Henry Hill's on-the-spot discharge was more emphatic, 'The Bearer hereof Henry Hill soldier of the 2 Virginia detachm't. Captain Stribling's company and having served Eighteen Months being the term for which he was engaged is hereby discharged from said detail in which we certify he hath behaved as a brave and faithfull soldier. Given at Salisbury [NC] the 18 day Janry 1782 S[igismund]. Stribling Capt S[mith]. Snead Maj'r Com't'. Prior to his late-war service, Hill enlisted in Captain Reuben Lipscomb's company, 7th Virginia Regiment in February 1778 for one year; in September 1778 he was noted as a 'Negro & Bowman [officer's servant]'. In December he was transferred to the 5th Virginia, until his February 1779 discharge. By his own testimony he was in the battles of Monmouth, Guilford Courthouse, the Ninety-Six siege, Hobkirk Hill, Eutaw Springs, 'and some of less note'.[18]

John Redman served only in the war's last years, at least part of that tine as an officer's waiter. John Jenkins recalled, 'that he knew John Redman during the Revolutionary war and that he served 2 years at least in the 1st Virginia Redg't of light Dragoons Comanded by Col'n [Anthony Walton] White as a Wa[i]ter to Lieutenant Vincent Howel in the Company comanded by Capt [James Gun …'. Redman was in only one small battle, though a singular one. He noted in his 1823 account, 'that he enlisted in Winchester in Virginia about Christmas of the year [1780] for and during the War that he marched from thence with other recruits under Lieutenant Vincent Howell to Richmond in the spring of said year and was put into the regiment of horse commanded by Colonel [Henry] Lee and marched from Richmond … with a detachment … under Captains [John] Hughes & [James] Gun [both of the 1st Continental Light Dragoon Regiment] & said Lieutenant Howell to the South that he was in … service & lay in North Carolina at the time Cornwallis was taken [in October 1781]. That he was in no battle except one in the neighbourhood of Savannah with the Indians under their Chief, Sago'. The 1st Continental Light Dragoons were part of a force Brigadier General Anthony Wayne led into Georgia to interdict loyalists and Indians attempting to enter Savannah. As of 27 April 1782, Wayne's troops consisted of the 1st and 4th Continental Dragoons, Colonel James Jackson's Georgia Legion cavalry and infantry, Major Thomas Posey's Virginia Detachment, and Georgia militia, plus an artillery company. The action he referred to was the 23 June 1782 incursion by Upper Creek leader Emistisiguo and some 300 of his warriors. As they were attempting to enter Savannah, they surprised Major General Anthony Wayne's camp at the small hamlet of Ebenezer. Wayne quickly rallied his forces and counterattacked, killing Emistisiguo and approximately 30 others. Savannah surrendered less than a month later.[19]

17 Graves and Harris, Southern Campaign Pension, James Nickens/Nickins (S38262) John T. Brooke affidavit.
18 Graves and Harris, Southern Campaign Pension, Henry Hill, 'Negro' (S41639).
19 Graves and Harris, Southern Campaign Pension, John Redman, 'Free Colored Person' (W5691), deposition of John Jenkins; NA (US), Compiled Service Records, John Redman/Redmund,

'THEY WERE GOOD SOLDIERS'

Private, 1st Continental Light Dragoon Regiment, 1780–1783. The trooper wears a horsehair crested leather helmet, blue coat with green facings, and leather breeches. Artwork by Don Troiani (Courtesy of the artist, www.historicalimagebank.com). Reuben Bird was with the 1st Regiment Light Dragoons from 1780 to 1783, acting as bowman (servant) to Lieutenant William Gray. Bird stated he 'enlisted for and during the war … in April or May in the year 1780 in Hillsborough in North Carolina in the Company commanded by Captain James Guinn in the Regiment of Dragoons commanded by Colo [Anthony Walton] White of Virginia … he was in no battle, he being a colored man, and kept as a Bowman, although he was very near the ground where several were fought …' John Redman was a trooper with the same regiment in South Carolina and Georgia in 1782. National Archives (United States), Revolutionary War Pension and Bounty-Land Warrant Application Files (National Archives Microfilm Publication M804), Records of the Department of Veterans Affairs, Record Group 15, Washington, D.C., reel 243, Reuben Bird (S37776); reel 2013. John Redman (W5691).

Three veterans were teamsters. Thomas Campbell served in the 4th Virginia and testified:

> about the month of September 1776 … he enlisted for three years under one Captain Wilson [John Wilson, ensign 4th Regiment 1776, lieutenant, April 1778, killed at Eutaw Springs] of the County of Culpepper … Virginia where this applicant then resided believes the enlisting orders were presented to him by … Captain Wilson of the Fourth Virginia regiment. The Colonels name … was Naval [John Neville], of the said Fourth Virginia Regiment, General [Charles] Scotts Brigade. … about six days after he enlisted they were mustered and marched Immediately to a place called Whitemarsh in the state of Pennsylvania … they

---

Captain John Hughes 5th Troop, 1st Continental Light Dragoons; Nathanael Greene to John Barnwell, 'Head Quarters [Round O, S.C.] January 11th 1782, Conrad, Dennis M. (ed.), *The Papers of General Nathanael Greene*, vol. X, 3 December 1781–6 April 1782 (Chapel Hill and London: University of North Carolina Press, 1998), pp.180–181. NA (US), Revolutionary War Rolls, folder 136, item 222, 'Return of the Troops in Georgia, Commanded by the Honorable Brigadier General Wayne Camp Ebenezer April 27th 1782'. 'Return of Non–Commissioned Officers and Privates of the State of Pennsylvania now actually Serving in the Southern Army …,' Edward Hand, 19 March 1782, Hazard, Samuel, (ed.), *Pennsylvania Archives*, vol. IX (Philadelphia: Joseph Severns & Co., 1854), p.517. The Battle of Ebenezer, 23 June 1782, 'American Revolutionary War', https://www.myrevolutionarywar.com/battles/1782-skirmish/. Harrington, Hugh T., 'Anthony Wayne's 1782 Savannah Campaign', 9 October 2014, Journal of the American Revolution, https://allthingsliberty.com/2014/10/anthony-waynes-1782-savannah-campaign/.

there joined the main Army under General Washington … from White Marsh they were marched to a Place called Valley forge … in the State of Pennsylvania where he remained with the Army … from sometime in December 1777. through the Winter until June 1778 when the army was marched to Monmuth where he was engaged in the Battle which was there fought and there in consequence of being over heated and worn out with fatigue he was taken sick and was put in the hospital where he remained some weeks very sick … after he recovered so that he could walk the Doctor who took care of him let him go to live in a family near that place and the army was marched from there he does not know to what place.[20]

Mr Campbell's 1833 application recounted,

at the time I enlisted … I was a slave to Colonel Martin Picket of Virginia who gave me my Choice Either to remain a slave as I was or to go into the Army and I chose the latter and entered as stated in my … Declaration. In the Battle at Monmouth I was with the Artillery and Drove the horses … from & after the Battle of Monmouth in consequence of being over heated and fatigued I was sick and for not less than six months was unable to perform any service whatever … he has never entirely recovered from said sickness occasioned by being over heated.[21]

Thomas Campbell was listed on an October 1777 roster of 'Lieut. John Wilson's new recruits [enlisted for the war] belonging to the 4th Virginia Regiment'. Two privates of that name are mentioned in two different companies, but they seem to be the same man. The one in Captain John Brent's company in November 1777 was noted as being on command with the artillery. In December he transferred to Captain Jason Riddick's company and over the ensuing months was several times recorded to be working as a wagoner. His extant service records end at May 1778.[22]

Soldiers were pulled from the ranks for a number of extra duties; most were temporary, but some received permanent assignments. One such was Daniel Williams, who was a wagoner for the length of his enlistment. Williams noted,

he was drafted into the service of the Continental Army in which he served near five years as a Waggoner, and had charge of a Waggon & 2 Horses and remained in that Station until the close of the War … he was at the Battle of Brandywine, Germantown, Monmouth, York Town [siege] (and many others) during the War … when he left the service he received from his Commanding officer an honourable Discharge which he has mislaid and Lost.[23]

A fellow veteran supported Williams' application:

---

20 Graves and Harris, Southern Campaign Pension, Thomas Campbell, 'a black man' (R1609).
21 Graves and Harris, Southern Campaign Pension, Thomas Campbell (R1609).
22 NA (US), Compiled Service Records (Virginia), Thomas Campbell.
23 Graves and Harris, Southern Campaign Pension, Daniel Williams, 'Coloured Man' (R11569).

Alexander More [former 8th Virginia private] … being duly sworn saith he is now aged 81 years, that he received from the US a pension. that he is well acquainted with Daniel Williams a Coloured Man who was a Waggoner in the Continental Army during the Revolutionary War – that deponent was a Private in the Army under Genl Washington, was in the Battle of Brandywine, Germantown, and at the Battle of Yorktown, that he well rem[em]bers the said Daniel Williams being … attached to Waggon department driving team and continued with them until the close of the war … deponent removed to Philad'a from Virginia soon after the War where he has resided ever since … he has know[n] Daniel Williams residening in Philad'a for many years and knows him to [be] the same person Discribed above.[24]

Daniel Williams concluded his submission with a poignant plea:

he never has at any time received from the United States compensation for his services except Rations and Cloathing … after the war he returned home to accomack [Virginia] and remained there for several years and then removed to the State of Maryland where he resided 13 years and then came to Philad'a. where he has resided 27 years during which time he has been blessed with health sufficient to enable him by his industry to support and provide for himself and family … he is now old poor and infirm and requires some aid from the Government he has in the Prime of Life faithfully served.[25]

In the end Williams was denied a pension, it being determined 'He did not serve in a military capacity'. To the contrary, enlisted wagoners and other support personnel were in fact eligible and with sufficient proof of service did become pensioners.[26]

Daniel Strother was another black army wagoner denied a pension, but his service and testimony further emphasizes the importance of these unsung veterans:

on the 8 day of January 1781 he joined the Continental Army then at Charlotte County Virginia which was under the command of General [Nathanael] Greene as a waggoner of which army Samuel Edmondson … was Wagon Master General … he was ordered to assist in taking provisions to Head Quarters which were then in Guilford County North Carolina. after arriving at head quarters the detachment of which this deponent was one was employed in transporting damaged catridges

---

24 Graves and Harris, Southern Campaign Pension, Daniel Williams (R11569), deposition of Alexander More. NA (US), Compiled Service Records (Virginia), Alexander Moore/More. Three Virginia soldiers with that name, all serving with the 8th Regiment, are listed: Corporal, Captain James Knox's company, noted as serving from 25 April 1776 to 30 May 1777, sick in Virginia May 1777. (Perhaps the same Moore in Croghan's company). Private, Captain William Croghan's company, this Moore/Moor, 'on furlow' in May 1777, served as a wagoner in July 1777, was wounded at Brandywine (11 September 1777), and was discharged 5 January 1778. Private, Captain Thomas Berry's company, first muster roll noted September 1777, last noted as on command in February 1778.
25 Graves and Harris, Southern Campaign Pension, Daniel Williams (R11569).
26 Graves and Harris, Southern Campaign Pension, Daniel Williams (R11569).

&c and drafted into the heavy baggage accompanying the Army this was just before the battle at Guildford Court House which took place in March 1781. and they were ordered across the Dan River – after the battle of Guildford C House he was ordered with others by Col John Thornton commanding the Culpepper [Virginia] Militia to drive stock for the Army which orders were obeyed … in September 1781 he went again with the Militia to York town in Virginia w[h]ere they joined General Washington and remained there untill the British surrendered and Lord Wallis (Cornwallis) was made a prisoner … he was honorably discharged after each tour of service but has unfortunately lost his discharge.[27]

Peter McAnelly, former Virginia militia soldier, deposed he:

had been long acquainted with the above named Daniel Strother – that their first acquaintance commenced near Yorktown in Virginia in the year 1781 in the following manner … on the morning before Cornwallis surrendered a waggoner belonging to the detachment in which he McAnnally served run away … from the Virginia Regiment the Captain then ordered this deponent to take his place and ordered him up to the public stores for a Barrell of Rum, at which place he saw and became acquainted with the aforenamed Daniel Strother … Strother was when he first met him as aforesaid selected by the officer of the public Stores as a waggoner for the army and he believes the officer's name was Major Thomas Minor [aide to Virginia militia general Edward Stevens].[28]

As C. Leon Harris notes, the reason for denying Strother's pension claim was that he "'did not serve six months in a military capacity,'" apparently because his service was mostly as a wagoner. This rejection is not consistent with the Pension Office's own regulations, which excluded wagoners only if they were "occasionally employed with the army upon civil contracts".[29]

Many soldiers never applied for a pension and their stories are lost. For some a tantalizing outline of their service can be traced via muster rolls and other documents, often coalesced in the Federal compiled service records. One such was Cesar Black, whose file shows him to have begun his military career as a drummer (and sometimes fifer) in the 10th Virginia Regiment, Captain David Laird's company, commencing on 3 December 1776. He endured the 1777 summer and autumn campaigns in New Jersey and Pennsylvania, and entered the Valley Forge winter camp at year's end. In June 1778 he was listed as 'Sick Valley Forge', and in August, now a drummer in Captain Nathan Lamme's 6th Virginia company, was noted as 'Left at V. Forge'. From that point on the records show him to be on command (detached service) at Philadelphia, up to November 1779, after which we lose track of him.[30]

---

27 Graves and Harris, Southern Campaign Pension, Daniel Strother, African American (R10275).
28 Graves and Harris, Southern Campaign Pension, Daniel Strother (R10275), deposition of Peter McAnelly; *Ibid.*, Peter McAnelly (S16467).
29 Graves and Harris, Southern Campaign Pension, Daniel Strother (R10275).
30 NA (US), Compiled Service Records (Virginia), Cesar Black.

17

North Carolina: 'The men sent on Board of Prison Ships – myself among them …'

At the end of August 1775 the North Carolina Provincial Congress resolved to raise 1,000 state troops, enlisted for as little as six months up to a year, with the expectation they would eventually be accepted into Continental service. To embody those soldiers, on 1 September they authorized the formation of two North Carolina Regiments (commanded by Colonels James Moore and Robert Howe). That November the Continental Congress ordered the 1st and 2nd North Carolina reorganized as Continental regiments; a third regiment was approved in January 1776, and two more the following March. With promotion of Moore and Howe to brigadier general, the five North Carolina regiments in 1776 were commanded by Francis Nash, Alexander Martin, Jethro Sumner, Thomas Polk, and Edward Buncombe, and enlistments were extended to two and a half years. In May a sixth regiment was formed under Alexander Lillington. A contingent of North Carolina troops was sent to Charleston, South Carolina, when that city was threatened by British forces in late May 1776, but only the 1st Regiment took part in the defensive operations on the outer islands. That July Savannah, Georgia, was thought to be in danger and Brigadier General Robert Howe marched south with the 3rd North Carolina, in company with Virginia and South Carolina troops. By October Howe had under his command in Georgia some 300 men of the 1st, 2nd, and 3rd Regiments.[1]

September 1776 saw the creation of the 7th, 8th, and 9th North Carolina Regiments, a result of the Congressional 88 battalion resolve. The new units were commanded by Colonels James Hogun, James Armstrong, and John Williams. In April 1777 the state legislature created Colonel Abraham Sheppard's State Regiment, added to the Continental establishment in July of that year. That unit was designated Sheppard's Additional Regiment, but more commonly called the 10th North Carolina. Soon after, Brigadier general

---

1   Wright, *Continental Army*, pp.71–72; Hugh F. Rankin, *The North Carolina Continentals* (Chapel Hill: University of North Carolina Press, 1971), pp.62–63, 70–83.

Francis Nash began to gather the North Carolina regiments at Halifax, several just returned from South Carolina, in preparation for marching them north to join Washington's army. By May they were en route, with a three-to-four-week hiatus at Alexandria, Virginia, to inoculate those men who never had smallpox. Two hundred already-immune men continued north under Colonel Sumner and Lieutenant Colonel Archibald Lytle, reaching Morristown, New Jersey, by mid-June. Nash's men marched first to Philadelphia, serving there and in the vicinity until early August when they were ordered to take post at Trenton, New Jersey, where Lytle's men re-joined the brigade. Leaving Trenton on 24 August, the North Carolina troops joined the main army at Wilmington, Delaware, on the 28th. The North Carolina brigade participated in the battles of Brandywine and Germantown. Francis Nash was mortally wounded in the latter action, and in mid-December Georgian Lachlan McIntosh replaced him as brigade commander. Enduring the Valley Forge winter, the North Carolinians served in the June 1778 Monmouth campaign, and remained with Washington's army until they marched south to join the Charleston garrison in late 1779.[2]

At its greatest, North Carolina's contribution to the Continental Army consisted of ten foot regiments, all of them understrength during most of their service. By 1778 the units were so reduced that the remaining men were concentrated in the 1st and 2nd North Carolina while officers were sent home to recruit and form four new regiments, with mixed success. Supernumerary officers, too, were sent back to North Carolina to raise a new regiment of nine-months levies. That unit, the 3rd North Carolina, was sent north to work on the West Point fortifications, and was mustered out in spring 1779. Following the May 1780 loss of Charleston, South Carolina, including North Carolina's three remaining Continental regiments, the state struggled to raise new units to replace their loss. The British occupation of North Carolina hampered that effort, and the lack of commissioned officers only exacerbated the situation. In April 1781 Major Pinkethan Eaton, formerly of the 3rd and 5th North Carolina Regiments, led an ad hoc Continental unit of 170 drafted men, enlisted for 12 months, to join Major General Greene's forces in South Carolina. Twenty-five men were detached for service with Lee's Legion, and that unit, along with Eaton's North Carolinians, plus a force under Lieutenant Colonel Francis Marion took part in the capture of Fort Motte, Fort Granby, and Augusta, as well as the siege of Ninety-Six. Cornwallis's army having moved to Virginia, by mid-June 1781 Brigadier General Jethro Sumner had organized one North Carolina regiment with volunteers and drafts funneled to High Rock Ford on the Haw River. With a second regiment in progress but still unformed, and having only 200 of his 500 troops armed (those consisting of 'delinquents & old Continental Soldiers'), Sumner moved on 1 July to join Greene's force. On the 14th the command, now at Salisbury under Colonel John Baptiste Ashe, received 300 muskets and cartridge pouches, but no bayonets. Ashe's 1st Regiment continued their march south

2   Rankin, *North Carolina Continentals*, pp.87–148; 'Jacob Turner's Book', Walter Clark (ed.), *The State Records of North Carolina*, XII, 1777–1778 (Wilmington: Broadfoot Publishing Co.,1993), pp.485, 495.

on 14 July while Sumner remained at Salisbury to form the gathering levies into a second regiment (Colonel Ashe incorporated into his corps a group of draftees from the Salisbury district, and those men remaining from Major Eaton's command). By early August Sumner with the 2nd Regiment joined Greene and Lieutenant Colonel John Armstrong was given command. Both regiments (possibly combined into one unit) participated in the Eutaw Springs action on 8 September. The day before that battle a small force of North Carolina Continentals under Major Reading Blount had joined the army; a leavening of experienced men was added to Blount's levies and formed into a 3rd Regiment. In spring 1782 expiring enlistments and scant numbers of new enlistees led to a reduction of the North Carolina line to two regiments, then in winter 1783, to a single unit, soon to be disbanded.[3]

North Carolina Soldier Narratives

North Carolina's African American soldiers enlisted early-on and saw extensive service. 'Free mulatto' John Butler was an early-war soldier, recalling in 1820:

> [H]e enlisted on or about the 4th day of May 1776 for the term of two years and six months in Windsor Bertie County N Carolina in the Company commanded by Captain Jeremiah McLayn or McLean [likely John McLane, 4th Regiment] in the regiment commanded by Colonel Thomas Polk [4th North Carolina] … he continued to serve until the expiration of the [enlistment term] … when he was discharged at Halifax N.Carolina … he was in the battle of Charleston S. Carolina [Sullivan's Island, 28–29 June 1776] …[4]

William Stewart served through the 1777–1778 Philadelphia and Monmouth campaigns, returning south in late 1779.

> [H]e was born in Brunswick County State of Virginia and is now in his seventy sixth year of age, he removed to North Carolina, Northampton County where he enlisted in the year 1777, under Major Hardy Murphy [Murfree, 2nd Regiment] a Continental recruiting officer in the month of June, he was then marched to Halifax North Carolina, and from that to Alexandria in Virginia, where there were assembled fifteen hundred new recruits where those who had not the smallpox were inoculated, and in the last of September of the same year we were marched to a place called the White Marsh in New Jersey [actually Wilmington, Delaware] and there joined the headquarters of General Washington, where the detachment

---

3 Rankin, *North Carolina Continentals*, p.16. For the 1778 North Carolina levies see, Rees, 'The pleasure of their number', Part I. 'Filling the Regiments by drafts from the Militia'., http://tinyurl.com/blz2gjw. For post-Charleston North Carolina regiments see, Rankin, *North Carolina Continentals*, pp.218–220, 328–333, 341–351, 387–388.
4 Graves and Harris, Southern Campaign Pension, John Butler, 'free Mulatto' (S41463); Paul Heinegg, 'List of Free African Americans in the Revolution: Virginia, North Carolina, South Carolina, Maryland and Delaware (followed by French and Indian Wars and colonial militias)', http://www.freeafricanamericans.com/revolution.htm.

was placed in the company of Captain Robert Fenns [Fenner] in the Second Regiment North Carolina line our Colonels were Colonel John Patton & Colonel Harney. We there wintered and in the spring marched to … the Valley Forge on Schulkill River and from thence to West Point on North River and was there at the time the British took Stoney Point, Declarant was marched among other places to the White Plains, Pyramus [Paramus], Hackensack & Long Island … was in the Battle of Monmouth, under the command of General Hogans [James Hogun], we marched to various places in jersey and finally marched, through Baltimore, to North Carolina under the command of General Hogan, and was discharged in the month of June in the year 1780 in North Carolina, his discharge was signed by General Hogan, having served three years the full term of his enlistment, He preserved his discharge for many years until it was worn out, & lost … After his discharge he remained in Northampton County North Carolina until about 27 years ago when he removed with his family into Pennsylvania, and has for the last 21 years resided in Westmoreland County, Pennsylvania, Declarant is a colored man but was free born.[5]

Martin Black enlisted the same year and, barring a brief hiatus, did not leave the army until late 1782.

he enlisted at New bern and was marched with others under the Command of Colonel Ben Sheppard [Abraham Shepard] as a part of the tenth Regiment as he believes to Georgetown on the Potomack [River] at which place the soldiers were inoculated for the small pox. From Georgetown he marched to Valley Forge in Pennsylvania where the American Army were encamped under General Washington, while the enemy were in Philadelphia. He was in the battle at Monmouth [28 June 1778], at the Storming of Stoney point [New York, 16 July 1779] and at … West point. from West point he went … in the Brigade of General Hogan [James Hogun] to Charleston. He was a prisoner at Charleston with the army surrendered there [12 May 1780] but escaped on the seventh day & returned to New bern North Carolina. From his first enlistment as above mentioned to the return to Newbern, he served three years. After remaining at home a few days he enlisted as a soldier in Captain Benj. Colemans [2nd North Carolina, captured at Charleston] company as an Eighteen months man in the Continental line … marched to Charleston where he remained with the army there encamped until the Peace, when the army entered the City as the British evacuated it [14 December 1782], & in a few weeks after was discharged. His discharge is long since lost. At Valley Forge (during the first term of service) the men were distributed to make up deficiencies in the regiment & he passed from the tenth to the second North Carolina Regiment, and from the Company Commanded by Silas Sears Stevenson [Silas Ayres Stevenson] to the Company Commanded by Captain Clem Hall [Clement Hall].[6]

---

5   Graves and Harris, Southern Campaign Pension, William Stewart, 'colored man but was free born' (R10173).

6   Graves and Harris, Southern Campaign Pension, Martin Black, 'free Negro' (S41441).

In 1820 Joseph Case claimed he enlisted in '1777 … in Captain William Goodman's company of the 5th Regiment, Commanded by Col Gideon Lamb, in the line of North Carolina …'.[7] Due to his mention of service in several different companies this clarification was submitted a year later:

> Case enlisted under Capt Wm. Goodman [4th Regiment, killed at Eutaw Springs in 1781] in the … in the State of N. Carolin … Capt Goodman marched him to Stono in South Carolina he was there put under Capt Ramsey and did belong to Capt [Matthew] Ramseys Company [4th Regiment] on the day of the battle of Stono [Ferry, 20 June 1779] which Battle he was in … he continued under Captain Ramsey for some time and marched with him from Stono to Charleston and soon after general Hogan [James Hogun] arrived in Charleston he was Removed from Capt Ramseys Company and put under the command of Capt G[ee]. Bradley [3rd Regiment] … he was made Captain Bradleys waiter … [and] was in Charleston during the siege … was made a prisoner at the surrender of Charleston with Capt Bradley … he continued a prisoner to the enemy for 14 months still with Captain Bradley … he & Captain Bradley was both exchanged at the same time and … some time after their exchange Captain Bradley give him a written discharge in the City of Richm'd, which discharge he hath lost …[8]

William Casey spent most of his military service (1777–81) in the 4th Virginia Regiment, spending the winter at Valley Forge and taking part in the June 1778 action at Monmouth Courthouse. Casey recalled of his southern service:

> After being some months in the north, we were marched back to the South – and passed all the streams on the ice – untill we reached James River at Richmond, where after waiting a few days for a thaw, we crossed in Boats. We were then by a hurried march carried through Petersburg and Hix's ford in Virginia to Halifax N.C. where we crossed the Roanoke – thence by the most direct Rout to cross Creek, now the site of Fayetteville N.C. – thence through Camden and Geo[rge]. Town So. Carolina to Charleston, which place we entered the 11th April as well as I recollect in 1780 – and were there besieged by the British under the command of Gen'l. [Henry] Clinton – Lord Cornwallis & Colonel [Banastre] Tarleton – which was continued untill, I think, 12th May – when the American forces surrendered. I recollect at this place [Brig.] Gen'l. [Lachlan] McIntosh & [Lieutenant] Colonel Wm. Henderson [3rd South Carolina Regiment] – also [Brig.] Gen'ls. [Charles] Scott and [William] Woodford & [Lieutenant] Colonel [John] Nevill [4th Virginia]. The officers taken Prisoners were paroled and the men sent on Board of Prison Ships – myself among them – we were detained on Board I think more than a year – when we were carried Round by water to the James River, and up the River to James Town in the latter part of the summer 1781, where they

---

7 Graves and Harris, *Southern Campaign Pension*, Joseph Case, 'other free' (i.e. non-white) (S41472).

8 Graves and Harris, *Southern Campaign Pension*, Joseph Case (S41472); Patrick O'Kelley, *Nothing But Blood and Slaughter: The Revolutionary War in the Carolinas* (Lillington, N.C.: Blue House Tavern Press, 2004), Vol.1, pp.291–299.

were released – having been exchanged as he understood for Burgoyne's men — we were then march'd to Williamsburg where, having performed my full term of four years, I was discharged – my discharge was signed by Colonel John Nevill – but is lost or mislaid so that I cannot produce it. At the time I was discharged I understood Cornwallis & his troops were surrounded at little York in Virginia. After my discharge I came home to Southampton & remained but a short time, when I moved and settled in No. Carolina in the County of Bute [sic] in that part of it which now constitutes the County of Warren. I was again enlisted by Captain Dixon Marshall of the [1st North Carolina] Reg't. commanded by Gen'l. Jethro Sumner and was shortly after taken by Gen'l. Sumner to wait upon him – in which capacity I served thirteen months and eight days when I was discharged by Gen'l. Sumner. This discharge is also lost or mislaid. For this latter service I received from No. Carolina a Land warrant for 640 acres.[9]

John Womble served with Lieutenant Colonel Robert Mebane's 3rd North Carolina Regiment for one eventful year:

[O]n or about the first of June in the year [1779] … at the town of Halifax … he enlisted as a private soldier under Major [Thomas] Hogg of the 10th [actually 3rd] Regiment of the North Carolina Line … From Halifax he marched with Major Hogg's recruits to Kinston (N.C.); at which place he was put under the command of Capt [Michael?] Quinn of the … [3rd] Regiment commanded by … field officers Colonel Robt. Mebane & Major Hogg – From Kinston he marched to Cross Creek … as a place of Rendezvouz, thence he marched in the summer of the … year to Charleston S.C. where soon after his arrival he was transferred to the company under the command of Capt [John] Campbell of the said … Regiment … He remained in Charleston under the same officers till some time in August in the year [1779] … when the American Forces under the command of [Maj.] Gen'l. [Benjamin] Lincoln were called to make an attack on Savannah [besieged 24 September to 19 October 1779]; he then left Charleston & marched to assist in the … attack; but Gen'l. Lincoln being unsuccessful in his attempt on Savannah, the army returned to Charleston – soon after his return to Charleston he was placed under the command of Captain Maun [?] of the said … Regiment … sometime in May in the year [1780] … he assisted in the defence of Charleston, when attacked by the British Forces under Sir Henry Clinton; & in the unfortunate capture of that City he was taken prisoner & sent to Haddrell's Point … he well recollects that Capt Singles[?], then acting Brigade Major & Doctor Lumus [Jonathan Lumos, 3rd North Carolina] Surgeon were among the captured & paroled officers. The battle, he remembers from circumstances that will never be effaced from his memory– according to the articles of capitulation, the officers & their servants were to be paroled & their persons & property held sacred; he embraced the opportunity as to avoid going on board the Prison Ships, immediately became Doctor Lumus servant & was with the Doctor dismissed on parole. He attended the Doctor to Washington (N.C.) & there remained some time, the residue of the

---

9   Graves and Harris, Southern Campaign Pension, William Casey (Kersey), 'Free Colored' (W29906.5).

time till the end of the War, he passed on the Banks of the Tar River on his Parole having never been exchanged & therefore not regularly discharged ...[10]

Given the status of African Americans in the United States. Drewry Tann's account is perhaps not as odd as it first appears:

> ... he inlisted under Captain [Joshua] Hadley [1st North Carolina Regiment] ... and states the manner he came in the service as follows, that being born free in the county of Wake he was stolen from his parents when a small boy by persons unknown to him, who were carrying him off to sell him into Slavery, and had gotten with him, and other stolen property, as far as the mountains on their way ... his parents made complaint to a Mr. Tanner Alford who was then a magistrate in the county of Wake state of N. Carolina to get me back from those who had stolen me, and he did pursue the Rogues & overtook them at the mountains and took me from them & my parents agreed that I should serve him (Tanner Alford) untill I was twenty one years old, when he had served Alford several years (six years) it came Alfords time to go in the army (or he told me so) and told me if I would go in the army he would set me free on which condition I readily listed under Captain Hadley for eighteen months ... and marched to Charleston & thence to James's Island where he served out his tour of inlistment ... he had a discharge and was about returning home when a Captain Benjamin Coleman [2nd North Carolina] who told me he lived in Bladen County N. Carolina took his discharge from him and tryed to compell him to remain in the service & be his waiting man ...he listed volluntarily in the army under Capt Hadley. he served as before stated on James island near Charleston S. Carolina where there was some English prisoners & he was sometimes stationed as a guard over them ... [11]

In 1834 North Carolina Secretary of State William Hill noted that, 'Drury Tan a private in Captain Hadley's Company of the 10th Regiment, enlisted on the 1st day of August 1782 for 18 months and that nothing more is said of him on said rolls'.[12]

The 1782 southern campaign is little known or written of. Zachariah Jacobs served in South Carolina under Major General Greene at a time when Crown forces were hemmed in at Charleston, and pressure was building on the British at Savannah, Georgia. No great battles were fought, but men on both sides were killed and wounded in a number of small actions. Jacobs testified,

> That he enlisted in the army of the United States in the year 1781 in the month of October with Captain James Mills, and served in, as he believes, the eighth regiment of the North Carolina line under the following named officers: Gen Green, Colonel [Archibald] Lytle [6th North Carolina], Major Robert Raiford [2nd Regiment], Major Griffith McKee [McKree, 3rd Regiment], Adjutant Curtis Ivey [3rd Regiment], Captain James Mills [1st or 10th Regiment], Richard

---

10 Graves and Harris, Southern Campaign Pension, John Womble, 'free colored person' (S42083).
11 Graves and Harris, Southern Campaign Pension, Drewry Tann, 'a Free man of Colour' (S19484).
12 Graves and Harris, Southern Campaign Pension, Drewry Tann (S19484), William Hill statement.

Fenner 1st Lieut [2nd Regiment], John Slade 2nd Lieut [likely Stephen Slade, 2nd Regiment] … Major [Reading] Blount [1st Regiment] commanded … he left the service in December 1782, having enlisted for & served twelve months … when he entered this service he resided in Brunswick County N. C … he was in a skirmish near Dorchester in S. C. between Gumbee Creek & Bacon bridge, it being an attack on a Row galley in Ashley River, which was upset & the men on board taken prisoners [Jacobs likely confuses some of his chronology, as the only known incident matching this attack is the 19 March 1782 capture of the British armed galley *Alligator*] … he [had] marched from Wilmington which he left the 10th of March 1782, through Brunswick County N.C. into S.C. through Georgetown across Santee at Strawberry ferry, on to the Eutaw Springs, thence to a place called Round O, thence to Ashley Hill about fifteen miles from Charleston, where he was stationed and remained till his term of enlistment was out, and continued a month or two longer, then marched to Wilmington and was disbanded the week before Christmas …[13]

Mr Jacobs earlier militia campaigns were more harrowing than his Continental service.

He served three months in the militia under Colonel [John Alexander] Lillington, Captain Joseph Wood, also under Gen [John] Ashe entered in the last [weeks] of 1778 … he was drafted; he resided in Brunswick County when he entered this service, was in the battle at Briar Creek in Georgia which he thinks was in February 1779 [3 March 1779] … he marched out of Brunswick County through S. C. into Georgia and was surprised and defeated by the enemy at Briar Creek, this applicant made his escape home & his time being nearly out did not enter again, a great many of the americans were drowned in crossing Briar Creek. He was again drafted for the militia service for nine months and served a little over two months, was in the battle at Guilford Court House [15 March 1781] and wounded in the leg, carried to the hospital and remained till somewhat recovered & then started home & on his way was taken prisoner by the tories and kept tied & made to go with them ten or twelve days, then delivered to the British at Colonel Brown's in Bladen County, below Carvers Creek, and took a parole from Major [James Henry] Craige, rather than be hung or sent to the provough [provost] in Wilmington; cannot recollect his officer's names; he marched out of Brunswick County, through Bladen on towards Guilford & joined Gen Green's army beyond Big Pedee [Great Pee Dee River] …[14]

Most states at least once during the war, some a number of times, enacted a levy from the militia to fill their Continental regiments on a short-term basis. The service of the drafted men ranged from as low as six months to a high of 18 (the latter term in the war's later years). In 1778 North Carolina drafted men for nine months. A portion of these levies served with Colonel James Hogun's reconstituted 3rd North Carolina Regiment at West Point,

13 Graves and Harris, Southern Campaign Pension, Zachariah Jacobs, 'free Negro' (W5304).
14 Graves and Harris, Southern Campaign Pension, Zachariah Jacobs (W5304); O'Kelley, *Nothing But Blood and Slaughter*, Vol.4, pp.45–46.

New York, and Philadelphia. The service of many levies was delayed until late 1778 or early 1779; they fought in several actions against British forces in South Carolina and Georgia.[15]

Descriptive rolls for 67 Granville County, North Carolina, levies revealed that 54 were white, five black (one with no trade), four mulattoes (three with no trade), and one half-Indian. Their descriptions were as follows:

- 'Lewis Simms a black man 33 years of Age 5 feet 10 inches high well made a Planter'.
- 'William Pettiford a black man slim made 5 feet 6 inches high 17 years old thin visage'
- 'Gibson Harris 17 years of age 5 feet 6 inches high a black man a Planter'
- 'Jeffrey Garns 20 years old 5 feet 9 inches high a black man, a Planter by Trade in the room of William Edwards Cook'
- 'Joseph Allan a well made Molatto 22 years of age 5 feet 6 inches high short hair & dark Eyes a Planter'
- 'Abraham Jones a Molatto about 44 years of age 5 feet 6 Inches high'
- 'Jonathan Jones a Molatto 17 years of age 5 feet 8 or 9 inches high'
- 'Jenkins Gowan a Molatto about 17 years of age 5 feet 5 or 6 inches high'
- 'David Hunt a black man 30 years of age 5 feet 7 inches high a Planter'[16]

The service record was ascertained for only one of these men. William Pettiford (described in a September 1820 deposition as 'a man of colour') testified when applying for a pension in 1819:

> [H]e ... enlisted, in June 1781, in Granville County in the State of North Carolina, in the Company Commanded by Captain [Thomas] Donoho of the second regiment, as he understood, in the North Carolina line ... for the term of twelve months ... he continued to serve in said Company, & in Captain Walton's Company, to which he was afterwards transferred, until the end of his said enlistment, when he was discharged from service at Salisbury ... [17]

An addendum to above stated, 'Wm. Pettiford ... on this 19th. day of April 1819, further declares on oath, that he had forgotten & mistook the company to which he was transferred from Donoho's – That it was Captain [William] Saunders's company & not Captain Walton's – That he served nine months in the Continental service ... in the North Carolina line, previous to the said twelve months service as an enlisted soldier under Captain Farrar, & part of the time under Captain Walton – that he was regularly discharged from

15 Rankin, *North Carolina Continentals*, p.16. For the 1778 North Carolina levies see, Rees, 'The pleasure of their number', part I. 'Filling the Regiments by drafts from the Militia'., http://tinyurl.com/blz2gjw., and part II, 'Fine, likely, tractable men', http://tinyurl.com/cttrxe8.
16 North Carolina State Archives (Raleigh), Military Collection, War of the Revolution, Box 4, Continental Line, 1775–1778, Folder 40, 'A Descriptive List of the ... men raised under the Present Act of Assembly in ... Company' (fifteen sheets), Granville County, N.C., 25 May 1778. See also, Rankin, *North Carolina Continentals*, p.16.
17 Graves and Harris, Southern Campaign Pension, William Pettiford (S41948), 19 February 1819 and 1 September 1820 depositions, and 19 April 1819 addendum.

his nine months service on Stony Creek, near Salisbury, in North Carolina'. Another note stated his late war one-year service began on 14 June 1781.[18]

Another pension was found for David Hunt, but whether the man is our Granville County levy is uncertain. Bobby Moss and Michael Scoggins in their work indicate they are one and the same, and the service recounted by the pensioner fits with events.[19] In May 1819 the veteran noted,

> he ... enlisted for the term of Nine Months sometime in the Year 1778 in the County of Edgecombe ... in the Company commanded by Capt John Baker of the third Redgiment commanded by Colonel Hogan in the line of North Carolina ... he was discharged from service in Hallifax North Carolina by order of Lieutenant Colonel commd. Robert Mebane of the third Regt. ... he was marched during the said period to the state of New York and stationed for some time at Westpoint ... was in no Battle during his service ...[20]

The pension papers contain no mention of Hunt's race.

Discharge certificate for Prince Danford, 2nd New York Regiment. Signed by George Washington, it notes that Danford 'has been honored with the BADGE of MERIT for six Years faithful Service'. To qualify, veterans needed to have an 'uninterrupted series of [years of] faithful and honorable services ... and a man who has deservedly met an ignominious punishmt. or degredation cannot be admitted a Candadate for any honorary distinction, unless he shall have wiped away the stain ... by some very brilliant achievement ...'

National Archives (United States), Revolutionary War Pension and Bounty-Land Warrant Application Files (National Archives Microfilm Publication M804), Records of the Department of Veterans Affairs, Record Group 15, Washington, D.C., reel 735, Prince Danford (S43472). General orders, 7 August 1782, John C. Fitzpatrick (ed.), *The Writings of George Washington from the Original Manuscript Sources 1745-1799*, vol. 24 (Washington: Government Printing Office, 1938), pp.487–488. General orders, 11 August 1782, ibid., vol. 25 (1938), pp.7–8.

18 Graves and Harris, Southern Campaign Pension, William Pettiford (S41948).
19 Bobby Gilmer Moss and Michael C. Scoggins, *African-American Patriots in the Southern Campaign of the American Revolution* (Blacksburg, S.C.: Scotia-Hibernia Press, 2004), p.126.
20 'Hunt was listed as a black man in 'A Descriptive List of the ... men raised under the Present Act of Assembly in ... Company', NC Archives,. Military Collection, War of the Revolution, 'A Descriptive List of the ... men raised under the Present Act of Assembly in ... Company' (fifteen sheets), Granville County, N.C., 25 May 1778. Graves and Harris, Southern Campaign Pension, David Hunt (S41671).

Prince Danford and other veterans who were eligible for the 'Badge of Merit' for six years' service served would have been entitled to wear a single chevron, an 'Honorary [badge] of distinction', on his left coat sleeve. The non-commissioned officer standing next to his officer (above) has such a badge on his arm.

National Archives (United States), Revolutionary War Pension and Bounty-Land Warrant Application Files (National Archives Microfilm Publication M804), Records of the Department of Veterans Affairs, Record Group 15, Washington, D.C., reel 735, Prince Danford (S43472). General orders, 7 August 1782, John C. Fitzpatrick (ed.), *The Writings of George Washington from the Original Manuscript Sources 1745-1799*, vol. 24 (Washington: Government Printing Office, 1938), pp.487–488. General orders, 11 August 1782, ibid., vol. 25 (1938), pp.7–8. Library of Congress (Prints and Photographs Division Washington, D.C.), DRWG 1 – L'Enfant, no. 1, Pierre Charles L'Enfant' (artist), 'Encampment of the Revolutionary Army on the Hudson River' (painting of West Point and dependencies, August 1782), detail of part of a group of Continental soldiers, http://www.loc.gov/pictures/item/2004678934/.

18

'They had a great frollick … with Fiddling & dancing': Small Things Forgotten

Revolutionary veterans' pension files contain wartime letters and journals, discharge papers signed by Washington and other officers, pages from family Bibles, and needlework samplers with family information. As we have seen, the depositions themselves include not only service narratives, but an assortment of personal and soldier-life details. The depositions also provide insights into African American society, both free and enslaved.

Several black veterans mentioned serving under a name different from the one they had before or after the war. To confirm a man's military career the authorities examined surviving muster rolls and other records, so providing the moniker used during the enlistment period was important. Connecticut veteran Jack Freeman's situation was typical. He first applied for a pension in July 1833 under the name Freeman. In February the year following William Sanford, brother of his former master, recounted:

> Gideon Tomlinson returned to me the Pension papers made out for Jack Freeman and gave the reason why he could not obtain a pension viz, that there was no name of Jack Freeman on the Roll in Captain Ezl. Sanford's Company in Colo. Bradley's Ridgment, I sent for Jack, he came to see me, I told him the reason as above stated, he readily answered, I was called Jack Rowland when in the service, he then said Captain [Ezekiel] Sanford [Jack's master] sd. he should be called Sanford & asked who was his former Master [before Sanford] he told him one Rowland of Fairfield (he the Captain) then said you shall be called Jack Rowland.[1]

Sanford then asked, 'do you know that you was called Jack Rowland when the Roll was called[?] – he answered yes I know I was / question 2nd why did you not tell of … this before[?] / answer. I did not think any thing about it I have been called Jack Freeman so long'.[2]

---

1   NA (US), Pension, reel 2093, Jack Freeman (S17058), deposition of William Sanford.
2   NA (US), Pension, reel 2093, Jack Freeman (S17058), deposition of William Sanford.

Other pension applicants had the same experience. Devonshire Freeman, who served in 1775 and 1776 under Colonel Charles Webb, was supported by neighbor David Hawley, who stated that Freeman was 'sometimes called by the name Devonshire Kersey'.[3] Samuel Fayerweather testified for his former fellow-solder Cato Tredwell:

> I am well acquainted with Cato Treadwell... I knew him well in the army ... and have known him ever since ... in the year AD 1780 he enlisted as a private soldier in the Company commanded by Captain Wright in the Regiment commanded by Colonel Heman Swift ... he served faithfully ... for three years ... he was a good soldier, and was often called in the army by the name of Cato Freeman, & I think it probable that he was by that name entered on the muster roll, but I then knew his name was Cato Treadwell.[4]

Cezar Shelton related that 'at the time he went into the Army he resided in Bridgeport [Connecticut] ... with a Family by whom he was brought up by the name of Shelton. He was then and during the term he was in the Army call'd Ceasar Negro or Ceasar Nig'. As has been previously seen, many black Americans lived under names specifically associated with their color, and duplication of names, while inevitable, must have caused some confusion. For example, former 4th Connecticut soldier David Gardner noted concerning Caesar Clark, 'He believes he [Clark] was on the Rolls by the Name of Caesar Negro ...'. Gardner recalled, too, 'There was a Number of Blacks belonging to the [4th] Regiment – most if not all of whom had been Slaves and obtained their Emancipation by Enlistment – Some retained the Names of their former Masters – Some assumed new Names for themselves – and some had Names imposed on them by their Officers ...'. Involuntary name change for black men and women was a symbol of servitude or inferiority; for newly-freed African Americans the ability to choose for themselves was a small but overt symbol of liberty.[5]

William Tracy's identity experience was likely not much different from that of many enslaved Americans. Silas Goodale stated, 'he was a Lieutenant in Col John Durkees Regiment in the year 1776 ... [and] recollects ... Will a black Man to have belonged to ... that Regiment ... he saw him in October or November 1776 off against Fort Washington in New Jersey [possibly referring to Fort Lee] ... he believes he saw him at the battle of Trenton ... he also understood & verily believes that he enlisted for ... one year ... He was called Will – Will Tracy or Will Huntington'. Former sergeant Andrew Griswold related, 'he was ... in the regiment commanded by Col John Dirkee ... ... he well knew ... William Tracy otherwise called Will Primus a black Man ... he had been a slave in a family ... by the name of Tracy & afterwards

---

3 NA (US), Pension, reel 1021, Devonshire Freeman, African American (S36519), deposition of David Hawley.
4 NA (US), Pension, reel 1021, Cate Tredwell, 'a free negro man' (S35358), deposition of Samuel Fayerweather.
5 NA (US), Pension, reel 2168, Cezar Shelton (S19764). Ibid., reel 550, Caesar Clark (S37871), deposition of David Gardner.

he belonged to a family of the name of Huntington. Which name he enlisted by he cannot tell but he was called Will or Will Primus …'. Lastly, in July 1818, 'C. Goddard' wrote a letter regarding Tracy's petition: 'Sir, I take the liberty to inclose the cases of two … black Men of whose circumstances or service there is no doubt – One of them is intelligent reads & writes – the other has been a slave is very old and very ignorant & it is not to be expected that he can recollect the name by which he was enlisted other than Will a Negro –' So, for one man at different times going by William Tracy, Will Huntington, Will Primus, or merely 'Will a Negro', identity and personal autonomy went hand-in-hand.[6]

Another aspect mentioned in pensions was marriage. In 1845 William Chavens provided a nice insight into civilian celebrations, stating 'he was at [black veteran] William Casey's Weding, when he intermarried with Mary Evans in Seventeen hundred and Eighty Six in the month of December, at the house of Thomas Evans in the County of Mecklenburg, Virginia, & he thinks that the Parson that Married them was John Marshall, the reason that he recollects all about the wedding, because they had a great frollick on the day with Fiddling & dancing &c'.[7] Jacob Francis's widow Mary Francis said of their 1789 Amwell, New Jersey wedding:

[S]he was married at the House of Nathaniel Hunt her old master while a slave … her marriage ceremony was performed by a coulored man named Cato Finley who was in the habit of solemnizing marriages & who married most of the coulored people in that vicinity … this deponent has heard that Cato was previous to that time the property of old Doctor Finley & was sent by him to solemnize the marriages of coulored people and that it was in this way he came so generally to be called on [to] perform [the] ceremony for people of coulor … one Philis Duncan and Mr. Samuel Hunt the son of her old master was present at her … marriage … at the time … it was not customary for white persons to perform the marriage ceremony for people of coulor, but that so far as she knows it was always done by persons of their own coulor.[8]

In February 1840 Samuel Parsons of Hartford, Connecticut pleaded the case of Ruth Maguira, writing the Commissioner of Pensions concerning the lack of any marriage record:

[I]n the case of Negroes who were married and unmarried without much ceremony, it cannot be supposed that the parties would be particular in causing a record of the fact to be made – more especially in this case, where the husband was an ignorant African who could not have appreciated its importance nor have anticipated that its omission would at some future period, deprive his beloved spouse of the benefit of his services as a soldier of the revolution.

6   NA (US), Pension, reel 2407, William Tracy (S35362), depositions of Silas Goodale, and Andrew Griswold, and C. Goddard (letter).
7   Graves and Harris, Southern Campaign Pension, William Casey (Kersey) (W29906.5).
8   NA (US), Pension, reel 1015, Jacob Francis (W459), deposition of Mary Francis.

> The applicant being very poor & unable to incur much expence in looking up further testimony, and the witnesses already adduced being certified to be respectable, I hope she may soon receive the pension to which she is most undoubtedly entitled.[9]

Parsons' use of the derogatory term 'ignorant' was, in part at least, based on Ruth's dead husband's illiteracy. Titus Thomas stated, 'Peter Maguira was born in Africa & never learnt to read or write'.[10]

Occasionally, an old veteran's reminiscence shed light on regional differences among the men who made up the Continental army; in this instance an archaic term still used by some Massachusetts soldiers at the war's beginning. Moses Stout related:

> I am acquainted with Jacob Francis … I recollect being out and serving a tour of duty of one month in the militia … Jacob was out and served with us that month – we went first to bound brook and from that to Pompton & Pyramus and lay there some time I recollect while we lay there there was a scouting party of 50 or 60 men turned out to go down to Hackensack & toward the English Neighbourhood as we called it. [D]own toward Bergen & Paulus Hook Jacob went as one of the party … [learned] at that time that Jacob had been out in the New England service among the Yankeys as we then called them. Jacob called his, nap-sack 'snap-sack', we told him it was 'nap sack' he said that they called it snapsack in the New England troops that he had been with.[11]

The first United States pension legislation was passed in August 1776, awarding half-pay to Continental army and navy officers merely for the fact of their wartime service, and to enlisted men for the duration of any disability resulting from a service-related injury. Only those unable to earn a living as a result of their injury were eligible. Over the ensuing years additional resolutions provided half-pay for serving officers; stipulated in 1778 to continue for seven years after the war's end, in 1780 extended to half-pay for life, and, finally, in 1783, changed to full pay for five years. In August 1780 widows and orphans of officers who died during military service were allotted seven years' half pay. Six years after the turn of the new century the Revolutionary War invalid pension laws were amended to include militia and state troops, as well.[12]

In March 1818 Congress passed the first all-inclusive veterans' pension act; the only requirements were service of nine months or more and that the applicant was in financial need. Subsequent amendments required pensioners and future applicants to submit a detailed list of their income and possessions (1820), and allowed veterans removed from the rolls to reapply

9 NA (US), Pension, reel 1615, Peter Maguira (R6830), Samuel Parsons to J.L. Edwards, February 1840 (letter).
10 NA (US), Pension, reel 1615, Peter Maguira (R6830), deposition of Titus Thomas.
11 NA (US), Pension, reel 1015, Jacob Francis (W459), deposition of Moses Stout.
12 Anon., *Index of Revolutionary War Pension Applications in the National Archives* (Washington, D.C.: Government Printing Office, 1976), pp.ix-xiii.

with new proof of need (1823). The last service-pension act, in June 1832, expanded eligibility and provided full pay for life to veterans who spent two years or more in Continental or state service; lesser allotments for those who served under two years but greater than six months. Legislation in the years following allowed pensions for soldiers' widows, the last of those was passed in 1878.[13]

The grandson of slaves, free black Pennsylvanian James Forten was a drummer and powder-boy aboard the privateer *Royal Lewis* commanded by Stephen Decatur, Senior. After capturing a British brig-of-war on their first cruise, the frigate *Amphion* forced Decatur's ship to surrender and the crew became prisoners. Forten survived this ordeal and returned to the Philadelphia sail loft he worked at prior to the war, eventually being promoted to foreman. When the loft's owner Robert Bridges retired in 1798 he wished that Forten retain his position. Mr Forten soon owned the business outright, at one point employed almost 40 workers, and went on to become prominent in local and national politics, as well as in the abolitionist movement. Forten's military experience was not unique, though his post-war career was, and because of that success he never applied for a pension. Most of his fellow old soldiers and seamen were not so fortunate, and their pension accounts provide insights into their later lives.[14]

Because of injuries incurred in military service, Rhode Island veteran Prince Vaughan had received a monthly pension in 1786, the certificate for which is in his Federal pension file. He submitted this register in June 1820:

Real Estate None
Personal Estate as follows to wit (necessary clothing & bedding excepted)

3 Chairs	$0.30
1 sea Chest (old)	$0.50
6 plates	$0.12½
1 Trunk	$0.30
6 Knives & forks	$0.12½
1 Spider	$0.25
1 Pitcher	$0.18
1 oyster knife	$0.12
2 Tumblers	

… declarant is a shoe black by occupation, he at present follows that business & keeps an Oyster stand when he is able, deponent has been sick, for four years past he has and he has just recovered and does but very little at his business.[15]

13   Anon, *Index of Revolutionary War Pension Applications*, pp.ix-xiii.
14   Kaplan, Sidney, *The Black Presence in the Era of the American Revolution, 1770–1800* (Greenwich, Ct.: New York Graphic Society, Ltd. in Association with the Smithsonian Institution Press, 1973), pp.46–47; James Forten, 'Black Past', https://blackpast.org/aah/forten-james-1766-1842.
15   NA (US), Pension, reel 2455, Prince Vaughan, African American (S42603).

New Jerseyian Adam Pearce provided this 'Schedule of the property … taken June 22nd. 1820 …', total value: $84.27: '2 Chests', 'Lot of Dishes', 'Dressers', '2 bags', '3 Chairs', 'Drawing knife', 'Saw & chisel', 'Sweeping Brush & brooms', 'Stillyards' [steelyard, a scale used to weigh objects], '2 hatchetts', '2 Iron Potts', 'Tea Kettle & Spider', '1 Dutch Oven', '3 pales', '3 [Crates?]', illegible item valued one dollar, 'Shovel & tongs', '3 trammels', '3 Flat Irons', 'lot of Sundries' valued at one dollar, '1 axe', 'table', '1 Gun', '3 Barrels', '1 lot[?]' one dollar value, '1 Lot of wool', 'Saddle &c', '17 sheep', '2 Cows & Calves', '3 pigs', '2 [Cots?]' five dollars value. He closed, 'And I do further swear that my family Consists of myself age as above specified [a sixty-four-year-old laborer] unable to work being very Infirm having totally lost the use of my right arm by the Erysipolas [Erysipelas is a skin infection, a form of cellulitis] my wife Doreas aged 55 years very infirm & my son Matthias aged 17 years being the only person we Got to have to look for support or maintenance'.[16]

Sixty-three-year-old Cato Fisk wrote in July 1820;

> … he enlisted in the spring of the year 1778 into the Company commanded by Captain William Rowell of the Second New Hampshire Regiment … commanded by Colonel George Reid for during the war … he served the full term of his enlistment and was discharged in June 1783 … My occupation is that of a Labour[er] but am not of sufficient ability to pursue it as formerly by reason of age and infirmities / I have in family residing with me my wife aged 53 years Two sons James & Ebenezar / James is aged About 28 years & is non compis Mentis [not of sound mind]. Ebenezar aged about 34 years who has been sick for several weeks confined to his bed and a grand daughter Louisa aged three years. Their capacity to contribute to their support is nothing but their personal labour …
>
> Schedule Containing the whole estate and income of Cato Fisk …
>
> A small hut & small Bark [shelter?] standing on another mans land 40.00

1 Cow	15.00
1 Pig	3.00
8 Old chairs	1.50
2 Old Tables	1.00
Iron ware	1.50
Crockery knives & forks	0.75
Syth & Sneath [handle]	0.75
One old Ax	0.67
	64.17[17]

Occasionally we find a former soldier with a larger estate, but sill in need of assistance. Rhode Islander Reuben Roberts stated in 1820, 'A SCHEDULE of Property and Income (necessary clothing and bedding excepted) … viz one Acre of land in … Warwick together with a small one Story house unfinished thereon, 1 pig, 6 Chairs, 2 tables, 6 Knives & forks, 2 pots 1 Kettle, 1/2 dozen cups & saucers, 6 plates, 1 dish, other than the above he has no property of any description except as above excepted … he is a Labourer & would when

---

16 NA (US), Pension, reel 1933, Adam Pearce (Pierce/Percey), mulatto (S34468).
17 NA (US), Pension, reel 982, Cato Fisk (Fiske), 'a colored man' (W14719).

he is able – but having his leg broken while in the Army – is confined for six weeks together in consequence of said Misfortune …'.[18] Marylander Lazarus Harman submitted the following:

> … 28th day of July 1820 … I do solemnly swear that I was a resident citizen of the United States on the 18th day of March 1818 and that I have not since that time by gift sale or in any manner disposed of my property or any part thereof with intent thereby so to diminish it as to bring myself within the provisions of an act of congress … Schedule hereto annexed and by me subscribed. [two or three illegible words] interest in one hundred and thirty acres forest land Two old horses two yoke of oxen Four cows. Three yearlings & two Calves one sow and eight shoats twelve sheep one ox cart 2 Plows 2 Harrows 4 old chairs 6 plates 1 Pewter[sic] 4 Pewter spoons Iron pot 1 Tea kettle 1 dutch oven 1 coffee pot 6 cups and saucers 4 knives and forks 2 Tables 1 old Loom 4 old [illegible word] 1 on chain 2 Bolts and chains[?] This declarant has five in family that he is a labourer and quite infirm that his wife Betty is old and infirm that he has two sons John eighteen years old and Joseph who is twelve years old. That there is due and owing from this declarant four hundred and forty four dollars eighty seven cents … [19]

Some, perhaps many, veterans – of all races – were extremely destitute. Richard Potter enlisted in May 1777 in the 1st Rhode Island Regiment and may have served the previous year in the Colonel James Varnum's 9th Continental Regiment. Potter fought at Fort Mercer in 1777 and Monmouth in 1778. His pension was denied, likely due to his deserting the army in July 1780, but Justice Amos Cross attempting to assist his plea wrote, 'I hope I shall not obtrude when I take the liberty to mention … the situation of this Indigent applicant / He is now very meanly Clad, so much so as not to appear decent and has no means of subsistence except what he can derive from the little labour he is able to perform …'.[20]

Occasionally applicants went to great trouble to garner support. Charles Cuffey was an 18-month veteran of Colonel Abraham Buford's 1780–1782 Virginia Regiment. In September 1830 he wrote Pension Commissioner James Edwards from, 'Princess Anne Court House … Sir I have now the honour to acknowledge the receipt of your Letter of the 15th of June last and to enclose you the affidavits of Robert Page and W. A. Patterson which I hope will prove satisfactory. I will just add that to obtain these papers I had to beg my way on foot from this place to the County of Chesterfield and back a distance of upwards of Two hundred and fifty miles and am now almost weighed down by the journey'. Bristol Budd enlisted in March 1777 in Colonel Charles Webb's 2nd Connecticut Regiment, and served until 1783, by his own account seeing action at Whitemarsh, Monmouth, and Stony Point. In June 1821 Mr Budd testified that he was, 'A poor old blind Negro,

---

18 NA (US), Pension, reel 2059, Reuben Roberts, African American (S39834).
19 Graves and Harris, Southern Campaign Pension, Lazarus Harman, 'Free Colored Person' (S34911).
20 Popek, *They fought bravely*, pp.176, 272, 303, 698. NA (US), Pension, reel 1960, Richard Potter, African American (R8380), Amos Cross to the War Department, February 1822 (letter).

who was led by his son, aged 14, four hundred miles, to obtain the Certificate of his Captain (a respectable Man, of New Canaan, Connecticut) that he did not <u>desert</u>, but served to the end of the war ...'.[21]

African American Revolutionary veterans were occasionally cited in the newspapers. Some, such as Oliver Cromwell, received notice while still living, while Ned Hector and others were only recognized after their passing. Jacob Francis, veteran of a 1776 Massachusetts Continental regiment and later in the New Jersey militia, died in 1839, and the 5 August *Newark Daily Advertiser* republished this notice from the *Flemington Gazette*:

> Another Hero of the Revolution.— In this village, on Tuesday the 26th of July, JACOB FRANCIS, a colored man, in the 83rd year of his age. He has resided in this place thirty-five years; has been an orderly member of the Baptist Church for thirty years; he has raised a large family, in a manner creditable to his judgement and his Christian character, and lived to see them doing well; and has left the scenes of this mortal existence, deservedly respected by all who knew him.
>
> Jacob Francis was a soldier of the Revolution—he served a long tour of duty in the Massachusetts militia, and was some time in the regular army in New Jersey; and we have learned from those who knew him in those days of privation of peril, that his fidelity and good conduct as a soldier were the object of remark, and received the approbation of his officers. For the last few years he received a pension from the government; an acknowledgement of his services to his country which, though made at a late day, came most opportunely to minister to his comfort in the decline of life, and under the infirmities of old age.[22]

As John L. Bell notes, 'This was by far the longest death notice in that issue of the *Daily Advertiser*, and it was reprinted at least as far away as Cleveland'.[23]

The rising generations continued to serve, sacrifice, and contribute to the welfare of their country. Eighty-one-year-old Judith Lines, wife of a Connecticut veteran, related in 1837, 'my youngest son died of a wound recd in the last war [War of 1812], his name was Benjamin, the wound was recd. at the Battle of Chippewa'.[24]

---

21 Graves and Harris, Southern Campaign Pension, Charles Cuffey (Cuffee), free black (W9402). NA (US), Pension, reel 398, Bristol Budd, 'Negro'(W253054).

22 Bell, John L., 'Boston 1775', 9 January 2018, http://boston1775.blogspot.com/2018/01/pvt-jacob-gulick-and-pvt-jacob-francis.html.

23 Bell, 'Boston 1775', 9 January 2018, http://boston1775.blogspot.com/2018/01/pvt-jacob-gulick-and-pvt-jacob-francis.html.

24 NA (US), Pension, reel 1567, John Lines, 'a black man' (W26775), deposition of Judith Lines.

19

'Life, Liberty, and the Pursuit of Happiness': Post-War Societal Attitudes, the Black Experience, and Slavery

We hold these Truths to be self-evident, that all Men are created equal, that they are endowed by their Creator with certain unalienable Rights, that among these are Life, Liberty, and the Pursuit of Happiness.

Declaration of Independence, July 1776.

What, to the American slave, is your 4th of July? I answer: a day that reveals to him, more than all other days in the year, the gross injustice and cruelty to which he is the constant victim.

Frederick Douglass, 5 July 1852.[1]

Society's general attitude towards African Americans and the effect of slavery on free blacks is reflected in a number of pension accounts. We began this story with white Virginian James Redd's objection to James Harris receiving a pension. Harris had served as a North Carolina Continental in 1776, later with the militia, and participated in the actions at Charleston in the war's second year, and Gates's defeat at Camden. Redd noted that Harris 'is as Black as half of the Negroes in this county nothing promps me to make this inquiry but to know if that class of the community is entitled to pensions and to detect fraud if there should be any …'. One suspects there was more to Mr Redd's query than mere fraud. Included in Harris's file are what seem to be rebuttals to Redd's contesting letter, two of which are appended:[2]

---

1 Frederick Douglass, 5 July 1852, 'What to the Slave Is the Fourth of July?' https://www. thenation.com/article/what-slave-fourth-july-frederick-douglass/.
2 Graves and Harris, Southern Campaign Pension, James Harris, 'A Free Negro' (W11223), James M. Redd to Patrick C. House, 13 February 1836 (letter).

I Thomas Hale of the county of Franklin and state of Virginia do swear that it is my opinion that free men of Colour did serve in the Revolution in the state of North Carolina and believe that & know that free men of colour were regularly enrolled in the state of South Carolina

[signed] Thos Hale [3]

To Mr. James Edwards Pension Officer [War Department] Washington City

Sir In answer to your letter of this day – I have to inform you that from the information of members of Congress – I have no doubt that until … 1814 free people of colour served in the militia and had the right of suffrage in the state of North Carolina I infer from the act of assembly of North Carolina passed in 1814 – which you will see in the 2nd Vol Rec'd book of Laws of that state pages 1290 & 1291, that no distinction was made before as to militia service performed or to be performed – but you will see that after the passage of that Law the Captains and other returning officers in making their returns – were to put in seperate columns the white & coloured militia men. The book is in the library and the case is clear – and I consider the information I have received and the inference I draw from the Law of 1814 that people of colour before had allways in N Carolina been subject to Militia Service is conclusive and I hope that you will see this matter on looking at the Law ref'd to as I do I am Sir yr mo obt

Washington 4th Feby 1837 N[athaniel] H Claiborne [Virginia Congressman]. [4]

There is no record of a reply, if any, to Mr Redd, but James Harris retained his pension to the end of his life.

Another North Carolina veteran's papers provide an interesting comment on that state's integrated units. A white veteran's testimony supporting former militia solder Holiday Hethcock's claim noted:

Personally appeared before me one of the Justices of the peace in and for said County / William Bryan … doth on his oath declare … that in the times of our Revolutionary War free negroes and mulattoes mustered in the ranks with white men in said State – at least in that part of the State in which he then resided – and in which Holiday Hethcock then resided – to wit in the County of Johnston. This affiant has frequently mustered in company with said free negroes and mulattoes … That class of persons were equally liable to draft – and frequently volunteered in the public service. ~ This affiant was in the army a short time at Wilmington at the time Craig was near that place [Lieutenant Colonel James Henry Craig, British 82nd Regiment; he was at Wilmington, North Carolina the entirety of 1781] and remembers that one mulatto was in his company as a common soldier whose name Archibald Artis — This affiant has always known the said Holiday Hethcock – and has always understood that he was in the army of the Revolution

---

3   Graves and Harris, Southern Campaign Pension, James Harris (W11223), deposition of Thomas Hale.
4   Graves and Harris, Southern Campaign Pension, James Harris (W11223), Nathaniel H. Claiborne to James Edwards, 4 February 1837 (letter).

Sworn to and subscribed this 21st day of November 1834 … [signed] William Bryan.[5]

In November 1832 white North Carolinian John Ferrell applied for a pension, but had only one witness, who he thought would be considered unreliable. Ferrell noted, 'he has no documentary evidence that he can prove his service by & … knows no man now living who was with him but old Arthur Toney a Coloured man & whose evidence (being a Colored man) would not be good Testimony'.[6]

One man seems to refer to restrictions and necessary precautions imposed on black citizens when travelling out of their community. This note was found in Virginian James Cooper's pension file:

The State of Virginia Octob'r 1787 The Bearer James Cooper, a Molatto Free Man, Being Desirous to Travel in … States [of] Carolina and Georgia, its Recommended that he doe pass unmolisted so long as he Behaves himself well, he being an old Soldier in bluforts [Buford's] defeat he served fathful [page torn; signature illegible]. [7]

Some veterans, or their families, only belatedly received what was due them. Holiday Hethcock's application for a pension was rejected in the 1830s. Twenty years later his son David Hathcock reopened the case. The following letter was included in Hethcock's file:

Washington D.C. April 5th 1854
Hon. L. P. Waldo Comr,. of Pensions

Sir On examining the case of Holliday Hethcock, of N. C. for pension under act of June 7th 1832, we find that his services and identity are fully proven by three witnesses, and that his case has been suspended merely because he was a free man of color. As we understand that several cases of this sort have been admitted you will oblige us by having it admitted.

Respectfully &c. Thompson J[?] Venable [8]

Racial prejudice was one burden Americans of color suffered under, but slavery was the overwhelming encumbrance that affected even free blacks. Philip Savoy, 'a man of Collour', who had served in the 4th Maryland Regiment, noted in his 1818 pension application, 'I have a family but they are all slaves. I am myself free and ever have been'. Another former Maryland Continental, Michael Curtis, testified in 1821, 'I have no wife and the children

---

5   Graves and Harris, Southern Campaign Pension, Holiday Hethcock (Hathcock), 'a free man of color' (R4812), deposition of William Bryan.
6   Graves and Harris, Southern Campaign Pension, John Ferrell (S6836). Ibid., Arthur Toney (W4835).
7   Graves and Harris, Southern Campaign Pension, James Cooper (S39362).
8   Graves and Harris, Southern Campaign Pension, Holiday Hethcock (Hathcock) (R4812), Thompson Venable to L. P. Waldo, 5 April 1854 (letter).

born by my wife dec'd. are slaves'.[9] Several other old soldiers told similar tales, as in these 1820 depositions:

- Thomas Mahorney, 2nd Virginia Regt. 1777–78/79, 'declares that he is a planter on a little farm not his, and is rendered unable to pursue it by reason of his age and infirmity and that his family residing with him are as follows: Viz: his wife Maima[?] and his son Jack both of which are slaves, he the said Thomas Mahorney being a free man of colour who served in the war of the Revolution, and is unassisted by the labour of his family'.[10]
- Drury Scott, 10th Virginia Regt. 1777–83(?), 'My occupation is that of a rough carpenter, but I can get but little work and if I had more I could not do it my wife is all my family, but being a slave can render me no assistance'.[11]
- Andrew Pebbles, 15th Virginia Regt. 1778–82, '… by Occupation I am a Miller … from the infirmities of old age increased by the wounds received in the revolutionary War I am not able to render much service to my employer … I am a free Mulatto … my wife and child who live at the Mill where I do are Slaves … my wife's name is Rachel aged between 50 & 60 years and my Child's name is Ursula aged 11 years …'[12]

Undoubtedly, other black Revolutionary veterans shared these men's experiences.

Black chattel slavery was a fact during and after the war, despite the enlightened platitudes of the July 1776 Declaration of Independence and the wishes of many Americans, north and south. Still, progress was made towards limited abolition and the seeds were sown for eventual emancipation in all the northern states.

During the war enslaved blacks submitted a number of petitions or engaged in legal actions for their freedom, most notably in Connecticut, Massachusetts, and New Hampshire, and these had some effect. By 1783 Massachusetts' slavery was in its 'death throes' following positive outcomes to a series of lawsuits brought by slaves. The rulings resulted in relegating the case to Judicial Review by the state's Supreme Court. In effect this meant the justices were to rule on the validity of the new state constitution, which contained a clause crucial to the legal actions, that 'all men are born free and equal, and have … the right of enjoying and defending their lives and liberties'. Because of those cases, along with changing economic circumstances and civic attitudes, the Massachusetts 1790 census listed no slaves in the state. Connecticut and Rhode Island passed gradual abolition acts in 1784, though in the former state black bondage continued until 1848, in Rhode Island

---

9   Graves and Harris, Southern Campaign Pension, Philip Savoy (S35057) Ibid., Michael Curtis (S39398).
10 Graves and Harris, Southern Campaign Pension, Thomas Mahorney, 'a free man of colour' (S38166).
11 Graves and Harris, Southern Campaign Pension, Drury Scott, African American (S35644).
12 Graves and Harris, Southern Campaign Pension, Andrew Pebbles, 'free Mulatto' (S38297).

until 1842. Other states followed, all with statutes providing for gradual emancipation. One of the most touted wartime laws was Pennsylvania's 1780 'Act for the Gradual Abolition of Slavery'. As with other such laws it did not entirely rise to its promise. Not one slave was immediately freed, and the original stipulation to free female slaves at age 18 and males at age 21, was amended that all slave children 'born after the law became effective [be] consigned to servitude until age 28'. As Gary Nash notes, 'Thus it was possible for a female child born on the last day of February 1780 [before the law went into effect] to live out her life in slavery and, if she gave birth to children up to her fortieth year, to bring into the world in 1820 children who would not be free until 1848'. Despite those drawbacks, Matthew White discovered that some Pennsylvania justices used the law to seize and free slaves whose owners brought them into the state, claiming that without proof of ownership the nominal slaves were considered free. Further south, Virginia barred slave importation in 1778 (a ban many believed would bring about the end of slavery there), and in 1782 repealed a 1723 law barring private slave manumissions. Numbers of slaves, too, were freed who served as soldiers or performed other important service during the war, but that was the limit of Virginia's progress.[13]

The following table shows changes in slave numbers for the original thirteen states in the early 19th century; in 1810 slaves totaled 1,191,364, by 1850 the total United States enslaved population was 3,204,313. As shown below, by 1810 two northern states, New Jersey and New York, still contained relatively large numbers of enslaved blacks, but northern enslavement was dying while the southern economy thrived on human bondage.

Table 5: Numbers of Slaves in the Thirteen Original States, 1800 and 1810[14]

	1800	1810
New Hampshire	8	0
Massachusetts	0	0
Connecticut	915	310
Rhode Island	380	18

---

13 Quarles, *Negro in the American Revolution*, 47–49. 'Massachusetts Constitution and the Abolition of Slavery', https://www.mass.gov/guides/massachusetts-constitution-and-the-abolition-of-slavery. Nash, *Race and Revolution*, 34–35. Menschel, David, 'Abolition Without Deliverance: The Law of Connecticut Slavery 1784–1848', *Yale Law Journal*, vol. 111, no. 1 (October 2001), pp.183–222. Rhode Island, 'Manumission Act, 1784', http://sos.ri.gov/virtualarchives/items/show/71. 'An act for preventing the farther importation of Slaves', October 1778, Hening, *The Statutes at Large Being a Collection of all the Laws of Virginia*, vol IX (1821), pp.471–472. 'An act to authorize the manumission of slaves', May 1782; 'An act directing the emancipation of certain slaves who have served as soldiers in this state, and for the emancipation of the slave Aberdeen', October 1783, ibid., vol XI (1823), pp.39–40, 308–309. Matthew C. White, ''Under the Influence of the Excitement Then Universal': Pennsylvania's Missouri Crisis and the Viability of Anti-Slavery Politics' (conference paper, February 2019), 'A Fire Bell in the Past: The Missouri Crisis at 200', Kinder Institute on Constitutional Democracy, University of Missouri.

14 1800 Federal Census, https://en.wikipedia.org/wiki/1800_United_States_Census. 1810 Federal Census, https://faculty.weber.edu/kmackay/statistics_on_slavery.htm. 1850 United States Census, https://en.wikipedia.org/wiki/1850_United_States_Census.

	1800	1810
New York	20,613	5,017
New Jersey	12,422	10,851
Pennsylvania	1,706	795
Delaware	6,153	4,177
Maryland	103,312	111,502
Virginia	346,968	392,518
North Carolina	133,296	168,824
South Carolina	146,151	196,365
Georgia	59,699	105,218

American slavery would end only with the 1860s Civil War and the descendants of early inhabitants and later immigrants, white and black, free and newly-freed, would shed their blood to bring about its demise. Beginning in the summer and autumn of 1862 black volunteer and state regiments were formed, and in 1863, following President Abraham Lincoln's Emancipation Proclamation, the Federal government determined to raise regiments of United States Colored Troops. Despite their Revolutionary forebears' accomplishments on the battlefield the question was asked, 'Will they fight?' The first all-black Federal unit to participate in a large-scale action was the 1st Kansas (Colored) Regiment. At the Battle of Honey Springs in Indian Territory, 17 July 1863, some 60 miles west of Fort Smith, Arkansas, they saw heavy fighting and mauled the Confederate units opposing them. Following that action, their wounded commander Colonel James Williams, asked of Major General James Blunt, 'General, how did my regiment fight?' Blunt replied, 'Like veterans, most gallantly'. In a private letter Blunt noted, 'The question that negroes will fight is settled …'. Another Union soldier who fought at Honey Springs crudely and pointedly wrote, 'I never believed in niggers before, but by Jasus, they are hell for fighting'. Despite the racial epithet, the change of opinion is striking.[15]

Continental and militia forces that served during our Revolution were, with few exceptions, integrated, a practice that lasted up to the War of 1812. The American Civil War 'Colored' regiments were segregated, manned by black enlisted men and commanded by white officers. Change can be slow, but on 26 July 1948 President Harry S. Truman signed Executive Order 9981 enacting integration and non-discrimination in the American military. Even after the defeat of the Confederacy and ratification of the Constitution's 15th Amendment, black Americans continued as second-class citizens and were subject to atrocities by white citizens. The struggle still continues, but we have long since learned the answer to the question, 'Will they fight?'

---

15 Noah Andre Trudeau, *Like Men of War: Black Troops in the Civil War, 1862–1865* (Boston, New York, London: Little, Brown and Co., 1998), pp.37, 107–108. 'United States Colored Troops', https://en.wikipedia.org/wiki/United_States_Colored_Troops.

Benjamin Warner note and wartime knapsack. (Courtesy of the Fort Ticonderoga Museum Collection, Object AC-049)

Some former common soldiers retained mementos from their military service. Black veteran Artillo Freeman submitted a detailed list of his belongings, along with their value, totaling $15.75. At the end of the tally he added one more item, 'Revolutionary Uniform – Invaluable'.

White veteran Benjamin Warner's knapsack and accompanying note are the most striking to survive. His double-envelope linen pack is the only known existing wartime example of that design. As such it is invaluable, and the message he left with it stirringly echoes Revolutionary zeal and sentiment: 'This Napsack I caryd through the war of the Revolution to achieve the Merican Independence I transmit it to my oldest sone Benjamin Warner Jr. with directions to keep it his [for] oldest sone and so on to the latest posterity and whist one shred of it shall remane never surrender your libertys to a foren envador or an aspiring demegog. Ticonderoga March 27, 1837'. These keepsakes eventually found their way into the collections of Fort Ticonderoga in New York. Warner's headstone in a small Vermont graveyard bears a phrase that shows pride of service and again evokes the spirit of liberty, 'Revolutionary War Soldier and Friend of the Slave'.

Two other men, John McElroy and Aaron Thompson (both white), had been fifers in Continental regiments. The former wrote in 1820, 'I have my old Fife and knapsack yet', while David Crane, cousin of Thompson's wife, noted after the old soldier's death he, 'had heard him [Thompson], often say so, and mention, the fact of his, having mutilated his fife in order to prevent its being stolen and that he might preserve it, as a relic, of his services in that Struggle'. As far as we know, Freeman's, McElroy's, and Thompson's personal relics no longer exist. Former fifer Thompson's music book does survive, in the collections of Yale University.[16]

---

16 National Archives (United States), Revolutionary War Pension and Bounty-Land Warrant Application Files (National Archives Microfilm Publication M804), Records of the Department of Veterans Affairs, Record Group 15, Washington, D.C., reel 2373, Artillo Freeman, 'a black man' (S44853), Aaron Thompson (W19450); reel 1679, John McElroy (16192); reel 1021.

Afterword: 'They were good soldiers'

William Eustis was a surgeon in Gridley's Massachusetts Artillery Regiment in 1775, with Knox's Continental Artillery Regiment the following year, served in all the 1776 battles, including Trenton and Princeton, and became an army hospital physician from 1780 to the war's end. He was later James Madison's Secretary of War from March 1809 to January 1813. During the 1820 debates concerning Missouri statehood Eustis rose and spoke against,

that article in the constitution of Missouri, making it the duty of the Legislature to provide by law 'that free negroes and mulattoes shall not be admitted into that State' ... Those who contend that the article is not repugnant to the Constitution of the United States ground themselves on the position that blacks and mulattoes are not citizens of the United States and have repeatedly referred to the condition of those [barred from militia service] in Massachusetts to support the assertion. I invite the honorable member from Delaware, who has lately addressed you, with the honorable member from Virginia, who ... maintained the same position, to go with me and examine the question to its root.

At the commencement of the Revolutionary war, there were found in the Middle and Northern States, many blacks and other people of color, capable of bearing arms; a part of them free, the greater part slaves. The freemen entered our ranks with the whites. The time of those who were slaves was purchased by the States, and they were induced to enter the service in consequence of a law by which, on condition of their serving in the ranks during the war, they were made freemen. In Rhode Island ... they were formed, under the same considerations, into a regiment commanded by white officers; and it is required, in justice to them, to add, that they discharged their duty with zeal and fidelity ... The services of this description of men in the navy are also well known. I should not have mentioned either, but for the information of the gentleman from Delaware, whom I understood to say that he did not know that they had served in any considerable numbers.

The war over and peace restored, these men returned to their respective States. And who could have said to them ... after having shed their blood, in common with the whites, in the defence of the liberties of the country, You are not to participate in the rights secured by the struggle, or in the liberty for which you have been fighting? Certainly, no white man in Massachusetts.

The gentleman from Virginia says he must not be told that the term, we the people, in the preamble to the Constitution, means, or includes, Indians, free negroes, mulattoes. If it shall be made to appear that persons of this description, citizens at the time, were parties to, and formed an integral part of that compact, it follows, incontestably, that they are and must be included in it. To justify the inference of [that] gentlemen, the preamble ought to read, We the whitepeople. This was impossible; the members of the convention who formed that constitution, from the Middle and Northern States, could never have consented, knowing that there were in those States many thousands of people of color, who had rights under it. They were free – free from their masters? Yes, in the first instance; they also became freemen of the State, and were admitted to all the rights and privileges of white citizens. Was this admission merely nominal? This is answered by the fact that they did enjoy and did exercise the rights of free citizens, and have continued to exercise them, from the peace of 1783 to this day … It has been justly observed on this subject, by a gentleman on the other side, that facts and practice are better than theory. Here, then, we offer incontrovertible facts, proving, not from theory, but from actual and long continued practice, that black men and mulattoes, in Massachusetts at least, are citizens, having civil and political rights, in common with the whites. If we are asked for evidence of their being in the exercise of these rights, it is answered, that a knowledge of the history and practice of the State for more than forty years past, will show that they have been in the constant exercise of them. To vote in the election of town, county, and State officers, the same qualifications of residence and property are required from them, as from the whites, and, having these qualifications, they have a voice in the election of all state officers … By whom, and for whose use and benefit, was the Constitution formed? By the people, and for the people, inhabiting the several States. Did the Convention who formed it go into the consideration of the character or complexion of the citizens included in the compact? No, sir; they necessarily considered all those as citizens who were acknowledged as such at the time by the constitutions of the States.[1]

In 1824 and 1825 former Continental Army Major General Marie Joseph Paul Yves Roch Gilbert du Motier, Marquis de Lafayette, returned to the United States. At New Orleans, Louisiana, he met with a group of African American veterans who fought at the Battle of New Orleans in 1815. John Mercier, their former commander, addressed Lafayette, saying in part, 'the Corps of men of Colour who so eminently contributed to the defense of this Country … felt that they should first offer to one of the Heroes of the American Independence, their tribute of respect and admiration'. The *Courier of New Orleans* recorded that:

---

1   Philip B. Kurland, and Ralph Lerner (eds.), The Founders Constitution, document 14, William Eustis, Admission of Missouri, House of Representatives, 12 December 1820, *Annals of Congress: The Debates and Proceedings in the Congress of the United States*, vol. 37 (42 vols. – Washington, D.C.: Gales & Seaton, 1834–56), pp.35–38, http://press-pubs.uchicago.edu/founders/documents/a4_2_1s14.html?fbclid=IwAR18oU55JGG7zZeAsIdkM2ehZeuVdZ0oeml04sE7iMhyrSS2Pcqf09kA4eE. Courtesy of Matthew C. White.

[T]he General received the men of colour with demonstrations of esteem and affection, and said to them: "Gentlemen, I have often during the War of Independence, seen African blood shed with honor in our ranks for the cause of the United States. I have learnt with the liveliest interest … what a glorious use you made of your arms for the defense of Louisiana. I cherish the sentiments of gratitude for your services, and of admiration for your valor. Accept those also of my personal friendship, and of the pleasure I shall always experience in meeting with you again." The General then kindly shook hands with them all, and thanked the Governor for the opportunity he had given him to become acquainted with them.[2]

Service in the War of the Revolution was a mark of pride for black veterans to the end of their days. On 17 July 1820, Artillo Freeman claimed to be 99 years of age and

resident in the City of New York … he enlisted at Roxbury in Massachusets in the Summer of 1776 to serve during the War, in the 3rd Regt. in the Massachusets Line … commanded by Col Hull [likely William Hull, captain 19th Continental Regiment in 1776; major 8th Massachusetts as of January 1777; lieutenant colonel 3rd Massachusetts, August 1779] in Captain Lummens [unidentified] company, he was then transfer'd to Col Tuper or Col Glovers 4th Regiment, he is not sure which in Captain Williams [unidentified] Company, he was in the battle of White Plains [28 October 1776], Monmouth [28 June 1778] and the Siege of little York in Virginia and in a Number of little engagements, he has a Wife Aged 88 Years and One Daughter a Cripple under his care aged 30 Years, named Hester, he has no Trade, but Picks Oakum for a living when he is able to work, he is in Indigent Circumstances and requires the Aid of his Country or Individual Contributions for support …

In 1818 Mr Freeman testified that 'he was engaged in the Contest of Throgs point [14 April 1781], White plains, Pines brige [14 May 1781] Morrosena [22 January 1781]…' He again claimed to have enlisted in 1776. There is no record of Artillo Freeman serving prior to 1781, when records indicate he enlisted in mid-April. The only engagement he could have served at was the May 1781 Pines Bridge action, but as of 20 May 1781 he was listed as 'Colo[nel's] Servant Absent With the Colo at Boston'. Despite some discrepancies in his testimony, Mr Freeman leaves us with proof of the honour he attached to his military service. In July 1820 at the behest of the War Department Artillo Freeman submitted a tally of his belongings. With no real estate or fixed income, Freeman noted, 'he has no Trade, but Picks Oakum for a living when he is able to work …'. Mr Freeman's possessions

---

2   *Courier of New Orleans*, 19 April 1825, Web exhibit drawn from the Spring 2001 Special Collections & College Archives exhibit 'Lafayette and Slavery', curated by Diane Windham Shaw, Lafayette College, Easton, Pa., http://academicmuseum.lafayette.edu/special/specialexhibits/slaveryexhibit/onlineexhibit/meetings.htm ; see also, 'The Almost Chosen People' (Blog), https://almostchosenpeople.wordpress.com/2010/05/05/the-marquis-de-lafayette-and-the-black-veterans-of-new-orleans/.

included 'Bed & Beddings', '4 Chairs', 'Crockery', 'Pots Kettles pans', '1 Coat', '3 shirts', '1 Chest & Trunk', his 'Wife & Childs Clothes', a small quantity of personal apparel, and '1 Pig', in total worth $15.75. At the end of the list he added one more item, 'Revolutionary Uniform – Invaluable'.[3]

Former private Henry Hallowell, Colonel Rufus Putnam's 5th Massachusetts Regiment, gave this simple but fitting tribute to the African–American soldiers, free and slave, who served the Revolutionary cause in a number of roles: 'In my … company [there] was 4 negroes named Jeptha Ward, Job Upton, Douglas Middleton, and Pomp Simmons … part of them called on me after their time was out. They were good soldiers'.[4]

3   NA (US), Pension, reel 1021, Artillo Freeman, 'a black man' (S44853); Compiled Service Records (Massachusetts), Artillo Freeman.
4   Henry Hallowell, 'A Narrative of Henry Hallowell of Lynne, Respecting the Revolution in 1776, 1777, 1778, 1779 to January 17, 1780', Howard Kendall Sanderson, (ed.), *Lynn in the Revolution* (Boston: W.B. Clarke, 1909), p.64. Jeptha Ward served six years, enlisting on 15 April 1778 for three years, and reenlisting for the war in 1781; Job (Jube) Upton enlisted 25 May 1777 for three years, was discharged 15 May 1778; Douglas (Duglas) Middleton enlisted 10 April 1777 for three years, was discharged 10 April 1780, and Pomp Simmons (Simons or Simonds) served six years, enlisting 19 March 1778 for three years, and reenlisted for the war in 1781. Simmons went south to Virginia under the Marquis de Lafayette; a 5 April 1781 notation recorded, 'On comd. with the [light] Infantry'. Compiled Service Records of Soldiers who Served in the American Army During the Revolutionary War, National Archives Microfilm Publication M881, Record Group 93. 'Clothing Acct. for 1777', 5th Massachusetts Regiment (1778–81), Revolutionary War Rolls (National Archives), folder 7, frames 265 (Pomp Simons); 266 (Duglas Midleton); 267 (Jube Upton).

Appendix I

'Being a coloured man he was taken as a waiter': Overview of Soldiers as Officers' Servants

In August 1779 Continental army surgeon Jabez Campfield wrote, 'How hard is the soldier's lott who's least danger is in the field of action? Fighting happens seldom, but fatigue, hunger, cold & heat are constantly varying his distress'. In the same vein, 18th century common soldiers spent much more time preparing meals, digging fortifications or latrines, chopping and hauling wood, and myriad other mundane tasks, than facing the enemy in battle. One of the lesser-known roles for a soldier was acting as servant to one or several officers.[1]

Officers of both sides during the War for American Independence were allowed one or more personal servants, also called waiters, but the practice was regulated. November 1776 Continental army orders stipulated, 'No Boys (under the idea of Waiters, or otherwise) or old Men, to be inlisted …' Waiters (also called servant, batman, or 'bowman') accompanied their masters wherever they went. Directions for making unit field returns in March 1779 mentioned, 'Under *Rank and File* in the first column are to be inserted all men fit for duty, in which number are to be included all officers waiters belonging to the Army (who are ever to go on duty with their Masters, making part of the detail)'. Furthermore, soldier-waiters were expected to carry arms during drill and in line of battle, though, in reality, that did not always occur. On 4 May 1779, Washington directed that the army's brigades practice Major General Friedrich Wilhelm de Steuben's new manual of discipline and maneuver, 'and as a single man's being ignorant of the principles will often cause disorder in a platoon and sometimes in a battalion, no waiter or other soldier is to be exempted from this exercise'. This was reversed in May 1780, 'The Commanding officers of regiments are to be answerable that no Waiter or other person absents himself from the Exercise on any pretence and the

---

1   Journal of Surgeon Jabez Campfield, Spencer's Additional Regiment, 4 August 1779, *Journals of the Military Expedition of Major General John Sullivan Against the Six Nations of Indians in 1779* (Glendale, N.Y.: Benchmark Publishing Co., Inc., 1970), p.53.

Generals and Inspectors of Brigades will visit the regiments and see that this order is strictly obeyed'. At month's end, the commander-in-chief noted: 'No Arms to be delivered to Waggoners, Waiters of the General Field or Staff officers but only to those men who are to appear in Action'. Walter Stewart, Northern Army Inspector, gave his opinion of officers' waiters in July 1782, 'The … Servants to the Genl and field officers of our Army … are generally the most clean and lively Soldiers belonging to the Regiments. It is a pitty some Mode could not be fallen on to remove this Evil which is much more extensive than can be exhibited in Returns for altho the Company Officers Servants appear under Arms, yet it is very evident they loose much in their Discipline and Appearance as Soldiers …'.[2]

No official allotment of servants to officers prior to 1782 is known. One early intimation dates from November 1778, to the commander of Sheldon's 2nd Continental Light Dragoons, 'A field officer is to be allowed forage for four horses only including his servants. A captain forage for 3 horses including his servants, and a subaltern forage for two horses including his servants'.[3] This likely alludes to one servant per officer, with the additional mounts being pack horses for baggage. Near the end of the war, the commander-in-chief laid out the authorized allowance:

Head Quarters, Philadelphia, Saturday, January 19, 1782 … Commanding Officers of Regiments or Corps are not in future to furnish Servants or Waggoners from their Corps on any pretext whatever, without an express order from the Commander in Chief or Officer Commanding the Army. Officers actually belonging to regiments or Corps and serving with them are to be allowed servants from their respective Corps in the following proportions: Infantry, Artillery and all Corps serving on foot viz.

Lieutenant Colonel Major Two each One with Arms one without Arms
Captain Subalterns Surgeon Mate each one Servant with Arms
Cavalry Colonel Lt Colonel Two without Arms

And to each regimental Waggon is to be allowed one Waggoner without Arms. Field Officers of Regiments or Corps may take one servant with them on Furlough, but no other regimental Officers to take one from their Regiment on any Account.

No Officer or Doctor to take a Convalescent from the Hospital for a servant on pain of being Tryed by a Court Martial.

The General and Military staff and officers not belonging to Corps are to be allowed Servants in the following proportions, and when they are not otherwise provided may take them from the Army viz.

2   General orders, 10 November 1776, Fitzpatrick, *Writings of George Washington*, Vol. 6, pp.262–263; General orders, 11 March and 4 May 1779, *ibid.*, Vol.14, pp.224–225, 488; General orders, 12 May 1780, *ibid.*, Vol.18, pp.349–350, 407; Morristown National Park Library, Lloyd W. Smith Collection, Doc. #LWS 155, Walter Stewart, Inspection Report, Continental Army, West Point, 31 July 1782.
3   George Washington to officer commanding Sheldon's Dragoons, 26 November 1778, Fitzpatrick, *Writings of George Washington*, Vol.13, p.339.

Major General four Servants
Brigadier General four do.
Colonel Two do.
Lieutenant Colonel One do. without Arms.
Major One do.
Captains One do.
Aid decamp One do.
Major of Brigade one do.

The servants carrying Arms are to be exempt from Guards and other Camp duties, but are to appear under arms whenever the Regimt. Parades and are to Mount guard with the Officer on whom they wait. The Servants without Arms are never to appear in rank and File, except at the Inspection. When a Regiment Marches and leaves its Camp standing One servant to each Company is to be permitted to remain; but on the Camps being struck and the Baggage Loaded they are to join their regiment.[4]

Both white and black soldiers served as officers' servants; given their societal status it may be that soldiers of color predominated in the role, but we have no certain proof. On a small scale, a study of muster rolls for the New Jersey regiments from 1777 to early 1779 reveals that 10 soldiers, all white, were listed as waiters from September 1778 to February 1779. These men served with officers absent from their company, or with regimental and brigade commanders. There must have been waiters attached to the other company officers; possibly the men were not identified as waiters as the officers they served were not on detached duty. In January 1781 a 'List of the Men of Colonel Spencer's Regiment belonging to the Jersey Line' contained 72 soldiers, 12 of whom were described as 'Waiters, Absent'; again, all were white. The colonel and major of the regiment each had two waiters, while two captains, four lieutenants, the surgeon and a major of the New Jersey brigade each had one waiter apiece. James Condon, 33 years old at the time of his enlistment in May 1777, recalled of his service, 'enlisted … for and During the war … in the Company Commanded by [Captain, later Major] John Hollinshead belonging to the second Jersey Regiment … he continued to serve … near six years and after the takeing of Cornwallis … was not in the battles … being a Waiter'. Reiterating the use of white servants, some not soldiers, Georgian Dr. William Read, traveling north to join Washington's army in June 1778, 'made some improvements in his arms and travelling equipments, discharged a drunken servant and employed a steady, respectable Englishman', named John Houston.[5]

---

4   General orders, 19 January 1782, Fitzpatrick, *Writings of George Washington*, Vol.23, pp.450–452.

5   LOC, Washington Papers, series 4, Israel Shreve to George Washington (enclosure), 'A List of the Men of Colonel Spencer's Regiment', 8 January 1781. NA (US) Pension, reel 623, James Condon (S34220). 'Reminiscences of Dr. William Read, Arranged From His Notes and Papers', Gibbes, R.W., *Documentary History of the American Revolution: Consisting of Letters and Papers Relating to the Contest for Liberty, Chiefly in South Carolina, From Originals in the Possession of the Editor, and Other Sources. 1776–1782* (New York: D. Appleton & Co., 1857), p.255.

In his painstaking work on the Rhode Island regiments Daniel Popek discovered no bias regarding black soldiers being assigned to serve as waiters after the integrated Rhode Island Regiment was formed in 1781. One document supports that contention. A March 1781 regimental return lists the 'Rank and File on Extra Service'. Of those listed as waiters, six were white and four were African American, as follows:

Private John Fones in Rhode Island with Major Thayer
Private John Jones in Rhode Island with Major Bradford
Private Rufus Chapman in Rhode Island with Colonel Angell
Private Job Franklin in Rhode Island with Colonel Angell
Private John Tuley in Rhode Island with Colonel Olney
Private Prosper Gorton [July 1778 slave recruit] with Colonel Olney
Private Cato Green [July 1778 slave recruit] with Colonel Olney
Private John Greer with Colonel Greene
Private Prince Childs [African American] with Colonel Greene
Private Henry [Harry] Morris ['Negro'] with Colonel Lawrence [6]

Despite their plebian reputation, even New England officers, a number of them tradesman in civilian life, took on a servant or two. Colonel Loammi Baldwin, 26th Continental Regiment, described his situation after the autumn 1776 retreat to the Delaware River: 'Dec. 16 … I have lived 14 days upon nothing but fresh beef without salt and dry flower (which we have cooked in the best manner we could without even so much as a camp kittle half the time). Except 1 day allowance of salt pork, a fowle or two and a few sasages my waiter bought of some of the inhabitants … & a little salt they beged'.[7] Lieutenant John Tilden, serving with one of the Pennsylvania battalions in 1782, told of servants in the field, writing from near the Edisto River in South Carolina:

> January 9. [1782] – Make an addition to our hut; very bad off for want of furniture. … Dispatch two of our valets to head quarters.
> January 10. – Spend the day in reading Spanish novels. Our valets arrive this afternoon-bring tents which relieve us very much.

[Then, operating against British forces occupying James Island in the Stono River.]

> January 13. – Move up two miles from [Stono] river, lay in ye woods all day and eat potatoes. Our boys [waiters] not coming down with our bedclothes, we pass the night horridly …
> January 14. – Our boys bring down something to eat … [8]

---

6   'Rank and File on Extra Service', Rhode Island Regiment return, 22 March 1781, 'Returns Book, Second Rhode Island Regiment/Rhode Island Regiment', May 1779 to April 1782, Rhode Island Historical Society, Mss. 673, Revolutionary Military Records, SG 2, sub-series A, box 1, folder 60.
7   Harvard University, Collections of Houghton Library, Baldwin, Loammi, to Mary Baldwin, 19 and 21 December 1776, http://www.rootsweb.com/~nbstdavi/baldwin1776.html.
8   'Extracts From the Journal of Lieutenant John Bell Tilden, Second Pennsylvania Line, 1781–1782', *Pennsylvania Magazine of History and Biography*, Vol.19, pp.218–219.

African American Continental Soldiers Who Spent Some Portion of their Service as an Officer's Servant

Northern Soldiers

New Hampshire
Pomp Sherburne, 1780–1783, 'a man of colour', cook or waiter to Lieutenant Colonel George Reid, 2nd New Hampshire Regiment.

Massachusetts
Primus Hall (Primus Trask), 1781–1782, African American, steward to Colonel Timothy Pickering, Quartermaster General.
Thomas Haszard, African American, servant to Lieutenant Colonel Ebenezer Sprout, 12th Massachusetts Regiment, later 2nd Regiment.
Quamony Quash, 1775, African American, waiter to Colonel Theophilus Cotton, Cotton's Massachusetts Regiment.
Prince Sayward, 'a man of Colour', waiter to Maj. Samuel Darby, 7th Massachusetts beginning in 1778, 8th Regiment as of January 1783.

Connecticut
Richard Fortune (Putnam), enslaved 'black man', servant to Major General Israel Putnam. Daniel Putnam wrote on 'June 22 1818 Sir, I received a line from you on Saturday last requesting information regarding the services of Richard Fortune (a black man) in the Army of the Revolution. This man, at the commencement of the War, was a slave, belonging to General [Israel] Putnam. In December 1775 he was ordered by his Master to Cambridge and entered as a soldier in [Colonel John] Durkees [20th Continental] Regiment at that time recruiting for the Continental service, he was taken from the Regt. into the [military] family of his master, as a servant, and continued with him till April 1777, remaining on the muster rolls, & drawing pay, as a soldier in that Regiment. Some time in April 1777, under the promise of freedom at the close of the war, he enlisted again, in the same Regiment [4th Connecticut], and continued as a servant in General Putnams family till about the first of April 1779, when he was discharged the service. When I state his services in Genl. Putnam's family, it is understood, his <u>military family in Camp</u>, when he served with such fidelity and good conduct, as to obtain not only an honorable discharge from the army, but also all future claims of his master. I state these facts from my own knowledge, having been myself an aid-de-camp to Majr. Genl. Putnam, & resided in his family most of the time he was in service ….'
John Lines, 1780–1783, 'a black man', servant to Zebulon Butler (2nd Connecticut, later 1st Connecticut, served to June 1783), Lieutenant Colonel Ebenezer Huntington (Webb's Additional Regiment to January 1781, then 1st Connecticut, served to November 1783), Lieutenant Colonel Isaac Sherman (5th Connecticut, retired January 1783) Colonel Samuel Wyllys (3rd Connecticut Regiment, retired January 1781). Line testified in 1818 'about the middle of October AD 1780 enlisted for

three years into the Army of the United States … and was honourably discharged … on the 15th day of November 1783 … he served in the company of Captain [Nehemiah] Rice in the 5th Regt Col [Isaac] Sherman Connecticut Line; that he then next served in Colonel [Zebulon] Butlers Regt. same Line in Capt Harts company … that he then next served in Colonel Huntingtons Regt. … as waiter to the Coll. & just before his discharge he was waiter to Colonel [Samuel] Wyllys … that prior to sd. enlistment he had served his country as a private soldier … by various detachments, about two years …' Peres Tracey recalled in November 1836, 'I was acquainted with John Lines a black man … nearly fifty years ago & until his death in 1828 also with his wife Judith Lines for nearly as long … my Father Peter Tracey was in the Army of the Revolution for the greater part of the War … I have heard my Father say he used to be acquainted with Lines in the Army & that he was waiter to Colonel or Gen. Sherman [Lieutenant Colonel Isaac Sherman, 5th Connecticut, 1781–1783] & that for a considerable time during one Campaign Lines wife was with him in Camp & said to work for sd. Sherman and others.'

Cuff Wells, 'coloured man', waiter to the surgeon of the 4th Connecticut Regiment.

New York

Marlin Brown (Marlin Roorback), 'slave', servant to Lieutenant Colonel John Fisher, Nicholson's New York Regiment.

Joseph Johnson (Thomas Rosekrans), 'coloured', waiter to Major James Rosekrans (Rosenkrans). Rosekrans was a captain 4th New York Regiment, 1775; captain 5th New York, 1776 to February 1780; major 3rd New York, March 1780 to January 1781.

New Jersey

Peter Williams, African American, 1781–1782, waiter to Captain Jonathan Dayton, 1st New Jersey Regiment

Pennsylvania

Levi Burns, 'negro', waiter, enlisted for the war, Lieutenant Colonel's company, 10th Pennsylvania Regiment.

William Lukens, 'negro', waiter, Captain Stake's company, Colonel Michael Swope's Pennsylvania Battalion of Flying Camp militia, captured at Fort Washington 16 November 1776. *Charles Stourman*, 'a molatto man', waiter to Dr. Charles McKnight, Continental hospital surgeon from Pennsylvania.

Southern Soldiers

Georgia

Nathan Fry, Colonel Samuel Elbert's 2nd Regt. 1775–79, 'a free man of Colour ', drummer and officers' waiter (batman) to Major General Friedrich Wilhelm de Steuben and Major General Arthur St. Clair.

South Carolina

Isham Carter, 1779–1783, 'a free man of colour descended from an Indian woman and a negroe man', matross and waiter to Colonel Bernard Beekman and Captain John Wickley, 4th Scout Carolina (Artillery) Regiment. Carter recalled, 'he was inlisted by Col Beckman soon after the defeat of Col Ash [Brig. Gen. John Ashe] at Brier Creek [Georgia, 3 March 1779] … he continued in the service until the war ended … he was in the battles of Stono [Stono Ferry, South Carolina, 20 June 1779] Savannah [9 October 1779] and Charleston [siege, spring 1780] – attached to the 4 Reg't. of artillery commanded by Col [Owen] Roberts – and that he at times attended on the person of Col Beckman and sometimes served in the Company of Captain Weekly'.

North Carolina

William Casey (Kersey), head of a 'Free Colored' household), waiter to North Carolina Brigadier General Jethro Sumner, 1st NC Regt. 1782. As a private in the 4th Virginia Regiment Casey was captured at Charleston, South Carolina in May 1780. He noted in his pension deposition, 'The officers taken Prisoners were paroled and the men sent on Board of Prison Ships – myself among them – we were detained on Board I think more than a year – when we were carried Round by water to the James River, and up the River to James Town in the latter part of the summer 1781, where they were released – having been exchanged as he understood for Burgoyne's men — we were then march'd to Williamsburg where, having performed my full term of four years, I was discharged … At the time I was discharged I understood Cornwallis & his troops were surrounded at little York in Virginia. After my discharge I came home to Southampton & remained but a short time, when I moved and settled in No. Carolina … I was again enlisted by Captain Dixon Marshall of the [1st North Carolina] Reg't. commanded by Gen'l. Jethro Sumner and was shortly after taken by Gen'l. Sumner to wait upon him – in which capacity I served thirteen months and eight days when I was discharged by Gen'l. Sumner'.

Virginia

James Cooper, enlisted in 1778 for three years, 'a Molatto Free Man', waiter to Colonel Abraham Buford (11th Virginia Regiment to February 1781, then transferred to the 3rd Regiment).

John Harris, 1778, 'a free man of Colour', servant to Major James Monroe, aide to Major General William Alexander, Lord Stirling from November 1777 to December 1778. C. Leon Harris notes, 'A size roll compiled at Cumberland Old Court House … includes the following: John Harris/ age 21/ height 5' 4½'/ black hair/ hazel eyes/ yellow complexion …' Harris recalled that in 'year 1777 he entered Captain [James] Harris's company … in the 15th Continental regiment Va. Line then commanded … by Colonel [Gustavus Brown] Wallace, that he was taken from that regiment, & made Servant to President Monroe, who was then Major of horse & Aid de Camp to Lord Stirling … he acted in these situations about thirteen months, that he then got a furlough & returned to Va. that he was again in the Army, at Chesterfield Ct. House, under Colonel Davies, & was discharged therefrom by him, on the 15th day of October 1780 …'.

James Hawkins, 'being a coloured man he was taken as a waiter', waiter to Colonel William Croghan (4th Virginia Regiment to late 1779, 2nd Virginia, December 1779 to May 1780; captured at Charleston, on parole to the war's end). Former lieutenant Elias Langham testified, 'he was well acquainted with the said James Hawkins as a Soldier … in the first regiment of Artillery … that being a coloured man he was taken as a waiter to Major Chrogham [Croghan] that the length of time he served as a soldier … he does not know … Major Elias Langhorn [sic] … states that he himself served as a Lieutenant in the first regiment of the Artillery …'.

William Jackson, 1781–1783, 'a free man of colour', waiter to several officers in Gaskins'/Posey's/Febiger's Virginia Regiment. '… he was a Waiter for a few weeks during his enlistment for Captain [John Boswell?] Johnston and Lieut. Wm. Trabur [Ensign John Trabue?] and to Adjut. Wm. Eskridge'.

Francis Pearce (Pierce), 1781–1783, 'a free man of colour', bowman to Lieutenant Colonel Samuel Hawes (6th Virginia Regiment, September 1778 to January 1783; 1st Virginia, January 1783 to the war's end).

Shadrach Shavers, 1778–1781, head of a household of 'Free Colored Persons', bowman (i.e., batman), 3rd Virginia Regiment. Shavers testified he, 'enlisted for the term of three years in the spring of the year 1778, at Valley Forge in the state of Pennsylvania in the Company commanded by Captain Cunningham, in the second Virginia Regiment commanded by Colonel Febecker [Christian Febiger, 3rd Virginia Regiment] … he continued in … the aforesaid Regiment & in the Companies of said Cunningham, [Samuel] Cobbs & John P. Harrison in the Company of the last of whom he was when he got injured in one of his ancles, which rendered him incapable of active service & consequently that he came to Virginia with said Harrison (about the year 1781) who promised to obtain his discharge but never did …' Former captain George Burroughs stated in 1820, 'he knew Shadrach Shavers in the Revolutionary War, that the first time he recollects to have seen him was acting as Bowman to Captain John P. Harrison of the 2nd Virginia Regiment at that time commanded by Colo Febecker … Harrison informed him that said Shavers was a soldier in his Company …'

Lewis Smith, 1779–1781, 'a free man of colour', 'Bowman' to Lieutenant James Covington (9th Virginia Regiment) or Adjutant William Covington (4th Virginia). Smith enlisted 'in the year 1779. while in service he was under the command of Captain Covington and General Mughlenburg [Peter Muhlenberg]; was first marched to Cumberland Court House and there remained for six months, at which place he acted in the capacity of Bowman for the said Captain Covington; After which he marched from Cumberland Court House to Charlestown and there remained in service acting as Bowman as aforesaid for Capt Covington until the expiration of the time of his enlistment (say 18 months) …'.

James Wallace, 1778–1780, 'a free man of colour', cook for Lieutenant Colonel Charles Porterfield, Porterfield's Virginia State Regiment, until the colonel's mortal wounding at the Battle of Camden, 16 August 1780.

Reuben Bird, 1780–1783, 'a mulatto boy', bowman to Lieutenant William Gray, Lieutenant Colonel Anthony Walton White's 1st Continental Dragoon Regt. 1780–1783. Mr Bird stated he 'enlisted for and during the war … in April or May in the year 1780 in Hillsborough in North Carolina in the Company commanded by Captain James Guinn in the Regiment of Dragoons commanded by Colo White of Virginia … he continued to serve in the said Corps until the peace came, when he was discharged from service in Culpepper county … Virginia … he was in no battle, he being a colored man, and kept as a Bowman, although he was very near the ground where several were fought …'. Gabriel Gray deposed in 1820, 'I do hereby certify that the bearer Reuben Bird was Boman for my brother William Gray while he was Lieutenant in the horse service under the command of Colonel White in the Southern Campain of 1780 and 1781'.

Mason Collins, 1777, 'an illiterate Mulatto', bowman, Major Holt Richardson, 7th Virginia Regiment.

Appendix II

'While at the camp I had the small Pox': African American Women with the Army

Hundreds of women followed the Continental Army, some African American. The best description of a woman of color known to have accompanied the troops is as follows:

Fifty Dollars Reward.
Ran away on the evening of the 7th inst. from Trenton ferry, a likely Mulatto slave, named Sarah, but since calls herself Rachael; She took her son with her, a Mulatto boy named Bob, about six years old, has a remarkable fair complexion, with flaxen hair: She is a lusty wench, about 34 years of age, big with child; had on a striped linsey petticoat, linen jacket, flat shoes, a large white cloth cloak, and a blanket, but may change her dress, as she has other cloathes with her. She was lately apprehended in the first Maryland regiment, where she pretends to have a husband, with whom she has been the principal part of this campaign, and passed herself as a free woman. Whoever apprehends said woman and boy, and will secure them in any gaol, so that their master may get them again, shall receive the above reward, by applying to Mr. Blair M'Clenachan, of Philadephia, Captain Benjamin Brooks, of the third Maryland regiment, at camp, or to Mr. James Sterret, in Baltimore. Mordecai Gist [colonel, 3rd Maryland Regiment].[1]

Another woman was purported to have gone to the army:

One Hundred Dollars Reward.
RAN AWAY from the subscriber, on the 16th day of June last, a Negro Woman named SUE; she is about thirty years of age, about five feet two or three inches high, is big with child; she is more darkly coloured than a Mulatto, though not so black as Negroes are in general. She wears high caps, and was dressed in a blue and white short gown and petticoat. It is suspected she went to camp with a white

---

1   *New Jersey Gazette*, 28 October 1778.

Untold numbers of women, some African American, followed the Continental Army. The 6th and 8th 1781 Rhode Island Regiment companies were the 'black' companies in that corps; each had one man serving as a wagoner and each contained two women. Those two companies were also the largest in the regiment. (56 black rank and file, and musicians in each, 112 total; plus 4 black privates and musicians in other companies; 27% of musicians, and rank and file in the regiment were black.) The return shows 27 sergeants, 16 musicians, and 338 rank and file present. One sergeant and 20 rank and file absent with Scammell's Light Battalion were not listed. The ninth (light infantry) company, with 5 sergeants, 2 musicians, and 51 rank and file (2 of those were black), was absent serving with Lieutenant Colonel Jean–Joseph Sourbader de Gimat's Light Battalion, the Marquis de Lafayette's corps. Total for the entire regiment was 33 sergeants, 18 musicians, and 409 rank and file: Popek, *They fought bravely*, pp.362–372, 472.) (Courtesy of the Rhode Island Historical Society, Negative RHi X17 3696, John Rogers Returns Book, p.28A. Wilmington, DE, 4 September 1781. Ink on paper. Manuscript, Mss 673 SG2 B1 F60.)

woman commonly called Captain Molly, who has a husband in the 4th regiment of Light Dragoons. Whoever apprehends the said Negro woman and secures her that the owner may have her again, shall have the above reward and reasonable charges, paid by EDWARD HAND.[2]

---

2   *The Pennsylvania Packet*, 15 July 1779.

John Lines' wife Judith also spent some time with her husband in the service. Lines enlisted in the 5th Connecticut Regiment in March 1781 for three years; part of his time was spent at West Point and other Hudson Highland posts. By Judith Lines' own testimony, they married in 1780. She recalled, 'the next summer after I married … he sent for me to come to him I think the place was called the Highlands at that time my … husband was a waiter for Colonel Sherman & while at the camp I had the small Pox. I think I staid about 3 or 4 months'. Peres Tracy deposed that he knew 'John Lines a black man' for over 40 years. Tracy's father 'was acquainted with Lines in the Army … & … for a considerable time during one Campaign Lines wife was with him in Camp & used to work for [Colonel] Sherman and others'. Mrs. Lines also noted, 'my sd. husband used to write to me when he was in the Army & I have one of his letters now & which I give to the magistrate who takes this my Deposition it is dated 11 November 1781 & is in the hand writing of … John Lines my husband'. Mr Lines' pension file contains the letter mentioned by his wife; as far as is known this is the only surviving letter by a black Revolutionary soldier:

November the 11 1781 i take this Opper tuna ty to send to you my deer and loveing wife to let you now that i am well and hopeing these lines may find you and the Children Well I am Pleased [several illegible words] I shold be very glad to hear from you my deer and loveing wife I Cant but think it hard that I havnt had one letter [several illegible words] from home and this is the six letter of [mine?] and I haven't received one I have seen my father and my mother [is] dead and one of my brothers mother died 3 [weaks?] a go brother died 2 days a go i have two brothers liveing and all my sisters father is very much pleased of you and he intends to Come and se[e] you this faal or the first of the winter it is about six Weeks since i seen father he gives his cind Com Ply ments to you and so does all my brothers and sisters they are at the north river a bout sixteen miles from fishkill o my deer and loveing wife [several illegible words] the love the Cind love that I have for you I have gon a [illegible words] for your sake and I Could not help it god bless your deep love [illegible] and his wife is well [Game (possibly short for Gamaliel) Phillingly?] was in Camp last week and he says they was all well belong to Carnol [Isaac] Shermans [5th Connecticut] Rg ment Capting [illegible] Compy ny we lay at fishkill now i should be ver[y] glad if you would take [two illegible words] and Send me a letter how you have lived this sum mer and [whether?] the house is dun and [whether?] you kill that cow or [whether?] you have got a nother i want to [k]now all these things very much i in tend to Come home this winter if I Can but dont [k]now if i can god bless your deer soul if I Could se you my self then I Could talk with you my deer wife as I like i have seen hard times [several illegible words] I have lived a-11-day With Bread [likely means eating only bread, with no meat or vegetables] i have the [illegible word] a good deal bad so I re mane your loveing husband un tel death John lines.[3]

3   NA (US), Pension, reel 1567, John Lines, 'a black man' (W26775), depositions of Judith Lines and Peres Tracey. Ibid., Compiled Service Records, (Connecticut), John Lines.

Lines not only evinces his affection for Judith and imparts some news, he also provides some hint of the tasks his wife assumed during his absence.[4]

One last woman must be mentioned. Hannah Till was a cook/servant for several years in General Washington's military household. She was married to Isaac Till, and they are recorded to have had seven children, the first born circa 1761, the last around 1785.[5] One son was born during the Valley Forge winter: 'Isaac Worley Till son to Hannah a free Nigroe woman in full Communion with the Church was born in Gen: Washingtons Camp Valey forge nineteen months ago and baptized in this 4th Sabbath of Augt. 1779'. Isaac's birth would have occurred in January or February 1778, at which time Hannah was likely about 40 to 45 years of age.[6] Her life was documented by John Fanning Watson, as follows.

> Hannah Till … a black woman whom I saw in March, 1824 … served her seven years … to General Washington and La Fayette, as cook, &c. I saw her in her own small frame house, No. 182, south Fourth street, a little below Pine street [Philadelphia, Pennsylvania] … She was born in Kent county, Delaware. Her master, John Brinkly, Esq. sold her at the age of 15 years, when she was brought to Pennsylvania. At 25 years of age she was sold to Parson Henderson, and went with him to Northumberland. At 35 years of age she was sold to Parson Mason, of New York, with whom she dwelt there until the war of the Revolution; she then bought her freedom, and with her husband was hired into General Washington's military family as cooks – serving with him in all his campaigns for six and a half years, and for half a year she was lent into the service of General La Fayette. With one or the other of these she was present in all the celebrated battles in which they were engaged … I inquired regarding the domestic habits of Washington and others: she said he was very positive in requiring compliance with his orders; but was a moderate and indulgent master. He was sometimes familiar among his equals and guests, and would indulge a moderate laugh. He always had his lady with him in the winter campaigns, and on such occasions, was pleased when freed from mixed company and to be alone in his family. He was moderate in eating and drinking. I asked if she knew that he prayed. She answered that she expected he did, but she did not know that he practiced it … I asked her if he ever swore; she answered, that ideas about religion were not very strict, and that she thought that he did not strictly guard against it in times of high excitements, and that she well remembered that on one provocation with her, he called her c—d [colored] fool. General La Fayette she praised greatly – said he was very handsome, tall, slender,

---

4   NA (US), Pension, reel 1567, John Lines (W26775), 11 November 1781 (letter). John Lines' letter is faint and hard to transcribe. I reached out for help and Philip Mead, Chief Historian and Director of Interpretation at the Museum of the American Revolution in Philadelphia, took up the challenge and produced a comprehensive transcription. With that in hand, I was able to fill in some of the missing parts, contribute some amendments, and add some judicious editing. My heartfelt thanks to Phil for his kind help.

5   C.R. Cole, (with Charles L Blockson), "Hannah Till Mother of Isaac Woorley Till", (Daughters of the American Revolution, commemorative marker research, 2015), https://tinyurl.com/MotherofIsaacTill.

6   Cole and Blockson, "Hannah Till Mother of Isaac Woorley Till", Isaac Worley Till baptismal record, 2nd Presbyterian Church, Arch and 3rd Streets, Philadelphia, Pennsylvania, https://tinyurl.com/MotherofIsaacTill.

and genteel, having a fair white and red face, with reddish hair – that he spoke English plain enough – was always very kind. Her words were very emphatic: – "Truly he was a gentleman to meet and to follow!"[7]

Watson's sister visited occasionally with Mrs. Till:

> She says she received from her questions, such answers as these – "I well remember the arrival of the specie to pay the French army, for the house was so crowded that day that my pastry room was used to lodge the specie in, even while she still used the room. She continued with Washington till after Andre the spy was hung. On that day she saw many tears shed by our officers". General La Fayette called on her with Messrs. [Tench] Tilghman and [Clement or Nicholas] Biddle [in 1825]. To his question, Where was you when General Washington left Morristown? she answered, I remained more than six months with you, Sir, in the same house. He left her, promising to send her money by his son. The sequel was, that her house was embarrassed for arrear groundrents, and she was soon after informed to make herself easy, for La Fayette had cleared it off![8]

There are several references to Hannah and Isaac Till in Washington's wartime household accounts:

> 'Cash Paid to Servants Belonging to Genll. Washington's Family'
>
> 1776 – July: 15th, Negro Hannah, 16 shillings; 25th, Negro Hannah, 4 shillings.
> October: 15th, Negro Hannah, 2 pounds; Negro Isaac, 4 pounds.
> 1777 – February: 17th, Negro Hannah, 4 dollars; Servant Isaac, 6 dollars.
> April: 20th, 'To Cash Mr. Thompson paid Isaac', 5 shillings, 4 pence.
> June: 3rd, "To Servant Isaac & Hannah pay up to this day paid," 53 pounds, 7 shillings.
> 1778 – December: 19th, 'To Cash paid the Revrd. John Mason for Servant Hannah's wages in full as pr. Receipt', 30 pounds.[9]

Hannah Till was in fact a slave for much of the time she was in Washington's wartime employ, with her wages being paid to her master, the Reverend John Mason of New York, until at least the end of 1778. Mrs. Till may have purchased her freedom by June 1780, when at Morristown, New Jersey, she 'Received of Major [Caleb] Gibbs eight six dollars in full for two months wages at His Excellency General Washington's Family'. She signed, 'Hannah Till her mark.'[10]

---

7   John F. Watson, *Annals of Philadelphia, being a collection of memoirs, anecdotes, & incidents of the city and its inhabitants* (Philadelphia: For Sale by Uriah Hunt, 1830), pp.352–353.

8   Watson, *Annals of Philadelphia*, 352–353.

9   LOC, Washington Papers, series 5, Revolutionary War Household Expenses, Caleb Gibbs, and Mary Smith and Elizabeth Thompson (housekeepers), 1776 to 1780, images 3 and 125.

10   Justin Clement to the author, 22 April 2019 (email). Anon, 'The Mystery of Hannah Till & Isaac' (Valley Forge National Historical Park, manuscript).

Appendix III

'Peters is an East-India Indian ...': Compendium of Deserter Notices for Soldiers of Color

Appended are thirty-two newspaper notices, advertising men, mostly African American, who deserted from Continental and state regiments. Most are taken from Joseph Lee Boyle's invaluable two-volume work, 'He loves a good deal of rum ...': Military Desertions during the American Revolution, 1775–1783, vol. 1 (1775–June 30, 1777), vol. 2 (June 30, 1777–1783) (Baltimore, Md.: Genealogical Publishing Co., 2009). Lest anyone object to highlighting men of color who absconded from their enlistments, it must be said that Mr Boyle's collection contains 1,561 advertisements, showing that desertion was not only high-sport for American soldiers, but that the advertsiements for black soldiers are only two percent of the total (including white and Native American soldiers) published in 'He loves a good deal of rum ...' Add to that, outside of these notices, there are few personal descriptions of black soldiers, and these provide insights on their service, appearance, and, occasionally, their life away from the military.

For those notices gleaned from Mr Boyle's books, each is preceded by the volume and page numbers where they may be found.

Georgia
Snow Creek, Henry county, October 27, 1777.
DESERTED from Fort Salter's, in the New Purchase of the state of Georgia, the following solders, viz. ... [there follows a list of one sergeant, two corporals, and nine privates, likely all Caucasian, and after the end] Likewise **James Smith, and Wallace Dunston, mulattoes,** from Halifax. The above soldiers, being chiefly enlisted by Capt. John Baird of the state of Georgia, it is not I my power at present give a description of them, but expect they have mostly returned to their respective counties. I have in orders, from Col. Elbert, of the 2nd Georgia battalion of continental troops, to offer a free pardon o all deserters that voluntarily give themselves up to me and return to their duty; and I do further offer a reward of twenty dollars for each of the above mentioned soldiers, to

be delivered to me, or any other commissioned officer of the state of Georgia.

Shem Cook, Capt. 2nd Georgia battalion.

Virginia Gazette, 28 November 1777

North Carolina

Vol. 2, p.115.

HALIFAX, March 14

TEN DOLLARS REWARD

DESERTED from me the 12th instant on their march for Halifax, two soldiers belonging to the 5th battalion of this state, William Watson and Charles Peters, Watson has deserted five times, he has also cost the public twenty odd pounds for taking him up, and jail fees, he is about five feet ten inches high, dark complected, black hair, lives on or near Bay river, below Newbern. **Peters is an East-India Indian**, formerly the property of Mr. Thomlinson in Newbern. … BEN STEADMAN.

The North-Carolina Gazette, 1 May 1778; 8 May 1778; 15 May 1778.

Virginia

WILLIAMSBURG, June 6, 1777.

DESERTED from the troops of this state now in this city, on the 2nd instant, **Joshua Perkins, a mulatto**, about 5 feet 6 or 7 inches high, 24 or 25 years old, and is a straight well made fellow; had on a short striped jacket, a felt hat bound round with French lace, the remainder of his dress not remembered. Whoever apprehends the said deserter, and returns him to his company, shall have 5 DOLLARS reward.

WINDSOR BROWN, capt.

Virginia Gazette, 6 June 1777.

(Courtesy of Karen Harris.)

Vol. 2, p.118.

DESERTED from Capt. Nathaniel Fox's company of the 6th Virginia regiment, **JAMES ANDERSON, a black soldier**, six feet high, about forty years of age, rather spare made, and fond of liquor; had on when he went away, a light grey cloth coat and waistcoat: the coat faced with green, a pair of oznaburg overalls, and a small round hat with a piece of bear-skin on it: He took with him a pair of leather breeches which he had to clean, and also his firelock, cartridge-box, and new Dutch blanket. He is a ditcher by trade, and it is probable will endeavor to get employment in this State …

JOHN GIBSON, Col. 6th Virginia Reg.

Pennsylvania Packet, 13 May 1778

Vol. 2, p.227.

Philadelphia, January 12, 1780.

DESERTED from Captain Nathan Lamm's company, of the Third Virginia regiment, commanded by Col. Nathaniel Gist, viz.

JOHN MEREDITH, about 30 years old, 5 feet 10 inches high, born in the state of Pennsylvania, by trade a saddle-tree maker. …

CEASAR BLACK, **Negro drummer**, 35 years of age, 5 feet 7 inches high, well made, a shoemaker by trade, and has been employed in the public manufactory as an artificer in this city, making cartridge boxes for eighteen months past, and has been lately detected with a forged discharge.

ONE HUNDRED DOLLARS reward for each of the above deserters, if confined in any jail, and notice given of them to the Town-Major, or the subscriber.

CHARLES JONES, Lieutenant.

The Pennsylvania Journal; and the Weekly Advertiser, J 26 anuary 1780; 2 February 1780; 9 February 1780.

Delaware

Vol. 2, pp.294–295.

TWENTY-EIGHT DOLLARS REWARD.

DESERTED from the recruiting party belonging to the Delaware Regiment, the following recruits, viz. …

JAMES SONGO, **a Mulato**,[1] born in Kent County, Delaware State, 25 years of age, 5 feet 6 inches high, has been an old soldier, and is supposed to be gone to Maryland …

JAMES MOORE, Capt. D.R.'

Pennsylvania Journal; and the Weekly Advertiser, 26 June 1782; 4 July 1782; 10 July 1782; 3 August 1782.

Vol. 2, pp.298–299.

SIXTY-FOUR DOLLARS REWARD.

DESERTED from the DELAWARE REGIMENT, the following soldiers, viz.
…

JAMES SONGO, **a mulatto**, born in Kent County, Delaware State, 25 years of age, 5 feet 6 inches high, has lost some of his toes.

EPHRAIM HENDRICKSON, born in Maryland, 20 years of age, 5 feet 5 inches high, fair hair, plays upon the violin, is supposed to be near Sassafras Church, Maryland. …

THOMAS CLARK, **a mulatto**,[2] lives in Sussex County, Delaware State. …

JOHN WILSON, **a very white mulatto**,[3] born in Maryland, 21 years of age, 5 feet 5 inches high, stout made, can weave and make shoes; he may pass

---

1   James Songo (Delaware) Compiled Service Records (National Archives), enlisted 25 December 1781, mustered January 1782, age 25, height 5 feet 7 inches, farmer, born in Delaware, black hair, yellow skin, 'deserted was taken & deserted again 28 July 1782.

2   Thomas Clark (Delaware) Compiled Service Records (National Archives), on the rolls as of October 1777, a drummer, muster roll dated September 1780, Hillsborough, N.C., 16 August 1780 'missing in action,' as of January 1783 listed as prisoner of war.

3   John Wilson (Delaware) Compiled Service Records (National Archives), enlisted 24 June 1782, deserted July 1782, age 22, height 5 feet 5 inches, weaver, born in Maryland, black hair, yellow skin, 'enlisted as a substitute for James Messix'.

by the name of John Green, or Bray; he rode off from Dover [on] a small bay horse …

Any person securing the above deserters in any goal in the United Sates, shall have the above reward, or in proportion for any of them, and if delivered to any officer of said regiment in the State, or in Philadelphia, all reasonable charge, paid by me,

JAMES MOORE, Captain D.R. New Castle, 30 August [1782]'

Pennsylvania Journal; and the Weekly Advertiser, 14 September 1782.

Vol. 2, p.301.

Annapolis, September 10, 1782.

JACK BRAY, alias GREEN, [see John Wilson above]

THE slave of Mrs. ANN STEWART, of Ann Arundel county, ran away from his mistress about the first of June, then on a visit near Queenstown on the Eastern shore of Maryland. **Jack will pass very well as a whiteman, being a remarkable light mulattoe,** with grey or blue eyes, brown curling hair, and some freckles; tho' by attending to his dialect it may be discovered he has been much with negroes; he is 22 years of age, of a low stature, stout and well set, his face is rather large for his size, his nose stubbed; he carried a variety of clothes with him, but as he offered some for sale before he went off, 'tis probable he has disposed of most of them; he is a tolerable good weaver, rough shoemaker, and occasionally rode as a postilion, in which character he was when he left his mistress. It appears from an advertisement of the first of July, under the signature of Capt. James Moore, of the Delaware regiment, that Jack enlisted with a recruiting party at Dover, by the name of John Wilson, and had deserted and taken with him a small bay horse, old saddle and curb bridle. A Reward of TEN POUNDS (gold) and all reasonable charges, shall be paid to any person who will apprehend and secure him, so that the subscriber may get him. Any information which may be given of him to Mr. James Tilghman, of Queen Ann's county, will be immediately communicated to the subscriber.

CHARLES STEWART.

The Pennsylvania Gazette, 6 November 1782.

Massachusetts

Vol. 1, p.13.

Deserted from Prospect-Hill, late of Bolton, in the county of Worcester, James Bridges and John Chewen, of Capt. Hill's company, in Col. Phinney's regiment, in the new establishment, but of Capt. Hasting's company, in Col. Whitmore's regiment, in the old. James Bridges is an old countryman, about 5 feet 8 inches high, marked considerable in the face with the small pox, says he was a marine in the Somerset man of war, and deserted from Boston last March, has a large head of hair, almost black, and very long, which is commonly cued with a black ribband; had on when he went away, an old blue surtout, cloth-coloured coat and jacket; 'tis supposed he carried with him a pair of leather breeches, two shorts, tow and linen, two pair of yarn stockings, and two pair of new shoes. – **John Chewen is a molatto, but calls himself Indian**, about 5 feet 5 inches high, had on a dark coloured coat, and a pair of breeches something lighter; **has a wife at Holden, a proper Indian squaw**; he loves a good deal of rum. – It is to be hoped that every lover of his country will use his utmost endeavours to apprehend said deserters, and send them forthwith to Camp, or confine them in any of the continental gaols, and give information thereof to the subscriber, for which they will receive one dollar reward for each, and necessary charges paid by

JEREMIAH HILL, Capt.

New England Chronicle, from Thursday, 21 December to Thursday, 28 December 1775; from Thursday, 4 January to Thursday, 11 January 1776.

Vol. 1, pp.94–95.

DESERTED from Capt. Daniel Whiting's company, in the 6th regiment in the Continental service, **a mulatto fellow named JACOB SPEEN**, 5 feet 9 inches high, well built, short curled hair, had on a light brown coat, turned up with white, and leather-breeches, 23 years of age, belonging to Natick. Whoever shall take up said deserter and return him to said regiment, shall have Five Dollars reward and all necessary charges paid by D. WHITING, Captain.

New England Chronicle, 25 July 1776; 2 August 1776.

Vol 1, pp.234–235.

DESERTED from Captain Philip Thomas's Company, of Colonel Marshal's Regiment, the following Soldiers, viz. … [nine men, including] **Samuel Harding, a Negro**, of Malden. Whoever will apprehend either of the above Deserters, and secure them in and Goal in this State, and give Information to the Subscriber, shall have FIVE DOLLARS Reward for each.

Boston, March 26, 1777.

WARHAM WHEELER, Lieut.

The Independent Chronicle and the Universal Advertiser, 27 March 1777; 3 April 1777; *The Boston Gazette, and Country Journal*, 14 April 1777.

Vol. 1, pp.292–293.

DESERTED from Capt. Allen's Company, Col. Bailey's Regiment … **Jupeter Richards, a Negro Man**, 29 Years old, a tall likely fellow, speaks goof English, has been with one Mr. Kent, a Lawyer, inBoston, and has taken his Advice, which I believe is the Occasion of his absenting himself from my Company. Whoever will give Information to me the Subscriber, shall have SIX DOLLARS REWARD, paid by me,

JACOB ALLEN, Captain

The Independent Chronicle and the Universal Advertiser, 15 May 1777.

Vol. 1, p.333.

Deserted from Captain Oliver's Company, in Col. Greaton's Regiment, the following Soldiers …, **John Peprill, a Mulatto**, belomging to Kittery, 5 feet 10, was a soldier in Col. Poor's regiment the last campaign. George Feither, 5 feet 8, light complexion, a Hessian, speaks broken English …

ROBERT OLIVER, Captain.

The Boston Gazette, and Country Journal, 30 June 777; 14 July 1777.

Vol. 2, p.23.

DESERTED from Captain Joseph Wardsworth's Company, in Colonel Bradford's Regiment … **JOHN PARCE, a Molatto Fellow** aged about 35 Years. …

Boston, July 15, 1777.

STEPHEN NYE, Lieutenant.

The Independent Chronicle and the Universal Advertiser; 17 July 1777; 31 July 1777; 7 August 1777.

Vol. 2, p.38.

Postscript to a newspaper notice for Jackson's Additional Regiment:

'N[ota]B[ene]. … Deserted from my Company in Col. Micah Jackson's Regiment, John Harden, an Irishman, 25 Years old, 5 Feet 8 Inches high, light Complexion; **Peter Thomas, a Molatto**, 22 Years old, 5 Feet 9 Inches high …

JAMES VARNUM, Captain.'

The Independent Chronicle and the Universal Advertiser; 31 July 1777; 7 August 1777.

Vol. 2, p.128.

Deserted from Leicester, **a negro fellow named Sambo**, belonging to the continental army, he is a short well set fellow, thirty years of age, speaks bad English, and his left thumb is shorter and thicker by reason of a felon than the other. Whoever apprehends said negro, and confines him, and informs the subscriber, or return him to his corps, shall receive twenty dollars reward and all necessary Charges pad, by me

JAMES WHITTEMORE, Lieut.

The Massachusetts Spy: or, American Oracle of Liberty, 25 June 1778; 2 July 1778.

Vol. 2, p.132.

DESERTED from William Retter, conductor of a party of men engaged in the nine months service belonging to the Continental army in their march from the county of Worcester to Fish kill, at landlord Sco[tts] in Palmer, on the evening of the 5th instant, **a negro man** belonging to said party, from the town of Lacester, known **by the name of Sambo**, about five feet five inches high, well set, between 20 and 30 years of age, talks very broken English; had on an old Straw Hat, a dark coloured old Surtout and Leather Breches, has lost the joint of one Thumb. Whoever will take up said negro, and send him to Gen. Warner, at Fish kill, or confine him in any public goal, and give information of the same, shall have a handsome reward, and necessary charges, paid by me.

WILLIAM RITTER.
Connecticut Courant, 14 July 1778

Vol. 2, p.238.
Newtown, Bucks County, June 28, 1780.
TWO HUNDRED DOLLARS REWARD.
BROKE Goal last night … **a Negroe man, who calls himself JOHN,** an says he belongs to the Continental army, Colonel Bradley's regt. of New-England troops. He had with him, when committed, an old bay horse, about 13 and a half hands high, branded C.A. … The said Negroe is about 25 years of age, had on a red coat and waistcoat, wore threadbare, without lining, green breeches buttoned up the sides, a castor hat that has been turned, a pair of old pumps, one of hem tied, the other buckled. They [John and another prisoner] stole and carried off with them out of the goal yard, two shirts, one pair of new ribbed thread stockings, one pair of worsted ditto, and one linen handkerchief…
JAMES GREGG, Goaker.'
The Pennsylvania Packet, or the General Advertiser, 1 July 1780; 4 July 1780.

Rhode Island
Vol 1, p.89.
FOUR DOLLARS Reward.
DESERTED from the Company under my Command, in Col. Sage's Regiment, **a Negro Man, named Sambo Brown,** 5 Feet 7 Inches high, speaks broken, quick and loud, has lost Part of one of his Thumbs, and shews a Certificate of his Freedom, signed Samuel Brown, Justice of the Peace in Stockbridge. Had on when he went away a brown Sagathy Coat and Waistcoat, pale blue Broadcloth Breeches, white Thread Stockings, plated Buckles on Pinchbeck [a form of brass, an alloy of copper and zinc, mixed in proportions so that it closely resembles gold in appearance], and a Felt Hat in the Macaroni Taste.
Whoever takes up said deserter, and conveys him to the Subscriber, in Voluntown or New-York, or to Lieut. Abraham Sheppard, in Plainfield, shall receive the above Reward, and all necessary Charges, paid by
JOHN DIXON, Captain.
Providence Gazette; and Country Journal, 13 July 1776; 20 July 1776; 3 August 1776; 10 August 1776.[4]

Vol 1, p.250.
Deserted from his Post, in the Night, and carried with him his Gun and Cartridge-Bob, with seventeen Cartridges, one **Peter Coggary, a Molatto Fellow,** about five Feet and an Half high, stoops forward a little. Had on when he went away, a blue Shag Jacket, striped Flannel Trowsers, and an old Felt hat; he belongs to Capt. James Parker's Company, in Col. Talman's Regiment. Whoever will secure said Deserter, and give Notice

---

4   Brown apparently returned and deserted again, see advertsiement dated 14 September 1776.

to me, at Tiverton, shall receive Five Dollars Reward, and all necessary Charges, paid by

JAMES PARKER, Capt.

The Providence Gazette; and Country Journal, 12 April 1777; 3 May 1777.

Vol 1, pp.323–324.

Deserted from Capt. Tew's company, in Col. Angell's Regiment, **John Cook, a negro**, 24 years of age, about six feet high, well set, curled hair: Had on when he went away a chocolate coloured coat, with red facings…

EBENEZER MACOMBER, Lieut.

The Providence Gazette; and Country Journal, 14 June 1777; 21 June 1777; 5 July 1777.

Vol. 2, p.86.

Deserted from my company, in Col. Stanton's regiment, **Moses Hazard, a Mulatto**, about 5 feet 6 or 7 inches high, a sturdy, well built fellow, with long black hair…

MALACHAI HAMMETT, Capt.

The Providence Journal; and Country Journal, 15 November 1777; 29 November 1777.

Vol. 2, p.105.

Deserted from my company, in Col. Crary's regiment, about the middle of February last, James Allen, a likely, well-set Indian fellow, 22 years of age, 5 feet 5 inches high; he belongs to East-Greenwich. Also **Bristol Prime, a lusty Negro fellow**, 22 years of age, 5 feet 9 inches high; he belongs to Stonington, in Connecticut…

JAMES PARKER, Capt.

The Providence Gazette; and Country Journal, 28 March 1778; 4 April 1778; 18 April 1778.

Vol. 2, p.111.

Deserted from my company, and Col. Topham's regiment … **Sampson George, 20 years of age, 5 feet 7 inches high, a negro**…

WILLIAM WHIPPLE, Capt.

The Providence Gazette; and Country Journal, 18 April 1778; 25 April 1778.

Vol. 2, p.253.

Deserted. The following Recruits, inlisted for Col. CHRISTOPHER GREENE'S Regiment, viz. …Obadiah Wickett (Indian) a Native of Massachusetts, 27 Years of Age, 5 Feet 6 Inches high, is full faced; inlisted for North Providence. … **Jacklin (Negro)** born in Connecticut, 24 Years of Age, 5 Feet 5 Inches high, a Tanner by Trade; he is a likely well-made Fellow, sometimes wears a false Tail…

JEREMIAH OLNEY, Lieut. Col.

The American Journal and General Advertiser, 10 March 1781; 21 March 1781; 31 March 1781

Vol. 2, p.257.

DESERTERS.

DESERTED, the following Recruits, from Col. Christopher Greene's Regiment, viz., MICHAEL EPHRAIM, an Indian, a Native of Charlestown … RICHARD BOOTH, an Indian, a Native of Long-Island … **BENJAMIN ROGER, a Mustee**, a Native of Charlestown, 5 Feet 9½ Inches high, 21 Years of Age; inlisted for N. Kingstown. – CHARLES POCHATAUCH, an Indian, a Native of Charlestown … ISAAC ROGER, an Indian, a Native of and Inlisted for Charlestown …

JEREMIAH OLNEY, Lieut. Col.

The Providence Gazette; and Country Journal, 7 April 1781; 14 April 1781; *The American Journal and General Advertiser*, 11 April 1781; 14 April 1781; 21 April 1781.

Vol. 2, pp.263–264.

DESERTED from the Rhode-Island Regiment, the following Recruits, viz. … James Booney, an Indian (inlisted for South Kingstown) born in Westerly … **Levi Thurston, a Negro** (inlisted for Hopkinton) born at Tower-Hill, is 27 Years of Age, 5 Feet 6 Inches high, a well-set Fellow. – He deserted from a Party on their March to Head Quarters. … Peleg Dexter, an Indian (inlisted for Scituate) born in Cranston … Benjamin Fitch, an Indian (inlisted for East-Greenwich) a Native of Charlestown …

JEREMIAH OLNEY, Lieut. Col.'

The Providence Gazette; and Country Journal, 19 May 1781; 26 May 1781; 2 June 1781; *The American Journal and General Advertiser*, 30 May 1781; 20 June 1781; 23 June 1781.

Connecticut

Vol. 1, pp.99–100.

Deserted from Capt. Butler's Company, in Col. Nixon's Regiment, (from New-London, while the Brigade was on their March to New York) on the 20th of April last, **a Negro named JACK STRANG**, light Complexion, about 36 Years old, midling Stature, walks clumsy; It is said he has let himself to Labour for six Months. Whoever will take up said Deserter and return him to his Regiment in New-York, shall have Four Dollars Reward, and all necessary Charges.

New-London, July 11, 1776

SILAS WALKER, Lieut.

The New-London Gazette, 2 August 1776; vol. 13, issue 664.

Vol 1, p.138.

Lyme, Sept. 22nd. 1776.

Deserted from Capt. Simeon Martin's Company, in Col. Lippett's Regiment, one **Charles Prince, a negro** about six Feet high, well set, cross eyed, and William R[oh]an, about five Feet ten Inches high; had on blue Jackets; whoever will apprehend or secure either of the abovementioned Persons, in any of the Goals of the Thirteen United States of America,

so that the Captain shall have them or either of them, shall receive Five
Dollars Reward, and all necessary Charges paid

William Belcher, Lieut.

The New-London Gazette, 11 October 1776.

Vol 1, p.245.

DESERTED from Capt. William Ladd's Company, Col. Wyllys's Regiment,
one **Peter Thomas**, an inlisted Soldier, **a Molatto**, formerly an Inhabitant
of the Massachusetts State, but lately resided at Coventry, in the State of
Connecticut; five Feet nine Inches High, 23 Years of Age, very talkative,
and is fond of Company. Whoever will apprehend said Deserter, and
return him to the Subscriber in Hebron or to Mr. Adjt. Hart in Hartford,
shall have Five Dollars Reward, and all necessary Charges paid by

SOLOMON TARBOX, junr. Lieut.

*The Norwich Packet and the Connecticut, Massachusetts, New-Hampshire,
and Rhode Island Weekly Advertiser*, from Monday, 7 April to Monday,
14 April 1777; from Monday, 21 April to Monday, 28 April 1777; from
Monday, 5 May to Monday, 12 May 1777.

Vol 1, pp.306–307.

DESERTED from Capt. Woodbridge's company in Col. Swift's regiment,
about the 10th of April … **PETER JOHNS, an Indian molatto**, 28 years
of age, 5 feet 10 inches high, black hair, tied in his neck, one white eye
[perhaps a cataract?], is supposed to be near the State of Rhode Island,
in the east part of Connecticut…

REUBEN CALKIN, Lt.

Connecticut Courant, 26 May 1777

Vol 1, p.325.

DESERTED from me the subscriber **a Negro man servant, an enlisted
soldier, named BOSTON**, about 5 feet and 10 inches high; had on when
he went away a claret colour'd lappelled coat, brown jacket, brown cloth
breeches, an old felt hat and a check'd woolen shirt….

DANIEL ELDRIDGE, Lieut. in Col. Webb's regiment.

Connecticut Courant, 16 June 1777.

New Hampshire

Vol. 1, p.301.

DESERTED from Capt. Amos Emerson's company, in Col. Cilley's battalion,
– EBENEZER WILLIAMS, aged 26 years, about 5 feet 7 inches high, a
remarkable scar on his face. THOMAS WALKER, aged 33 years, about 5
feet 5 inches high, **GEORGE WALKER, a molatto-felow**, aged 26 years,
bout 5 feet 9 inches high; and **WILLIAM SHARPER, a negro-man**,
aged 48 years, about 5 feet 8 inches high. – Whoever will apprehend
said deserters, or either of them, and confine them in any goal and
advertise them in the public prints a Boston, so that their officer may
know where to find them, shall have FIVE DOLLARS reward for each,
and all necessary charges paid, by JONA EMERSON, Lieut.

Continental Journal, 22 May 1777.

Appendix IV

Analysis of the Chesterfield Supplement's Black Soldiers

Major General Friedrich Wilhelm de Steuben, commanding the Virginia Continental line, established his headquarters at Chesterfield, Virginia following the disastrous Battle of Camden, and called for the new recruits to join him there. A draft was held to rebuild the Virginia Continental contingent, and the result was the Chesterfield 'Size Roll', containing names and physical descriptions of all the conscripted men.

<u>African Americans on the Chesterfield List</u>: Lawrence Babits and Joshua Howard, in their book *Long, Obstinate, and Bloody: The Battle of Guilford Courthouse*, discuss the make-up of the 1781 Virginia regiments with Major General Greene, including African American soldiers. They note the possibility of as many as 110 blacks among the Chesterfield drafts, more than 12 percent of the total. C. Leon Harris in his online study and transcription of the Chesterfield roll puts the number of black soldiers at 53. This author, using criteria supplied by Messrs. Babits and Howard, totaled a possible high of 92 black men among the drafts, then narrowed that down using information available for individual soldiers and came up with a more conservative total of 57. Problems of identification remain; Evans Archer, described as having red hair, grey eyes, and a yellow complexion, was listed in the 1790 census as a 'free Negro'. His pension papers give no indication of race. Due to that and other identified men, all Chesterfield levies noted as having a 'yellow' complexion have been included as African American.

There are other minor discrepancies. In their article 'Revolutionary Ranks: An Analysis of the Chesterfield Supplement' authors Joseph A. Goldenberg, Eddie D. Nelson, and Rita Y. Fletcher tallied the number of men on the Chesterfield at 917. Babits and Howard put the Chesterfield levy data on an Excel spreadsheet, resulting in a total of 913 men.

For the purpose of this study 913 has been taken as the accurate figure.

Chesterfield Supplement total: 913 men (Babits and Howard)
Babits and Howard total of African American levies: 110 = 12% of total
Rees study, initial total: 92 = slightly over 10%
Rees study, final (conservative) total: 56 = 6.1%

As noted above, my initial number of black men listed on the Chesterfield list was 92. That was pared down substantially when the present author examined 37 men described as having black hair, black eyes, and dark complexion. Several men on the list under that description applied for pension, but none left any record they were of African American extraction. Furthermore, of the men under that description, two were born in France, two in Ireland, one in Italy, and one in England, further indication they were likely white. The proportion of blacks on the Chesterfield list also argues for the more conservative number. Taking 92 as the correct Chesterfield number would mean blacks were slightly over 10 percent of the whole. Considering that of the Virginia brigades listed in the August 1778 return, Muhlenberg's had the highest proportion of black troops, with 6.8 percent of the brigade. (Woodford's and Scott's were considerably lower, at 3.2 percent and 1.6 percent respectively), the proportion of 6.1 percent (56 African Americans) is still a relatively high number.

Descriptions of African Americans on the Chesterfield List

Conservative total: 56 (out of 913 men)

Black Hair, Black Eyes, Black Complexion – 22
(all but one born in Virginia)
Nathaniel Anderson, 39 years old, 64 inches tall, carpenter, deserted
Burrell Artist, 18 years old, planter, enlisted September 1780 for 18 months
Gim Ash, 18 years old, 57 inches tall, farmer, enlisted September 1780 for 18 months
Benjamin Branham, 40 years old, 65 inches tall, farmer, enlisted September 1780 for 18 months
Trade Brown, 18 years old, 63 inches tall, farmer, enlisted September 1780 for 18 months
Charles Charity, 24 years old, 66 inches tall, planter, enlisted September 1780 for 18 months
Robert Clarke, 20 years old, 70 inches tall, farmer, enlisted September 1780 for 18 months
Francis Cole, 25 years old, 70 inches tall, waggoner, enlisted August 1780 for the war
William Cuffy, 18 years old, 68 inches tall, farmer, 'a free man of Colour'
Lewis Fortune, 16 years old, 67 inches tall, planter, enlisted September 1780 for 18 months

Charles Freeman, 21 years old, 66 inches tall, planter, enlisted September 1780 for 18 months

Anthony Furman, 19 years old, 63 inches tall, planter, deserted

Joseph Langdon, 27 years old, 67 inches tall, blacksmith, enlisted August 1780 for the war

Berry Lewis, 23 years old, 69 inches tall, planter

Charles Morris, 17 years old, 62 inches tall, planter, enlisted September 1780 for the war

Godfrey Rickinson, 39 years old, 66 inches tall, blacksmith, enlisted August 1780 for 18 months

William Rowe, 28 years old, 66 inches tall, mason (born in Phila. Penna.), enlisted September 1780 for 18 months, deserted

Thomas Shall (Small), 37 years old, 64 inches tall, farmer, enlisted September 1780 for 18 months

Randolph Sly, 25 years old, 63 inches tall, planter, enlisted September 1780 for 18 months

Anthony Valentine, 33 years old, 68 inches tall, planter, enlisted September 1780 for 18 months

James Wallace, 28 years old, 63 inches tall, planter, enlisted August 1780 for the war

Charles Wiggans, 40 years old, 67 inches tall, farmer, enlisted October 1780 for 18 months

Black Hair, Black Eyes, Yellow Complexion – 22

(all but one born in Virginia)

Charles Barry, 18 years old, 65 inches tall, farmer, enlisted September 1780 for 18 months

Jacob Boon, 26 years old, 65 inches tall, farmer, enlisted September 1780 for 18 months

James Bowser, 50 years old, 66 inches tall, farmer, enlisted September 1780 for 18 months

William Buster, 22 years old, 68 inches tall, farmer, enlisted September 1780 for 18 months

William Carter, 22 years old, 69 inches tall, sawyer, enlisted September 1780 for 18 months

[?] Collins. 21 years old, 71 inches tall, sailor, enlisted September 1780 for 18 months

Francis Cypress, 30 years old, 66 inches tall, tailor, enlisted September 1780 for 18 months

Solomon Duncan, 39 years old, 68 inches tall, blacksmith (born in NC), enlisted September 1780 for 9 months, deserted

Joseph Dunston, 15 years old, 64 inches tall, farmer, enlisted September 1780 for 18 months

Dennis Garner, 26 years old, 66 inches tall, farmer, enlisted September 1780 for 18 months

Caleb Hill, 31 years old, 67 inches tall, planter, enlisted September 1780 for 18 months

William Holmes, 40 years old, 70 inches tall, planter, enlisted September 1780 for 18 months

William Jackson, 26 years old, 65 inches tall, groom, enlisted September 1780 for 18 months, 'a free man of colour'

Thomas James, 25 years old, 64 inches tall, deserted before serving

Francis Morris, 22 years old, 65 inches tall, ship's carpenter, enlisted September 1780 for 18 months

Richard Redman, 21 years old, 64 inches tall, planter, enlisted September 1780 for 18 months 'Free Colored Person'

William Scott, 28 years old, 66 inches tall, carpenter, enlisted September 1780 for 18 months

Edward Steveand (Steven), 15 years old, 63 inches tall, planter, enlisted September 1780 for 18 months

William Thomas, 21 years old, 67 inches tall, planter, enlisted September 1780 for 18 months, 'free colored person'

George Tyler, 23 years old, 66 inches tall, waiter, enlisted September 1780 for 18 months, 'Free Colored Person'

Edward Watson, 18 years old, 64 inches tall, farmer, enlisted September 1780 for 36 months

Jesse Wood, 16 years old, 58 inches tall, planter, enlisted September 1780 for 18 months, 'a free man of Colour'

Black Hair, Black Eyes, Mulatto – 2

Godfrey Bartlett, 26 years old, 65 inches tall, farmer, born in Va., enlisted for the war

Joseph Pierce, 45 years old, 66 inches tall, planter, born in Va., enlisted December 1780 for 5 months

Brown Hair, Gray Eyes, yellow/mulatto 1

Adderson Moore, 16 years old, 57 inches tall, planter, born in Va., enlisted for the war

'Negroe' – 1

[?] Hart, 16 years old, 63 inches tall, planter, born in Va., enlisted for the war

Black Hair, Hazel Eyes, Yellow Complexion – 1

Isaac Needum, 17 years old, 57 inches tall, farmer, born in Md., enlisted September 1780 for the war

Brown Hair, Hazel Eyes, Yellow Complexion – 1

John Caine, 23 years old, 63 inches tall, farmer, enlisted September 1780 for 18 months

Red Hair, Grey Eyes, Yellow Complexion – 1

Evans Archer, 25 years old, 64 inches tall, farmer, born in N.C., enlisted September 1780 for 18 months, marched to join Colonel Green

<u>Black Hair, Black Eyes, Swarthy Complexion – 5</u>
(all but one born in Virginia)
William Bowman, 30 years old, 66 inches tall, sawyer, enlisted September 1780 for 18 months
John Chavers, 26 years old, 69 inches tall, planter, 'free black'
William Melions, 22 years old, 67 inches tall, farmer, enlisted September 1780 for 18 months
William Parker, 24 years old, 64 inches tall, farmer, born in England, enlisted September 1780 for 18 months
Thomas Scott, 18 years old, 67 inches tall, planter, enlisted September 1780 for 18 months

Sources

'The Chesterfield Size Roll: Soldiers who entered the Continental Line of Virginia at Chesterfield Courthouse after 1 September 1780' (Library of Virginia citation: Joseph Scott. Roll of troops who joined at Chesterfield Courthouse since 1780. State government records collection. Also, 'Size-Roll of Troops join'd at Chesterfield Ct. House since Sept. 1 1780 Capt'n. Joseph Scott' and, 'This book is a Supplement to "Papers concerning the Army of the Revolution" Vol 1, Executive Depart. and in order, precedes Benjamin Harrison's Mission to Philadelphia by the Assembly. 1781'. Note by C. Leon Harris, 'The history of the size roll after the Revolutionary War is somewhat obscure. A sheet inserted into the book has … two notes in different handwritings'. Transcribed from bound photocopies, accession 23816.) Transcribed and annotated by C. Leon Harris, http://southerncampaign.org/pen/b69.pdf. A transcription of the entire Chesterfield supplement list, with accompanying notes, was provided by Joshua B. Howard and Lawrence E. Babits. Joshua Howard to author, 15 September 2010 (email).

Recommended Further Reading and Resources

Egerton, Douglas R., *Death or Liberty: African Americans and Revolutionary America* (Oxford and New York: Oxford University Press, 2009).

Grave, Will, and Harris, C. Leons, Southern Campaign Revolutionary War Pension Statements & Rosters, http://www.southerncampaign.org/pen/.

Grundset, Eric G. (ed.), *Forgotten Patriots: African American and American Indian Patriots in the Revolutionary War* (National Society Daughters of the American Revolution, 2008).

Heinegg, Paul, 'List of Free African Americans in the Revolution: Virginia, North Carolina, South Carolina, Maryland and Delaware (followed by French and Indian Wars and colonial militias)', http://www.freeafricanamericans.com/revolution.htm.

Heitman, Francis B., *Historical Register of Officers of the Continental Army During the War of the Revolution – April, 1775, to December, 1783*, New, Revised, and Enlarged Edition (Washington, D.C.: The Rare Book Publishing Company, Inc., 1914).

Jordan, Winthrop D., *White Over Black: American Attitudes Toward the Negro, 1550–1812* (Baltimore, Md.: Penguin Books, Inc., 1971).

Moss, Bobby Gilmer, and Scoggins, Michael C., *African-American Patriots in the Southern Campaign of the American Revolution* (Blacksburg, S.C.: Scotia-Hibernia Press, 2004).

Nash, Gary B., *Race and Revolution* (Lanham, Boulder, New York, and Oxford: Rowman & Littlefield Publishers, Inc., 2001).

Quarles, Benjamin, *The Negro in the American Revolution* (New York, London: W.W. Norton & Company, 1973).

'Revolutionary War Pensions', available on Fold3 (pay site), https://www.fold3.com/title/467/revolutionary-war-pensions/description; See also, *Index of Revolutionary War Pension Applications in the National Archives* (Washington, D.C.: Government Printing Office, 1976), copies of depositions and related materials in Revolutionary War Pension and Bounty-Land Warrant Application Files (National Archives Microfilm Publication M804), reel , 1199, Records of the Department of Veterans Affairs, Record Group 15, National Archives at Washington, D.C.

Christopher Ward, *The War of the Revolution* (2 Volumes, New York: The Macmillan Company, 1952).

Van Buskirk, Judith L., *Standing in Their Own Light: African American Patriots in the American Revolution* (Norman: University of Oklahoma Pres, 2017).

For information into the context of African American female followers' service see:

Rees, John U., "'The proportion of Women which ought to be allowed…': An Overview of Continental Army Female Followers,' *ALHFAM Bulletin* (Association of Living History, Farm and Agricultural Museums), vol. XXVIII, no. 4 (Winter 1999), pp.18–21, https://tinyurl.com/women-proportion.

Rees, John. U., "'The multitude of women": An Examination of the Numbers of Female Followers with the Continental Army,' *The Brigade Dispatch* (Journal of the Brigade of the American Revolution), three parts: vol. XXIII, no. 4 (Autumn 1992), pp.5–17; vol. XXIV, no. 1 (Winter 1993), pp.6–16; vol. XXIV, no. 2 (Spring 1993), pp.2–6. Reprinted in *Minerva: Quarterly Report on Women and the Military*, vol. XIV, no. 2 (Summer 1996), https://tinyurl.com/women-multitude.

Rees, John U., "'Spent the winter at Jockey Hollow, and … washed together while there …": American Revolution Army Women Names Project – Continental Army,' https://tinyurl.com/names-project.